D1568961

PUBLIC LIBRARY OF WINNIPEG
LIBRARY

DISCARDED

515 Portage Avenue
Winnipeg, Manitoba R3B 2E9

The Tragic Effect

PN
1899
.O3–
G713
1979

ANDRÉ GREEN

The Tragic Effect

The Oedipus Complex in Tragedy

TRANSLATED BY ALAN SHERIDAN

CAMBRIDGE UNIVERSITY PRESS

CAMBRIDGE

LONDON · NEW YORK · MELBOURNE

Published by the Syndics of the Cambridge University Press
The Pitt Building, Trumpington Street, Cambridge CB2 1RP
Bentley House, 200 Euston Road, London NW1 2DB
32 East 57th Street, New York, NY 10022, USA
296 Beaconsfield Parade, Middle Park, Melbourne 3206, Australia

Original French version © Les Editions de Minuit 1969
English translation © Alan Sheridan 1979

First published as *Un œil en trop* by Les Editions de Minuit 1969
English translation first published by Cambridge University Press 1979

Printed in Great Britain by
Western Printing Services Ltd, Bristol

Library of Congress Cataloguing in Publication Data
Green, André.
The tragic effect.
Translation of Un œil en trop.
Bibliography: p.
Includes index.
1. Tragedy – History and criticism. 2. Oedipus
complex in literature. I. Title.
PN1899.03G713   809.2′51   76–19629
ISBN 0 521 21377 0

If someone looks into the mirror, a man, and in it sees his image, as though it were a painted likeness; it resembles the man. The image of man has eyes, whereas the moon has light. King Oedipus has an eye too many perhaps. The sufferings of this man, they seem indescribable, unspeakable, inexpressible. If the drama represents something like this, that is why. But what comes over me if I think of you now? Like brooks the end of something sweeps me away, which expands like Asia. Of course, this affliction, Oedipus has it too. Of course, that is why. . .Life is death, and death is a kind of life.

Hölderlin, 'In lovely blueness. . .'

Contents

Foreword

BY FRANK KERMODE

Three-quarters of a century and more after the publication of *The Interpretation of Dreams* there is still strong resistance to the suggestion that analysts of literary texts have anything important to learn from psycho-analysis. Psycho-analysts have a well-developed apologetic, know all about resistance, and may be left to look after themselves. But literary critics – and metacritics, whose number increases with such interesting rapidity – need to consider what they may be missing. It is true that twentieth-century criticism, even when it is innocent of direct allusion to psycho-analysis, often betrays its generalized influence. Where the manifest sense may be left to the naïve or incompetent reader, the institutionalized expert deals primarily in the latent, and teaches others to do the same; and Freud contributed to this change, rather as the mythographers and allegorists helped to defend the hidden meanings of Renaissance literature. But full consciousness of this debt is rarely found in critics who are not doctrinaire Freudians. Others avoid it, and point, if challenged, to the obvious differences between their own practice and that of the psycho-analyst. For the latter, the approach to latent sense is by way of the analysand's free association; and only if the analysand honours his contract, and says everything, will there be uttered that which is heard by the third ear, that which reveals what is concealed. But although the critic must conduct some kind of dialogue with his text, and must hope to have an interpretative organ in some way comparable to that third ear (or that 'eye too many' of which Hölderlin spoke in the verses that form the epigraph of André Green's book and gave it its title in French), he is probably unwilling to allow that the only free association that can be super-added to his text – namely his own – is an equivalent source of information, so far as what is latent in the text is concerned.

Psycho-analysts have their own institutional constraints, and their discipline has, almost since its origin, been an arena of ferocious hermeneutical disputes. There are sects or parties, more or less clearly labelled. Critics, at any rate in Britain and the United States, are much less likely to proclaim so full a doctrinal adherence, though they are by no means such free agents as this might make them appear; and the constraints of their institution are more rigorous than many suppose. For example, it is still the common wisdom that criticism must 'respect' what the author of any work under consideration meant, or could have meant, to say in it. This position has been attacked on many different fronts over the past thirty years, but it remains the orthodox position. Consequently it has generally been assumed that such use as psycho-analysis may have in literary criticism depends upon its power to illuminate, using the evidence of the text, what was going on in an author. And this has given psycho-analysis a bad name among many, perhaps most, critics, who think of it largely as a fantastic or tedious supplement to biography, a quest, mechanically prosecuted, for evidence of what one disenchanted ex-practitioner has called 'the squeaking bedsprings of the primal scene', whether in Conrad's Congo or in Milton's Paradise.

For this state of affairs Freud, who left several examples of author-analysis, must certainly bear some of the blame. But his immense authority is not of the kind that excludes qualification, correction and development. His revolutionary approach to dream, to symptom and to parapraxis can be thought of as a preliminary to a fuller understanding of all discourse that one has reason to think less than transparent, which of course includes all literary discourse. Psycho-analysis cannot be a substitute for literary criticism; but they may be hermeneutical cousins, and it is worth asking whether the insights of psycho-analysis may not have a valuable application say to tragedy, and to particular tragedies, without regard to the psychical condition of Aeschylus, Shakespeare or Racine.

The isolated, defensive position occupied by modern American psycho-analytic criticism (there is very little, good or bad, in Britain) is almost certainly due to the way in which Freud has been transmitted to the critics. The over-confident positivism of the prevailing orthodoxy, ego-psychology, cannot appeal to the reader of today who finds himself engaged with the uncertainties of the literary text, with its negative modes of existence, with the problem of describing his precarious relationship to an object whose fundamental characteristic is that it 'is, and is not'. In England, there have been deviant schools of greater critical potential; one thinks of the work of Melanie Klein, of D. W. Winnicott, of W. Bion. But the potential has not been actualized. The adventurous critical employment of revisionist Freudian, or post-Freudian, approaches has been primarily the work of the French, who have perhaps benefited from the intermittency of Freud's effect on their own intellectual life. Whatever the reason, it is now commonplace that the *rifacimento* of Freud on the linguistic basis provided by Ferdinand de Saussure – the work, principally, of Jacques Lacan – has transformed French literary criticism. Associated with the school of Lacan, though very far from being a card-carrying epigone, is the author of the present work, Dr André Green.

Green is an analyst of international distinction, exceptional in his sensitivity to theoretical developments achieved by other schools than the French, and to relevant scholarship outside the limits of his own discipline. He also happens to have a lifelong interest in, and practical experience of, the theatre. It is from this conjunction of interests that the present book has grown. Its main purpose is to apply the methods of 'psychological hermeneutics' to tragedy – with a strong emphasis on tragedy in performance – and specifically to the *Oresteia*, *Othello*, and Racine's *Iphigénie*. He includes studies of other works, providing, for example, a brilliantly original treatment of *The Bacchae* of Euripides.

At the heart of these essays is the psycho-analytical doctrine which holds that 'the access to truth...can only pass through an examination of its distortions'. The truth is always in disguise; and for Green the tragic theatre is a peculiarly rich location of the enigmatic, the disguised, the secondary sense. It is precisely because tragedy came *after* myth and made it opaque that he values it so highly. The theme that constantly engages him is the *après coup*, the delayed meaning, disclosures made after the event. He seizes upon the least obvious text or figure as his leading clue, and pursues it unremittingly. The truth is for him inseparable from what he calls *méconnaissance*; 'the ways of knowledge and truth are set up in opposition'. Obviously he claims no finality for his own recognitions of truth, for they too are subject to further disclosures *après coup*. So, it might be said, are all literary analysis and interpretation; it is what such interpretation has in common with psycho-analysis, and a part of what the book has to tell us.

The interpretative essays on Greek, English and French tragedies are the heart of the book, but Green's more general purposes required a theoretical Prologue and Epilogue. The latter is an extended study of the Oedipus complex. Unlike most modern psycho-analysts, especially Americans, he is concerned with this complex in its full form, feminine as well as masculine, negative as well as positive – a structure to which every individual is heir, as a consequence of his/her psychical bisexuality. 'For that is the essential nature of this complex. It never exists in the simple state, but is always double. It never exists in an integral state, but survives only in a vestigial state. It never exists in a conscious state, but remains an unconscious state.' In short, it is a deeper and more tragic concept than we have grown accustomed to think it; and it is necessary to the studies of the tragedies that we should understand it in its fullest Freudian sense. It is in that sense that the Epilogue expounds it.

The Prologue forms a difficult entrance to the main body of the book. Its manner may well be unfamiliar to Anglo-Saxon readers,

but they should take courage from its subtle and unillusioned confidence in the value of psycho-analysis, and from the strength with
which the author juxtaposes the psycho-analytic and the tragic
scenes. The child, faced with the mystery of his origins and excluded
from any sharing in it, must seek it through interpreting his parents;
the spectator must interpret the dialogue, equally lacking in explicit
commentary, which he listens to in the theatre. But there is always
too much to interpret. And each requirement to interpret is complicated by the force of repression, which insists that truth may be
disclosed only as a hidden, an absent, truth. Beyond the physical
scene there is always that 'other scene'; the stage and the family are
alike tragic spaces. Moreover, to interpret is to distort, in order to
avoid the unpleasure that accompanies the revelation of the inadmissible. Truth endlessly repeated is endlessly deformed; every
interpretative act has an element of *méconnaissance*. In the course of
these preliminary deliberations, Green confronts many problems
familiar to us in other guises: of representation, of the pleasure we
find in tragedy, of the surprising interpretation which compels us to
disregard the simpler conventions of the critic's craft, the requirement, for example, of coherence. When we have followed him
through this long initiation we are ready for a genuinely psycho-
analytical reading of tragedy, and of individual tragedies considered
as representations of the phantasy or myth of the Oedipus complex.

Perhaps the matter is less familiar than at first appears, for we
are already aware of the existence of what Green, after Freud, calls
the 'other scene'. It is, in some form, a necessary hypothesis of all
speculative criticism, all criticism that does more than merely
'double' the manifest sense of its text. What Green has done, in his
interpretations of the *Oresteia*, of *Othello*, of *Iphigénie*, is not merely
to confirm the affinity between tragedy and myth, but also to afford
us means of understanding it. The radical instrument of this understanding is the full Oedipus complex, as, in all its complexity, its
doublings and inversions, it informs these studies.

Green's proposals are not made in a spirit of aggression or conquest; it is characteristic of his whole approach that he disowns the
desire to convince. Yet he is, boldly, a psycho-analyst, and rejoices in
the analyst's destiny, which is to have, like the artist, an eye too
many. I dare say he would be astonished if every one of his interpretations were to be found acceptable by his reader; I, for example,
reject some of his propositions on *Othello*; but I think my understanding of that tragedy is increased, not only by what I accept but
also by what I resist. So too with his effect on my general understanding of the problem of interpretation. For all that I demur at
some of the paradoxes proposed, I value what I have learnt from the

discussion, in the section on *The Bacchae*, of the transition from *plaisir* to *jouissance*, a Freudian variation that seems intuitively acceptable; and from what he says of 'disavowal' and *méconnaissance*. His book should alter our understanding of the spectator's response to tragedy, and modify, in a wholly beneficial sense, our thinking about the relation between the two kinds of analysis.

FRANK KERMODE

Author's Acknowledgements

This work owes much to many. My discovery of *living* tragedy dates from the years I spent in the Groupe de théâtre antique at the Sorbonne. Without this concrete experience of ancient tragedy, I would have learnt nothing *true* about it. Later, other groups contributed to my understanding. Among these, I should particularly like to mention the students who attended my seminar at the Institut de Psychanalyse, Paris. They gave me the opportunity for an exchange of views for which I am truly grateful.

A number of friends have helped me to bring this work to birth. My thanks must first go to Michèle and Christian David. I must also thank Claude Monod for the valuable help that she has unstintingly given. Bernard Pingaud has given me valuable advice. I owe an especial debt of gratitude to Muguette Green for her unflagging patience and meticulous care in preparing the final version of this book.

Lastly, I wish to thank Jean Piel for the confidence that he has shown in my work, both in the journal *Critique* and in the series of books bearing the same name.

A.G.

Translator's Note

In this English edition, footnotes have as far as possible been incorporated in the main body of the text. Where this would have resulted in an interruption of the author's argument, notes have been placed at the end of the book. I have added a few explanatory notes concerning certain psycho-analytic (and, more particularly, Lacanian) terms; these are contained within square brackets in the notes at the end of the book.

For works included in the Select Bibliography references are kept to a minimum: author, publication date and volume number where necessary, and act and scene or page number; e.g.:

Aristotle, 29
Delcourt, 1944, 23
Freud, *S.E.*, xxiii, 43
Bacchae, 186

In the case of the Racine play, the act and scene number are followed by a colon and the page number of the English edition: Racine, *Iphigenia*, ii, 5: 81. Details of the editions used are given in the Select Bibliography. Where no English version is cited there, the translations are my own.

Where quotations contain italics added by Green in order to emphasize a particular point, there is a note to this effect; otherwise italics may be assumed to be part of the text quoted.

Green's argument is occasionally based on a version of the Greek texts that differs considerably from the version used for the Penguin translation. The Greek has been retranslated to fit Green's argument where necessary.

A.S.

Prologue

The psycho-analytic reading of tragedy

Play is in fact neither a matter of inner psychic reality nor a matter of external reality...The place where cultural experience is located is in the *potential space* between the individual and the environment (originally the object).
...
I am assuming that cultural experiences are in direct continuity with play, the play of those who have not yet heard of games.

D. W. Winnicott, 1971, 96 and 100

I A TEXT IN REPRESENTATION: WAYS FROM IGNORANCE TO KNOWLEDGE[1]

There is a mysterious bond between psycho-analysis and the theatre. When Freud cites *King Oedipus, Hamlet* and *The Brothers Karamazov* as the most awe-inspiring works of literature, he notes that all three are about parricide; less importance has been attached to the fact that two of the three are plays. One naturally wonders whether, for all the interest he showed in the other arts, the theatre did not have a special significance for Freud – a significance that outweighed his interest in the plastic arts (despite Michelangelo's 'Moses' or Leonardo's 'St Anne'), in poetry (despite Goethe, Schiller or Heine), in the tale (despite Hoffman), in the novel (despite Dostoievsky and Jensen). Sophocles and Shakespeare are in a class of their own, especially Shakespeare; Freud recognized in him a master whose texts he analyses as if they were the discoveries of some illustrious precursor. But he seems to have had a special affection for the theatre in general.

Scene and other scene[2]

Why is this? Is it not that the theatre is the best embodiment of that 'other scene', the unconscious? It is that other scene; it is also a stage whose 'edge' materially presents the break, the line of separation, the frontier at which conjunction and disjunction can carry out their tasks between auditorium and stage in the service of representation – in the same way as the cessation of motility is a precondition

for the deployment of the dream. The texture of dramatic representation is not the same as that of the dream, but it is very tempting
to compare it with phantasy. Phantasy owes a great deal to the
reworking by the secondary process of elements that belong rather to
the primary processes, these primary processes being then subjected
to an elaboration comparable to that of ceremonial, in the ordering
of dramatic actions and movements, in the coherence of theatrical
plot.[3] But there are many differences between the structure of
phantasy and the structure of the theatre. Phantasy is closer to a
form of theatre in which a narrator describes an action occurring in a
certain place, but in which, though he is not unconcerned, he does
not himself take part. Phantasy is much more reminiscent of the tale,
or even the novel. Its links with the 'family romance'[4] reinforce this
comparison. In the dream, on the other hand, we find the same
equality, *de jure*, if not *de facto*, that reigns between the various
protagonists sharing the space of the stage. So much so that, in the
dream, when the dreamer's representation becomes overloaded, the
dreamer splits it into two and sets up another character to represent,
separately, one or more of his characteristics or affects. Broadly
speaking, it would be more correct to say that the theatre may be
situated *between* dream and phantasy.

Perhaps we should turn to the simplest, most obvious fact.
Does not the theatre owe its peculiar power to the fact that it is an
exchange of language, a succession of bare statements without benefit
of commentary? Between the exchanges, between the monologues,
nothing is vouchsafed about the character's state of mind (unless he
says it himself); nothing is added to these statements that refers to
the physical setting, the historical situation, the social context, or the
inner thoughts of the characters. There is nothing but the unglossed
text of the statements.

In much the same way, the child is the witness of the daily
domestic drama. For the *infans* that he remains long after his
acquisition of language, there is nothing but the gestures, actions
and statements of his parents. If there is anything else, it is up to
him to find it and interpret it. The father and mother say this or
that, and act in this or that way. What they really think, what the
truth really is, he must discover on his own. Every theatrical work,
like every work of art, is an enigma, but an enigma expressed in
speech: articulated, spoken and heard, without any alien medium
filling in its gaps. That is why the art of the theatre is the art of the
malentendu, the misheard and the misunderstood.

The space of the stage: the spectator in the spectacle

But this structure creates a space, is conceivable only in a space, that of the stage. The theatre defines its own space, and acting in the theatre is possible only in so far as one may occupy positions in that space. The spectacle presents not so much a single, overall view to be understood, more a series of positions that it invites the spectator to take up in order that he may fully participate in what is offered him on the stage. We have to consider, as Jacques Derrida does, the question of the 'enclosure' of representation. Just as the dream depends on the enclosure of the dreamer, the enclosure of sleep – beyond which there is no dream, but either waking or somnambulism – the limits of the theatre are those of the stage.

The theatrical space is bounded by the enclosure formed as a result of the double reversal created by the exchanges that unfold between the spectator and the spectacle, on either side of the edge of the stage. We may try to eliminate this edge; it is only reconstituted elsewhere. This is the invisible frontier where the spectator's gaze meets a barrier that stops it and sends it back – the first reversal – to the onlooker, that is, to himself as source of the gaze. But, since the spectacle is not meant to enclose its participants in a solipsistic solitude, nor to restrict its own effects by keeping its elements separate from each other, we must account for this in a different way. This return to the source has established a relation between source and object: the spectacle encountered by the gaze as it passes beyond the stage barrier. Nonetheless, the edge of the stage preserves its function of separating source and object. The spectator will naturally compare this with his experience of a similar encounter, where the same relation of conjunction and disjunction is set up, linking the object of the spectacle with the objects of the gaze that a different barrier, namely repression, places beyond his reach. It is as if those objects ought not to have been in full view, yet, by some incomprehensible paradox, will not allow the perceiver ever to escape them. They force him to be for ever subjected to their return, experienced in a form at once inescapable, unpredictable and fleeting. The permanence of the object seen in the spectacle is like the lure that tempts us to think that the solicitation might this time lead to the capture always denied hitherto. By arousing a hope that the secret behind the moment of disappearance of the repressed objects will be revealed, it allows the spectacle to unfold so as the better to surprise that secret.

This reversal on to oneself is always accompanied by a second reversal – the reversal into its opposite – whose meaning is more difficult to grasp. The first reversal enables us to measure, as it were, the fundamental otherness of the spectacle for the spectator. If the spectator allowed this otherness, he would either leave or go to sleep, and that would be the end of a spectacle that had never begun. But this otherness solicits him. Though unable to reject this otherness as totally alien, the gaze detaches itself to some extent from its object, otherwise the total participation of the spectator with the forces of the spectacle would merge them beneath the eye of a God bringing about from on high the coalescence of auditorium and stage. The gaze explores the stage from the point at which the spectator is himself observed by his object. The boundary between auditorium and stage is duplicated by the boundary between the stage as visible space and the invisible space off-stage. Together, these two spaces are opposed in turn to the space of the world, whose steady pressure maintains the space of the theatre between its walls.

The contradiction felt by the spectator is such that whereas the project of going to the spectacle initially created a break between the theatre and the world, the fact of being at the spectacle replaces the confrontation between the space of the theatre and that of the world (which has become invisible and so excluded from the spectator's consciousness) by the confrontation between the visible theatrical space and the invisible theatrical space. The world is the limit of the theatre and, to some extent, its *raison d'être*. But the relation of otherness between the subject and the world is replaced by the otherness of the spectator in respect of the objects of the gaze – an otherness no longer based simply on a boundary (the walls of the theatre, or the barrier formed by the edge of the stage), but on another space, one hidden from the gaze. As a result, there occurs a projection of the relationship between theatrical space and the space of the world on to the theatrical space, itself split into a visible theatrical space (the space of the stage) and an invisible theatrical space (the space off-stage). This latter space calls for exploration, for it is not only the space by which illusion is created; it is also that in which the false is fabricated. The space of the stage is the space of the plot, the enigma, the secret; the space off-stage is that of manipulation, suspicion, plotting. However, this space is circumscribable, since it is confined within the walls of the great chamber that is the theatre. (Its unlimited character in the cinema – here the chamber is the camera, but the entire world may be swallowed up in it – makes it impossible to explore these means as a lure for the cinema-spectator.) Thus the limit formed by the edge of the stage is extended to the limits of the space of the stage, this space offering itself as one to be transgressed, passed beyond, through its link with the invisible space off-stage.

This transgression is invited, therefore, by that which constitutes its second limit, a radically uncrossable limit, which denies the gaze of the spectator access to the invisible space off-stage. Since we have to renounce this second transgression as impossible, all that remains possible is the broadest incorporation of the stage space connoted by the term 'illusory', according to which what is incorporated is the opposite of the truth. That is the sense of the second reversal. By a shift of perspective, one might say, from veracity to veridicity, this reversal will affect the unsaid, the unspoken element, of the stage space: its unconscious, invisible problematic which, *qua* non-veridical, will be caught in the movement of return into its opposite, joining itself to the first reversal, which consists of a turning round upon oneself.[5]

So, whereas the spectacle takes place outside oneself, is alien to oneself, there is constituted the 'negative hallucination' of the unsaid of the stage on which all the said is inscribed. The hallucinatory value of representation, which the edge of the stage has materialized by the relation of otherness, both conjoint and disjoint, is inscribed on the opacity of the space off-stage in which the false is fabricated. Here the spectator finds himself in a place as metaphorical as that suggested by the appearance of those objects whose repression allows no more than fleeting residues to filter through. They too can be assembled into a constructed scenario. But this construction blocks, so to speak, the view of their original source, where the subject would have to recognize his own silhouette. This is like the negative hallucination in which the subject looks at himself in the mirror and sees all the elements of the setting around him, but not his own image. The impression that one sees without seeing, hears without hearing, speaks without making oneself understood, is also to be found, in a more fragmentary way, in dream space. This is not the result of some deficiency that weakens the living tissue of the dream, making it like a bloodless body – as is shown by the contrast to be found in some dreams between the effect of hyper-reality and the unintelligibility of their messages. The space off-stage frames this 'blank' of the stage on which the action is inscribed.

The conjunction of this double reversal makes possible that which is sent back to the spectator as his gaze, refused entry to the space beyond the stage. Out of this refusal is constituted the theatrical space in which outside and inside are no longer meaningful within the enclosure of the two reversals. Yet their two-sidedness – as in the figure constituted by the joining of the double reversal – which was once the expression of the opposition between the theatre and the world, has become the opposition in which the spectator is the theatre, and also the opposition between the said and the unsaid.

Text and representation

Such is the movement of this reading process performed by the spectator – a reading that is never made explicit, but solicited from some other point situated in the potential space between text and representation.

This space defines its objects: words and characters. The characters, heroes and heralds, exist only through what they say. What they say cannot be said in their absence; no one but they can say it. Once again, we are referred back to the text. Even the destruction of the text still leaves a text. Even its abolition in a theatre given over to action will refer us back to the notional text implied by the action. What is this text about? It is telling us about a reason that is the motive-force of the characters and which, by implication, must be ours. And yet, if we are interested in what is being said, it is because at this point an effect is created, not of reason, but of truth. From what point does this truth speak? It speaks from a point in which another reason, an 'other reason', is spoken.

This truth is heard with the sense of shock that one feels when made to face something previously dismissed out of hand, regarded as merely improbable, discredited as pure artifice or even trumpery. Phrases like 'It's pure theatre!' or 'How theatrical!' betray the contempt we are supposed to feel for the extravagant pretences of the counter-truth. The reasons why a spectacle does or does not succeed in achieving its effect, is liked or hated, are obscure. But when it happens, the truth is found not at the centre of the stage, but in the flies, where the lighting is placed. For the stage-hand who watches the actors from above and from behind the curtain, even the most tragic spectacle is just another show to be put on – *he* has seen it all before. When the truth is present – when the text speaks and when the hero speaks it with veracity – then even the stage-hand listens. But if he had to account for this, he would be as much at a loss as the spectator in the front row of the stalls. The comments of the initiate and the connoisseur are no more convincing. Writing about the theatre is, generally speaking, mere word-spinning or paraphrase. It throws no light on the spectator's reasons for participating in the spectacle.

We might even suppose that the theatre has its effect only in so far as its ways are misunderstood by the spectators. And they cannot but be misunderstood both because of the structure of the subject and because of the unfolding of the spectacle. The moment of truth is so dazzling and so short-lived that it has already passed while one is still waiting for it; or it tricks one's expectations so well that one thinks it has already passed when it is still to come. A reciprocal connection links the terms of a process occurring at two levels. One is that of the spectator's participation in what is taking place before him, which seems to drive the action constantly outside itself, by the very fact of that participation. The other is the internal articulation of the constituent parts that generate, by a logic peculiar to themselves, the ongoing movement of the drama. The paradox of this double process is that the empty place of the spectator is never more clearly seen than when the theatre is full – that is to say, when no other spectator can be admitted. This means that the representation can reveal an encounter with a pure testimony through the emergence of something addressed to no one specific person, but to the space occupied by the audience (a locus in constant displacement through its own multifariousness from stalls to gods). This encounter generates the sequence of actions in such a way that they follow on from one another of their own accord, as a result of the tensions that govern their conjunctions and disjunctions. No reading can be either that of the representation or that of the text, but only that of a text in performance, *in representation*.

Aristotle and Artaud

Reflection on the theatre extends from Aristotle to Antonin Artaud. Aristotle laid down canons that were accepted until fairly recently. The signifier/signified problematic is already to be found in the six elements that Aristotle distinguishes in tragedy. In this respect, the *Poetics* constitutes a composite whole that moves from thematic analysis, an analysis of the fable, to a linguistic analysis whose links with the preceding analysis are never made quite clear.

In his analysis of the fable, Aristotle notes the part played by phantasy and gives it precedence over reality: 'It is not the poet's business to tell what has happened or the kind of things that would happen – what is possible according to probability or necessity' (Aristotle, 29). The aim is simply to arouse fear and pity; and Aristotle declares, without further explanation that this result is never better attained than when illustrated by relations of kinship: 'When sufferings are engendered among the affections – for example, if murder is done or planned, or some similar outrage is committed, by brother on brother, or son on father, or mother on son, or son on mother – that is the thing to aim at' (Aristotle, 35).

The family, then, is the tragic space *par excellence*, no doubt because in the family the knots of love – and therefore of hate – are not only the earliest, but also the most important ones. But the fable must culminate in a recognition – a passage from ignorance to knowledge. Recognition by representation. The tragic space is the space of the unveiling, the revelation, of some original kinship relation, which never works more effectively than through a sudden reversal of fortune, a peripeteia.

It might be objected that this is taking things too literally. The theatre is the art of mimesis. What follows from this? If the theatre is the art of imitation – the art of the false, say its detractors – it is because Aristotle sees in imitation a specifically human characteristic: 'The impulse to imitate is inherent in man from his childhood; he is distinguished among the animals by being the most imitative of them, and he takes the first steps of his education by imitating. Everyone's enjoyment of imitation is also inborn' (Aristotle, 20). The psycho-analyst is delighted: Aristotle presents him with two of his favourite parameters, childhood and pleasure.

This remark will have a wider implication if one compares it with Aristotle's recommendation to take the bonds formed by kinship as material for the fable. For the climax towards which the fable is tending is recognition, which has its fullest effect only when it is wholly bound up with the sudden reversal of the action in the peripeteia. If we acquire our earliest knowledge through imitation, and if the passage from ignorance to knowledge (recognition) is effected by a sudden reversal, may we not think, from a more modern standpoint, that it is a question not so much of imitation as of identification? This sudden reversal would appear to centre on the relation of identification and desire, on the one hand, and, on the other, on the bipartite function of identification, since it is an identi-fication that contradicts the two terms of the parental couple. (And this more especially because catharsis presupposes identification, since its true meaning is not a purification of the passions, which is a Christian interpretation of tragedy, but the treatment of emotion by emotion, with the aim of discharging it. However, this discharge must not be conceived as some kind of antiphlogistic effect, since its action is more in the nature of an 'assuagement accompanied by pleasure', which implies a participation in which the Other[6] is involved.)

The series of examples given by Aristotle of kinship relations depicted in tragedy says nothing about any action between the parents, or about the effect of the father on his children (only the reverse case is cited). This is a strange omission in a text that refers so often to Orestes and Iphigenia, yet ignores the nature of the relations between their parents.

At the level of the signified, the kinship-relations model seems most effective in the matter of mimesis. At the level of the signifier, Aristotle observes that by far the most important thing is to excel in metaphors (Aristotle, 50). My remarks below are freely based on Lacan's notion of the paternal metaphor. It is a happy chance that links the kinship relation to metaphor. It is as if the kinship relation were metaphorical of all the others – and, within it, in the shadow in which Aristotle keeps it, the relation that unites the parents or the relation that expresses the effect of the father on his children to an even greater degree than the others; as if metaphor, at the level of the signifier in poetic creation, rediscovered at the level of language the creation about which the parental metaphor implicitly speaks.

A fable centred around kinship relations indicates not what has been but what might have been, as if it had occurred as the myths recount it. Dramatic art embodies these myths in speech. All theatre is embodied speech. The tragedy of Oedipus is impossible; how can the life of a single man pile up such a set of coincidences? It is not for the psycho-analyst to answer; but rather for the countless spectators of *King Oedipus*, who might say, with Aristotle, 'a convincing improbability is preferable to what is unconvincing even though it is possible' (Aristotle, 58).

In a prophetic text that is now more than thirty years old, Artaud calls for 'an end to masterpieces'. As a true man of the theatre, his concern is with the recipient of the work, the public. In the name of the public, Artaud demands the right to be involved, to be strongly affected. He does not hesitate to condemn and even to sacrifice on the altar of the theatre works of genius that no longer work today. 'And if, for example, the masses today no longer understand *King Oedipus*, I would venture to say *King Oedipus* is at fault as a play and not the masses' (Artaud, 114). Artaud is looking for a way by which we might recover the tragic *phobos*. If the appearance of the blinded Oedipus does not make us flinch, if it is powerless to arouse in us an emotion as violent as that which it aroused in the Greeks, if we are no longer capable of going into trance before such a vision, then we can only conclude that the representation of tragedy has become inoperative and that it must be dropped from the repertoire. We must rediscover the ways in which a relationship of enchantment and possession was created between a spectacle and its spectator. We must demand that theatre, to use his image, should affect us as music affects snakes, by a shudder that strikes us first in the belly and runs through our whole body. At the risk of our having to burn Shakespeare, Artaud calls for the advent of a theatre of flesh and blood.

How can we not approve of Artaud's intentions if it is a matter of giving back life and participation to the audience at a theatrical festival, so that new blood can flow once more in its veins? But what Artaud demands is more radical. He wishes to face the modern spectator with something in which the intelligibility of the spectacle is no longer, as in the past, related to its emotional resonance. He aims to provoke in the theatrical event, at any price, a *frisson* that shakes the spectator out of his passivity, out of the softening seduction that anaesthetizes him by way of the pleasant, the picturesque and the decorative. The theatre of diversion must give way to a corrosive theatre that will gnaw away at the shell that is constricting it and give us back a forgotten aspect of the spectacle. This is the theatre of cruelty.

Artaud often had to explain what he meant by 'cruelty'. It was far from any notion of sadism or bloody spectacle. One has only to read the 'Letters on Cruelty' and the two 'Manifestos' on the theatre of cruelty to understand that it involves something quite different. Artaud's revolt was no mere gesture: it aims at getting a particular result. This result is the restoration of a world always present in man, but covered up, buried – whose resurrection the spectator must live through. Artaud's virtue is that he gave back to the poetic world its face of carnal violence. It is a theatre that challenges verbal language, that appeals to a physicality of signs, to their cumulative effect, to their intensive mobilization around gestures and around the voice, which passes beyond the ordinary expressive range of speech. What the spectator sees must be totally absorbing, what he hears profoundly disturbing – an effect produced by the strangeness of the masks, the disproportion of their forms and the suddenness of their appearance. He alludes to dreams on several occasions, but always in a sense far removed from the sentimental affectation that usually accompanies writing on art and much closer to Freud's:

If theatre is as bloody and inhuman as dreams, it is. . .to demonstrate and to confirm in us beyond all forgetting the idea of a perpetual conflict, and of a spasm where life is cut through at every moment; where the whole of creation rises up against our state as finished beings. It is to give permanent, concrete and everyday form to the metaphysical sense of certain fables whose very atrociousness and vigour suffice to show that their source and meaning derive from essential principles.   (Artaud, 140–1)

It is not a matter of rejecting language; we must seek 'a directly communicative *language*'. Artaud rejects the form of speech that wants to subordinate all forms of communication to the 'intellectual dignity' of grammatical articulation, as a necesary condition of the circulation and exchange of meanings.

Can we even base a theory of writing on Artaud? The letter to Paulhan of 28 May 1933, which I quote, is evidence rather that Artaud attributes 'the ossification of speech' to the fact that the theatre, which reflects this degeneration, reduces speech to the level of writing, attributes the same value to the written and spoken word.

Western theatre only acknowledges as language, only allows the properties and qualities of language, only permits the name language to be applied (with the sort of intellectual dignity generally attributed to the word) to articulated language, grammatically articulated: that is to say, to spoken or written language, speech which whether spoken or not has no value greater than that of the merely written language.

(Œuvres complètes, IV, 141)

This reintroduction of the dimension of the body, this vibration of the organic, does not abolish language, but re-establishes language at its sources. For Artaud, these sources are quite unambiguously physical. To 'make grammatical' is to control this movement between bodily sources and objects of representation, at their points of inter-section, where they form a network in which they can give rise to one another, come together to form unstable, but nevertheless preg-nant matrices of meaning, subject to a certain order. This order cannot fail to make its presence felt: it cannot entirely dominate the material on which it works. It suggests what such an order in the modes of syntactic connection might be, but leaves out of account their relations of subordination. For Artaud, as for Freud, language is the completion of that other 'pre-language', to which many modifications must be made before it can be truly given the name.

This syntactic connection implies respect for the relations of subordination, utter intelligibility in the movement of these linked elements, the mapping out of the marks that govern the transforma-tions of the form to which the statement must eventually be reduced, the homogenization of its elements, which allows various ways of constructing or analysing words and propositions; it implies a narrow range of variation of articulated speech held in a register that seems to have been fixed within limits well short of its potential extent, by a concern for economy that enables it to cover an ever vaster domain, outside the confines of sense experience. All this has set itself up against a speech that may be less disciplined, but is more reveal-ing, because closer to its roots. What Artaud intends, therefore, is to add to language another language, rather than to dance on its corpse:

But if we were to make a movement of return, even a beginning, to the sources – in breathing, in creation, in activity – of language; if we were to relate words once more to the physical movements that gave birth to them; and if the logical and discursive side of speech were to disappear in favour of its physical and emotional aspect – that is to say, if words instead of being given a solely grammatical force were understood as sounds, were perceived as movements, and those movements themselves were related to other direct and simple movements such as we make in every circumstance of daily life, and such as actors do not make often enough – then the language of literature would take on a new form and come to life.

(Artaud, 181)

No lover of the theatre can remain unaffected by Artaud's radical challenge. And even if we have to recognize that the theatre of cruelty has been no more than a desperate and unsuccessful venture, we must also admit that everything significant in contemporary theatre owes something to the formidable shock that Artaud gave it. The lifting of the yoke that weighs down upon the stage is really a lifting of repression, an exposure of everything that is active, that is actively determined, that obeys rigorous necessity. The terms used by Artaud suggest the Ananke (necessity) of the ancients, except that determination is not a force to which one passively, obediently subjects oneself. There is no fatalism to be found in this conception. If there is determinism, each individual must participate in the movement of this determination by ceaseless defiance, as if it were the true dignity of man to stir up these forces and then to maintain as long as possible the answering force that they call up in him. The role assumed by physical language is not so far from the ancient notion found in Aristotle's *Poetics*, that elocution ranks equally with thought. Similarly, the stirring power of the chant formed a complement to the spectacle; and, to a different degree, it is the fable that causes the character to emerge from his apparently fixed identity.

But Artaud rejects this reference back from one language to another. It is not only their balance that he wishes to disturb but their very coexistence. If he wishes to remain in this carnal theatre, it is by a sort of initiation in which he would be both initiator and initiated. Artaud wants to force his way into the creative process of life itself. Every undertaking renews another already created; this fresh traversal of the space of creation follows a path determined by the principles that govern it, even if the individual making the journey is unaware of it. 'From a mental viewpoint cruelty means strictness, diligence, unrelenting decisiveness, irreversible and absolute determination' (Artaud, 154). The movement of the theatrical act shows us the transference of this governing determination on to the individual, who anticipates it and who, in accepting responsibility for it, shows himself to be determined (a reversal from the passive meaning to the active meaning) to bear it: to bear rather than assume, because although he arouses and provokes that state by which he determines himself, the performer in the theatre of cruelty does not master it. At most he relaunches this determination in the area of the theatre. And even if such an act never completely fulfils its function as purifying exorcism – and in this sense there is no difference between the strict meaning of catharsis and Artaud's aim – it restores a form to this determination (in both the objective and subjective senses). Failing to render that determination visible, since the various elements of the production are merely a mediation, the best that can be found, the theatrical act will render it transmissible, it will exhaust its power, at least in the first stage of elaboration, in its return towards the outside – but 'outside' only in the sense of a place occupied by a consumer who appears to have marked it out for himself as a zone of extraterritoriality. Yet Artaud has already dislodged him from it. Moreover, this term is intended only in the sense of a 'displacement' and the occupation of a channel, on the way to the spectator, who is from the first moment of the spectacle included in it as its very cause. To re-read the 'Letters on Cruelty' is to see that there is a kinship between Freud and Artaud that goes well beyond the limited question of the dream, and which extends to the much more general plan of the antagonism between the life and death drives in the relations that he adumbrates between good and evil.

What Artaud calls evil is what corresponds in Freud to that silent activity of the death drive, which one never actually grasps, but encounters only in the processes in which it is linked with Eros. Cruelty is the product of this fusion. Eros shows us that the process of connection, in so far as it has already appropriated the destructive force of death with no return, remains marked by this exclusion of the silence of death and has erected over its ruins ever larger built-up areas. Eros does not save death, does not simply stand as an adversary confronting it; it incorporates its destructive force as a force of possession aimed at whatever opposes its expansion:

I use the word cruelty in the sense of hungering after life, cosmic vigour, relentless necessity, in the Gnostic sense of a whirlwind of life eating up the shadows, in the sense of that pain, apart from whose inescapable necessity life could not continue.   (Artaud, 155)

Artaud speaks in terms that Freud would not reject, of that kernel 'ever more and more reduced, more and more eroded', of ever-lasting evil. The silence of the death drive, the absence that denies us any direct grasp of its manifestation, its access being only retro-spective and deductive, is clearly indicated in the following lines:

The desire for Eros is cruel since it consumes contingencies. Death is cruelty, resurrection is cruelty, since in all directions within a circular enclosed world there is no room for the true death, since ascension is a rending, finite space feeds on lives, and every stronger form of life passes through the others, and so eats them in a massacre that is a transfiguration and a good. . .Cruelty causes things to coagulate, causes the plans of the created to form.   (Artaud, 157)

Artaud's tragic quality derives from the fact that the monster of his
visionary endeavour devoured its author. Abandoned or misunderstood by his best friends, who faded away at his approach, he himself
seems to have been unable to bear the determination that he
demanded and desired. The further he advances in his project, the
more identification with the process of creation gives way to identification with the creator as the agent, rather than the actor, of his
creation. The further away one seems to move from the principle of
submission to the higher determinism that governs the individual
who practises the act of cruelty, the more imperious becomes the
wish for a proclamation in which Artaud claims to be not only each
of his progenitors, but the product of the generation or the single
progenitor engendering himself.

There is in the cruelty that we practise a kind of higher determinism to
which the executioner–torturer is himself subjected and which he must be
determined to endure if the time comes...The hidden god, when he
creates, obeys the cruel necessity of creation that he has imposed on himself.   (Artaud, 154–5)

At this point Artaud tries to get round the difference between the
sexes that he inevitably meets on this road. To remain in the neuter
is a temptation impossible to satisfy; the body has become the theatre
of the struggle between the masculine and feminine. The lure of a
direct access to what is hidden by repression through an approach
that would no longer be deductive, but provocative, was to lead in
Artaud to a possession of his body as a space of exploration and
transformation, a locus of attentiveness and receptivity where only
shadows move, and in which he was to find the true, absent death.

First the belly. Silence must start in the belly, left, right, at the spot where
hernial swellings occur, where surgeons operate...To know in advance
what points of the body to touch is to throw the spectator into magic
trances.   (Artaud, 223 and 206)

This localizing knowledge, with its inductive power, will now coincide with the incorporation of the space of the dream by the
dreamer:

> I cry out in dreams
> But I know I am dreaming;
> My will-power prevails
> On BOTH SIDES OF THE DREAM.   (Artaud, 223)

Derrida has rightly pointed out that the force of Artaud's assault is
'against the tyrannical possessor of the logos, against the father,
against the God of a stage dominated by the power of speech and
text' (Derrida, 345–99). The first manifesto of the theatre of cruelty

already indicated the direction of a movement that substitutes, for the duality of author and director, 'a kind of sole creator on whom falls the double responsibility both for the play and for the action' (Artaud, 142). From now on the father was challenged only to have his place usurped in the celebration of a unique, non-repetitive, ephemeral spectacle.

The localization of 'both sides of the dream' appears to express the imperceptible transition that turns the mere intention to follow the principle determining all creation into an ever more autonomous, demiurgic creativity, as Artaud became increasingly aware of the experience of the body, which provides the key for the forging of the magic chain by which every effect is produced: 'To be familiar with the points of localization in the body is to reforge the magic links' (Artaud, 206). It is to centre the site of the unique creator in the empty zone from which all space extends outwards. The vacuum of the body has now taken over a place homologous with the one Artaud once assigned to evil. But it is as if, as soon as this void was named or its limits fixed, it was bound to concentrate its own strength around it and hold on to it – having become an 'asphyxiated void'. The phallus forbids access to it.

Yet, this is the secret, as IN THE THEATRE. The power will no flow outward. The active masculine will be forced in upon itself. And it will retain breathing's forceful will-power. It will retain it for the body as a whole, while outwardly there will be a picture of the disappearance of strength which the SENSES WILL BELIEVE THEY ARE WITNESSING.   (Artaud, 221)

The effect of theatrical illusion is no longer that liberating expansion, that communicative flame that fires the audience; it is the process of evaporation of those things we were looking at, which are suddenly not there in the space of the stage. That is why Artaud calls on the spectator to forge that magic chain in which we now have to find the sequence of the images of an unconscious problematic.

The post-Freud theatre

The failure of the theatre of cruelty is perhaps less important than the effect it had on the theatre that survived. Even if contemporary drama cannot legitimately be said to be part of Artaud's prophetic vision, is it not the main thing that we have the new mobilization of the emotions that its creator demanded? An art of entertainment, of the picturesque or of decoration is giving way to productions that have a less seductive effect on the spectator.

Artaud's views counterbalance Aristotle's condemnation of the improbable, the uselessly wicked, the contradictory, the opposite of the requirements of art. All that Aristotle condemns, contemporary theatre has made its guiding principles: theatre of cruelty, theatre of disjointed language, theatre of the cry, theatre of unease and theatre of disturbance. This is our theatre: the theatre in our image. But, in the final analysis, is not all theatre, simply by virtue of the fact that it is a field vectorized by desire, a theatre with the characteristics listed by Aristotle? It is a question to be asked. It would be too simplistic to link it to the anxiety of the modern world, for the world has lived through other periods at least as anxiety-ridden as our own. It would be more correct to say that it is the post-Freud theatre. A theatre of desire, a theatre of the primary process, which tends towards discharge (hence the role of spontaneity, of the cry, of crisis), which is ignorant of time and space (theatre of ubiquity and non-temporality), which abandons the requirements of logic (theatre of contradiction) and, lastly, a theatre of condensation and displacement (theatre of symbolization).

This non-Aristotelian theatre could not fail, therefore, to be connected with a Freudian theatre. 'Freudian' does not mean a theatre that presents the discoveries of psycho-analysis, but a theatre that depicts the processes whose formal characteristics Freud has stated.

But it should be noted that although the distance to the affect is here reduced to a minimum, eliminating anything that could be an obstacle to personal reception, the reasons why we feel involved in the spectacle are still as opaque as the reasons why we feel moved by Sophocles or Shakespeare. What, then, becomes of Aristotle's recognition? Is it possible to say that a concern with recognition has been banished from our stage? This would be to deny that contemporary drama centres on the same fundamental obsessions that constitute the object of psycho-analytic investigation. This preoccupation supports my belief that a limited number of fables or myths serve as models and have the power to produce the variation that demonstrates the link with the underlying theme, constantly giving proof of their richness 'in essential principles', as Artaud says.

However, the more direct the approach, the more clouded the horizon against which it stands out, the more the reward of pleasure offered to the spectator has to be paid for by an equal measure of anxiety, as if to keep at bay any clear view of the underlying theme.

It is as if the mutation produced by the Aristotelian notion of 'recognition' has, by reducing the relation between ignorance and knowledge to a simple echo-relation lacking in true revelatory power, completely permeated the new formal peculiarities of contemporary drama. The modern theatre has found forms capable of expressing a type of signification quite different from that of the classical tradition, and closer to the unconscious. But behind this apparent progress, the meaning that emerges in this context seems like a miraculous effect, without explanatory force, referring only to itself, finding in itself the motives and effects of its action. The modern theatre has dealt with themes even more subject to taboo than those of ancient tragedy, and more evocative of the unconscious; but the emotional shock felt by the spectator is accompanied by no explanation as to why the representation produces this shock. This taste for strange and powerful emotions seems to testify to a desire for immunization, rather than for greater understanding. So it is left to science, through the exposition, even the diffusion, of psycho-analytic and other texts, to explain at the theoretical level the syntax of this discourse, provided that a respectful distance is kept from the work of art. Any attempt to link these two discourses – apart from a few historical examples that suggested the work of art was accessible to psycho-analytic discovery – any radical effort in this direction still produces the same gnashing of teeth that met the first theoretical development of psycho-analysis. The price to be paid for the acceptance of psycho-analytic investigations is always either a reintroduction of psycho-analytic thought into a larger frame of reference, or its restriction within an abstract formalization, such that the formalization cannot reveal what is banned, excluded, rejected by the manifest content of the text, but limits itself to reflecting the underside of which the work is merely the obverse. Or at least as if this exclusion, when it is admitted to exist, were merely the direct product of collective social censorship, where the relations between repressor and repressed are, as things stand, less understood than those that psycho-analysis has revealed in the case of the individual.

What we can say, however, is that there is a pre-Freudian and post-Freudian way of listening to the unconscious. The entry of psycho-analysis into the world of culture produced a change in the relation between the implicit and the explicit. Yet this new situation has in no way altered the link between the work and its effect so far as the passage from ignorance to knowledge of the unconscious is concerned. Far from shifting our attention away from the works of the past, these changes seem to bring us back to them. The sense of this return would seem to be one whereby a work not only speaks directly, but also, in the absence of any other source, provides knowledge. 'In *King Oedipus*, there is the incest theme and the idea that nature does not give a rap for morality. And there are wayward powers at large we would do well to be aware of, call them *fate* or what you will' (Artaud, 114). It is the privilege of masterpieces to be embodiments both of the power of the signifier and of the power of the forces that work upon it, to be the product of the work of the contradictions that they set in opposition. In the period we are discussing, there was no gap, such as exists today, between the discourse of works of art and the knowledge that science is articulating elsewhere, on another plane, so we are at least spared intellectual double vision. The import of the work is inexhaustible; it is not to be discovered through some vain attempt to get at an underlying reality by brutally tearing away its aesthetic veils.

The aim of a psycho-analytic reading is the search for the emotional springs that make the spectacle an affective matrix in which the spectator sees himself involved and feels himself not only solicited but welcomed, as if the spectacle were intended for him. Once this matrix is identified, it is necessary to analyse the elements that combine to make the recognition intelligible. The recognition is presented in a shifting mode, moving from ignorance to knowledge – whether on the part of the hero or the spectator – and remains opaque until we have unravelled the complexities of the means by which the opposed or collaborative forces have pierced the wall of repression. This penetration undermines the apperception of the spectacle, which then passes from the plane of overt monstration to that of a covert demonstration, whose different stages must be reconstituted.

II   TOWARDS A PSYCHO-ANALYTIC READING OF TRAGEDY

What right has the psycho-analyst to meddle in the business of tragedy? Freud proceeded with extreme caution in his search among the common stock of culture for examples of the expression of the unconscious. Today, when psycho-analysis is less concerned to seek validations outside its own field of practice, is it still proper to seek material for interpretation in works of art? Many people, including some psycho-analysts, believe that the period must now end in which psycho-analytic investigation turned to cultural productions, myths or works of art, to provide evidence for a possible mapping of the unconscious outside the domain of neurosis. Psycho-analysis has provided enough proof of its scientific character, and ought to confine its efforts to the strict framework, defined by its own rigorous parameters, of psycho-analytic treatment. The view is well founded; the field of psycho-analysis will always remain the locus in which the exchanges between analyst and analysand unfold. When the analyst ventures outside the analytic situation, in which he is in direct contact with the unconscious, as it were, he must proceed with caution. The work of art is handed over to the analyst; it can say nothing more than is incorporated in it and cannot, like the analysand, offer an insight into the work of the unconscious *in statu*

nascendi. It cannot reveal the state of its functioning through the
operation that consists in analysing by free association – that is to
say, by providing material that reveals its nature in the very act by
which it makes itself known. It does not possess any of the resources
that make analysis bearable: that of going back on what one has said,
rejecting the intolerable connection at the moment when it presents
itself, putting off the moment of an emerging awareness, even denying, by one of the many ways available to the analysand, the correct-
ness of an interpretation or the obviousness of some truth brought by
repetition to the front of the stage and needing to be deciphered.
The work remains obstinately mute, closed in upon itself, without
defences against the treatment that the analyst may be tempted to
subject it to.

It would be illusory to believe that one can use a work to provide
proof of psycho-analytic theories. Psycho-analysts know that this
enterprise is vain, since no degree of consciousness can overcome
unconscious resistance. In certain cases, it happens that a fragment
of psychical reality manages to overcome repression and seems to
emerge with exceptional ease. One then has regretfully to admit,
powerless to do anything about it, that the effect is usually followed
by a reactivation of the psychical conflict of which this fragment is
an integral part. Persuasion, whatever those unacquainted with
psycho-analytic experience may think, has never been one of the
analyst's instruments; however much he is tempted to use it to get
himself out of some impasse in a difficult case, its use will always
prove disappointing. The same can be said when the analyst presents
the results of his analytic work on some cultural object. If he does
not stay close enough to the lines of force that govern the architecture of his object, the truth that even a partly correct analysis
contains runs a strong risk of not being recognized, for all its right-
ness, because the factors opposed to crossing the barriers of the censor
find solid support in objections which, though superficial, are reinforced by rationalization. It is therefore particularly necessary to
be vigilant in the account of any such investigation. In psycho-
analytic treatment, the repetition compulsion again and again offers
to disclose the meaning of a conflictual organization, which one can
then approach in a fragmentary way. In the analysis of a work of
art, everything is said in a single utterance by whoever assumes the
task of interpretation, and no inkling is given of the long process of
elaboration that has made it possible to arrive at the conclusions
now advanced in connected form.

These few remarks are not intended to reassure those who fear the
intrusion of psycho-analysis into a domain in which it could have a
restricting effect. No interpretation can avoid constraining the work,

in the sense that it necessarily forces it into the frame provided by a certain conceptual approach. The work may then be seen from a different perspective, with a new meaning that enlarges it by inserting it in a wider frame of reference. To speak is above all to choose this restricted economy within the enclosure of discourse, in order to give oneself ways towards a development that is impossible if one says nothing.

These warnings are primarily intended to remind myself of the conditions that govern this venture of literary interpretation, that should guide my initial grasp of the work and the subsequent development of my analysis. In any case, the psycho-analyst has less need to defend himself against the charge of violating the work by imposing his version on it, in that a whole recent current of criticism makes it clear that no one is entirely free of this charge when he comes into contact with a work, that every work is itself a kind of reading, calling for a new reading that is the reader's only access to it. Any reading is by definition interpretative; an attribution of meanings is always going on even in the person who thinks himself the most humble of exegetes. Where is a tyrannical relation between reader and text most likely to become established: in the reader who admits his reading is a conjectural enquiry forcing the decipherer to find his way even as he attempts to draw the implicit map of the work, or in the reader who rules out any movement from his own position and merely repeats old schemata that he supposes to be eternal, though historical analysis would show that they are merely the fossilization of acquired knowledge? Who abuses cultural products most: he who seeks in them for a new vision that he supposes them to be still capable of producing, despite the accumulation of readings already in existence, or he who dispenses with radical questioning and brings to the works a mere paraphrastic commentary saturated with the presuppositions of common knowledge? It is just because psycho-analysis provides this radical questioning, this conjectural interrogation, this appeal to what is not given from the outset as cause of an effect, that it has a role in the renewal of criticism.

But even as part of this movement, its role will be a difficult one. Psycho-analysis will always be suspect. It will be criticized, for example, for setting up a relation between the author and the work, as if it were doing so in the spirit of the old biographical criticism, which saw the work as an extension of the experiences of the author's life. Yet psycho-analysis sees it in a relation of discontinuity with them. Biographical criticism saw the work as an echo or a reverberation of some event whose influence was measured in a relation of immediate understanding, according to an implicit scale of common feelings. The link established between author and work by psycho-analysis does not postulate a direct influence between the events of a life and the content of the work, but situates these historical elements in a conflict. These elements are set in the perspective of another problematic, which has been essentially misunderstood because it belongs to repressed childhood, the modes of combination of present and past no longer being accessible to the individual who experiences them, even though they may have a considerable conscious charge. So the work becomes the other network, by which rehandled modes of combination echo what has been reawakened of the unknown past by the present. This repeated past provides the material for a new relation, which keeps a significatory link with its roots that will help to illuminate it retrospectively. A hypothesis about the meaning of this relation for the author helps us to grasp the coherence of the work, which gains in comprehensibility without losing any of its mystery. The reawakening of some significatory constellation underlies this mobilization, which has transformatory power by virtue of its identity with the things from which it is separated by repression. This content is doubly articulated: by the original complexual organization and by the repetition manifested in the present 'event'. None of this puts the author at the mercy of his conflicts – at least, no more than anyone else, since each of us is the system of relations of the various agencies at work in the conflict.

Would it be possible, anyway, to show that there is no relation between a man and his creation? (This is not a thread I mean to follow here, but I must draw attention to the suspiciously passionate way in which any link between author and work is usually 'refuted'.) From what power could creation be nourished if not from those at work in the creator? The psycho-analytic point of view cannot accept that we have disposed of the problem of the genesis of works of art when we have invoked some absolute mystery of creation where the desire to create is not rooted in its unconscious ramifications. Nor can we be content with the idea that the work has the existential signification of a 'supersession' – a view, admittedly, expressed less often by the creator than by commentators on his production. The creator himself always remains aware of its character as a temporary halt on a journey whose aim is above all to ensure the stock of means that will enable him to continue the search.

In the last resort, what people fear most of all about the psycho-analyst is the threat that he will apply some pathological label to the creator or his creations. The keywords in the psycho-analytic vocabulary – though they have value only when placed in the structural ensemble from which they derive their coherence – continue to intimidate; no one feels secure from the unpleasant feeling he would have if, unexpectedly, this vocabulary were applied to him.

In our time, this fear has taken on a curiously paradoxical form. We all talk about the pervert and proclaim our potential brotherhood with him; but the mere mention of the word 'normality' is ruthlessly pounced on and denounced. Yet the psycho-analytic texts never postulate a norm – analysts have been attacked enough by physicians and psychiatrists for doing just that – except as a relative term that must be posited somewhere if we are to understand differences of degree or gradations between one structure and another. Resistance to psycho-analytic terminology makes itself felt as soon as it emerges from an unthreatening world of generalization, a world in which its resort to metaphorical terms allows us to harbour the secret hope that we are dealing with the language of some new mythology. It is easy to forget that psycho-analysis has been persecuted precisely for abolishing the frontiers between health and illness and showing the presence in the so-called normal man of all the potentialities whose pathological forms reflect back a magnified, caricatural image. It was Roland Barthes who wrote this condemnation of traditional criticism: 'It wishes to preserve in the work an absolute value, untouched by any of those unworthy "other elements" represented by history and the lower depths of the *psyche*: what it wants is not a constituted work, but a *pure* work, in which any compromise with the world, any misalliance with desire, is avoided' (Barthes, 37). These remarks can be applied to a good deal of the new criticism, or to those upholders of a theory of writing who defend a sort of literary absolutism.

When a psycho-analyst enters the universe of tragedy, it is not to 'pathologize' this world; it is because he recognizes in all the products of mankind the traces of the conflicts of the unconscious. And although it is true that he must not, as Freud rightly remarked, expect to find there a perfect correspondence with what his experience has led him to observe, he is right in thinking that works of art may help him to grasp the articulation of actual but hidden relations, in the cases that he studies, through the increased distortions that accompany the return of the repressed. Freud never thought that he had anything to teach gifted creators of authentic genius, and he never hid his envy of the exceptional gifts that allowed them, if not direct access, at least considerably easier access to the relations that govern the unconscious.

The exploitation of these gifts is directed towards obtaining the 'bonus of pleasure' that is made possible through the displacements of sublimation; this would tend to establish a relation of disjunction between the product of artistic creation and the symptom. For the first has the effect of negating the action of repression; but the second, because it is the expression of the return of the repressed, erupts into the consciousness only after paying the entrance fee of displeasure at the prohibition of satisfaction. Satisfaction, then, is indissolubly linked to the need for punishment associated with the guilt engendered by desire, whose symptom thus becomes its herald. The satisfaction of desire cannot be separated from submission to the sanction of the prohibition that weighs upon it.

This difference between symptom and creation now makes it possible to indicate their resemblance, if not their similarity. In both symptom and creation, the processes of symbolic activity are at work, as they are also in the dream or the phantasy. So artistic creation, 'pathological' creation and dream creation are linked by symbolic activity, their difference being situated in the accommodation that each offers to the tension between the satisfaction bound up with the realization of desire and the satisfaction bound up with the obser-vance of its prohibition. Neurosis, Freud would say, is the individual, asocial solution of the problems posed to the human condition. At the social level, morality and religion propose other solutions. Between the two, at the meeting-point of the individual and society, between the personal resonance of the work's content and its social function, art occupies a transitional position, which qualifies the domain of illusion, which permits an inhibited and displaced *jouissance*[7] obtained by means of objects that both are and are not what they represent.

Breaking the action of repression does not mean exposing the un-conscious in all its starkness, but revealing the effective relation between the inevitable disguising and the indirect unveiling that the work allows to take place. The unconscious sets up a communication between a sentient, corporeal space and the textual space of the work. Between the two stand prohibition and its censor; the sym-bolic activity is the disguise and the exclusion of the unacceptable, and the substitution of the excluded term by another less unaccept-able one, more capable of slipping incognito into the area that is closed to it. Indeed, if every text is a text only because it does not yield itself up in its entirety at a first reading, how can we account for this essential dissimulation other than by some prohibition that hangs over it? We can infer the presence of this prohibition by what it allows to filter through of a conflict of which it is the outcome, marked by the lure it offers, calling on us to traverse it from end to end. We shall often feel a renewed disappointment, faced by its refusal to take us anywhere except to the point of origin from which it took its own departure.

The trans-narcissistic object

The products of artistic creation are evidence of work. Every examination of them travels, however briefly, the route of their birth. These products set up in the field of illusion a new category of objects related to psychical reality. Their relation with the objects of phantasy enables us to understand their function more clearly. The objects of phantasy, which, on their admission to consciousness, had to undergo distortion and adjustments to make them compatible with conscious logic, remain, as I said above, occult; the reticence of their message testifies to the precariousness of this cover. But the veil that hides them also corresponds to another requirement. They are an integral part of an equilibrium in which the realizations of desire that are carried out through them are inseparable from a condition of appropriation by the subject, which is necessary to feed his narcissistic idealization. The unity of the phantasy is inseparable from the narcissistic unity that it helps to form. The types of objects to which artistic creations correspond are on the other hand characteristically objects of ejection, expulsion: objects put into circulation through disappropriation by their creator, who expects their appropriation by others to authenticate their paternity. The upsurge of desire that gave them birth is repeated at each new reception. This enables us to map out in such productions the narcissistic double of their creator, which is neither his own image, nor his own personality, but a projected construction, a configuration formed in place of the narcissistic idealization of the recipient of the work.

Thus the structures of phantasy face in two directions. First, towards the object, they sustain desire and help to form whatever serves in fulfilling it: dream, symptom or sexual activity – the means placed at the disposal of the discharge and the channels open to it. Second, they serve the search for an idealizing subjective unit involving the renunciation of the satisfaction of a complete discharge (aesthetic *jouissance* being subjected to the inhibition of the aim of the drive), but in which the narcissistic construction of the other is accepted. So the objects of artistic creation may properly be called *trans-narcissistic*: that is to say, they bring the narcissisms of producer and consumer into communication in the work. The communication of the two fields of this double orientation will give us a clue to whatever may arouse, as an after-effect, the desire phantasy, through the mediation of this narcissistic idealization.

The psycho-analytic approach to the work of art need not involve a study of the personality of the artist, but there is no need to exclude the possibility. It is enough to be aware of this narcissistic construction that is the artist's double, and to seek to map out the points of impact at which the desire phantasy is set in motion, even if this phantasy inevitably fails to satisfy its recipient. But, through the disjunctions so revealed, we may posit hypotheses concerning the mode of articulation that holds its parts together.

No doubt there is a risk – and adventurous hermeneuts have often been criticized for just this – that one may shape the work into a lock (or discover a lock in it) to fit one's own particular key. The objection need not be taken seriously. A work only allows itself to take the form of a lock if it can be so taken – if its material permits it to do so and if its form suggests it. The important thing is not that one should be able to insert a key, but that one should know what would be revealed by the door that one hopes to open. What one interprets of a corpus of work depends on the way in which one segments it – the originality of the segmentation is inseparable from the originality of what one discovers. And this discovery is not possible without the mode of segmentation proper to it and the body of references that supports it. Such an interpretation does not say everything about the work, but confines itself to the particular aspect of the work that concerns it, without bothering about the rest, without necessarily even touching on it; and the rest cannot be reached except by adopting another mode of segmentation.

Can one, then, say anything one likes about the work? No, for the discovery is set against the coherence of the system that corresponds to the interpretation, and the coherence of the work that may accept or reject this interpretation. It is not a question of reaching an infinity of juxtaposed and contradictory insights, nor of leaving the field open to the most extravagant and arbitrary interpretations, but of attaining a mode of reading that does not deny other modes of interpretation, but which takes as its aim the revelation of the unconscious effects of the spectacle.

It must be repeated, at the risk of being boring, that psycho-analytic interpretation is not exhaustive, but specific. No other approach can replace its particular discourse, just as this discourse cannot be substituted for any other. No doubt, one will come up against other competing interpretations – especially at the level of significations. This collision cannot be avoided. One must set the different readings side by side, and decide which provides most information, which is most revealing.

Our aim, therefore, is to rediscover, in a work whose specific nature is the labour of representation unfolding according to its own procedures, an analogue of what Freud described in his first intuitions about the functioning of the psychical apparatus. This process is the play of a pluri-functional system, which never progresses continuously and in a single direction; it goes back over inscriptions that have already been traced and slides away from obstacles; it reproduces its message with a distortion that forces us back to it; receives some new impulsion that overcomes a resistance; or breaks into fragments. It recomposes these dissociated fragments into a new message incorporating other elements from another fragmented totality, preserving at the essential level that nucleus of intelligibility without which no new crossing of the boundary can be made. It preserves itself from annihilation and consequent oblivion by a protective distortion which prevents it being recognized. The work of representation, which unceasingly maintains an effect of tension in the spectator, is the reconstitution of the process of formation of the phantasy, just as the analysis of the dream, through the resistance to the work of association and to the regroupings that this work operates, replicates the construction of the dream process.

This brings us, then, to our object: the psycho-analytic reading of a tragedy, a reading situated in the potential space between text and representation. Here a question inevitably arises: how are we to understand the *jouissance* felt by the spectator of a tragedy, when the spectacle arouses pity and terror? This question brings us back to Aristotle's problem, for which Freud tried to provide a new answer. The work of art, says Freud, offers an 'incentive bonus' to whoever experiences it. 'We give the name of an *incentive bonus*, or a *fore-pleasure*, to a yield of pleasure such as this, which is offered to us so as to make possible the release of still greater pleasure arising from deeper psychical sources' (*S.E.*, IX, 153). There is a discharge, then, but it is a partial discharge, desexualized by aim-inhibition and displacement of sexual pleasure. But we still have to account for the effect of tragedy.

How may we extend or replace the hypothesis of catharsis as a purging of the passions? Tragedy certainly gives pleasure, but pleasure tinged with pain: a mixture of terror and pity. But there is no tragedy without a tragic hero, that is, without an idealized projection of an ego that finds here the satisfaction of its megalomaniac designs. The hero is the locus of an encounter between the power of the bard, who brings the phantasy to life, and the desire of the spectator, who sees his phantasy embodied and represented. The spectator is the ordinary person to whom nothing of importance happens. The hero is the man who lives through exceptional adventures in which he performs his exploits, and who, in the last resort, must pay the gods dearly for the power he acquires in this way. Becoming a demi-god, he enters into competition with the gods, and so must be crushed by them, thus assuring the triumph of the father.

The spectator's pleasure will be compounded of his movement of identification with the hero (pity, compassion) and his masochistic movement (terror). Every hero, and therefore every spectator, is in the position of the son in the Oedipal situation: the son must become (move towards being) like the father. He must be brave and strong, but he must not do everything the father does. He must show proper respect for the father's prerogatives (his *having*), namely those of paternal power, sexual possession of the mother, and physical power, the right of life and death over his children. In this respect, the father, even when dead, indeed especially when dead, sees this power still further increased in the beyond: totem and taboo.

Tragedy, then, is the representation of the phantasy myth of the Oedipus complex, which Freud identified as the constitutive complex of the subject. Thus the frontiers between the 'normal' individual, the neurotic and the hero became blurred in the subjective structure that is the subject's relation to his progenitors. The encounter between myth and tragedy is obviously not fortuitous. First, because every history, whether it is individual or collective, is based on a myth. In the case of the individual, this myth is known as phantasy. Second, because Freud himself includes myth in the psycho-analytic field: 'It seems quite possible to apply the psycho-analytic views derived from dreams to products of ethnic imagination such as myths and fairy-tales' (*S.E.*, xiii, 185). (In his study of the structure of myths, Lévi-Strauss refers to the myth, without further explanation, as an 'absolute object'.) Freud rejects the traditional interpretation of myths as mere attempts to explain natural phenomena, or as cult practices that have become unintelligible. It is highly likely that he would have much to say about the structuralist interpretation. For the essential function of these collective productions was, in Freud's view, the assuaging of unsatisfied or unsatisfiable desires. This is my interpretation too; it finds support in the foundations of the Oedipus complex, which forbids parricide and incest and so condemns the subject to seek other solutions if he is to satisfy these desires. Tragedy is, at a collective level, one of these substitute solutions. The psycho-analytic reading of tragedy, therefore, will have as its aim the mapping of the traces of the Oedipal structure concealed in its formal organization, through an analysis of the symbolic activity, which is masked from the spectator's perception and acts on him unknown to himself.

Freud and his successors

The three essays that have become the three chapters of this book belong to the tradition, established by Freud, of psycho-analytic criticism. Indeed, Freud is my major point of reference, a reference extended by the new developments that have given fresh life to

Freudian thought. It is well known that since Freud's death, psycho-analytic thinking which in his work formed an organically linked whole has been split into various, sometimes contradictory, polarities. Thus the theoretical contributions of Melanie Klein and Jacques Lacan[8] provide two antinomian faces of psycho-analysis.

In the present grouping of the psycho-analytic world, one must, if one is not to condemn oneself to sectarianism, choose the group that includes the others, if I may borrow Euler's image. So it is sometimes surprising to observe that the ensemble that includes other ensembles bears a strange resemblance to the body of doctrine formed by Freudian theory, which has the advantages of completeness and balance. If one claims to be returning to Freud, one is under an obligation to respect the totality of his thought.[9]

In studying tragedy, one should not pay undue attention to the combinatory of signifiers (representatives of the drive), at the expense of the role of the affect. It is here that the reading between text and representation avoids the drawbacks of a disembodied formalization (the combinatory) or of a subjective construct (the emotional power of the spectacle).[10] The analysis of the text will stress its formalization: the reference to the representation–spectacle will emphasize its quasi-visceral role as discharge. There is a long-standing opposition between those who write about tragedy and those who act it or see it acted. The psycho-analyst must be attentive to the *text in representation* or the *representation of a text.*

Writing and representation

We often hear it said that the work cannot be reduced to its significations. The constitution of the signified by the action of the signifier is undoubtedly its essential nature. That which seems to elude psycho-analytic investigation forces us here to recognize its limits. But it is often a study of the latent signified, the relation of the manifest to the latent, that is most likely to throw light on the form of the signifier at any given point. In the long succession of signifiers in linked sequence which constitutes the work, the unconscious signified rises between two signifiers from the gulf or absence in which it resides and determines the difference between the 'natural' form of discourse and its literary form – not in order to express what has to be said, but in order to indicate, by veiling it, what needs to be hidden.

My constant concern will be to show the double articulation of the theatrical phantasy: that of the scene, which takes place on the stage, and is given an ostensible significance for the spectator; and that of the other scene that takes place – although everything is said aloud and intelligibly and takes place in full view – unknown to the spectator, by means of this chain-like mode and its unconscious logic.

But where does the operation of writing enter into this? This, it might be objected, is where the specificity of the work is to be found.

What about Aeschylus, Shakespeare and Racine as writers? This brings us to some of the crucial questions of contemporary criticism. In literature, should we allow privilege to the signifier or the signified? Why, for whom does one write? Put like that, the question cannot be answered. Signifier and signified are *relata* that necessarily refer back to one another, since the segmentation of the one cannot but affect the other by the same division. What is at issue, then, is not so much which has precedence over the other as the nature of the relation between them.

The resistance to the signified that is becoming so strongly marked in the present state of criticism is a sign of rejection and mistrust. Because it has for too long been linked with 'psychology', the signified has, so to speak, run out of breath. It is obvious that the work is not merely the signified that it overlays: it is the work of formalization without which there can be no work of art, but merely an expression of intention. If the work were merely what it signifies, what difference would there be between writing as literature and the writing of a treatise on psychology, a political manifesto or an advertising brochure? But this reference back to the specificity of the literary conceals a suspicion about the signified – especially, as I have said, if this signified is that of psycho-analysis.

It has recently been objected that psycho-analysis has turned away from 'the becoming literary of the literal' (Derrida, 340). The originality of the literary signifier appears to have been misunderstood by psycho-analytic criticism which, for the most part, remains an 'analysis of literary, or rather, non-literary signifieds'. Although it is true that literature sets out to be an exploration through the practice of the possibilities of language, it stumbles sooner or later upon the unspoken aspect of the work, on what we now call its 'unreadability', as the navel-cord from which it draws all its strength. Nothing appears to be external to this writing, whose links with representation have been undone. But what if writing *is* representation, as in the theatre? Do we not find here a defeat for that ambition, always present in non-theatrical literary forms, the ambition to be free of all direct reference to representation? It is facile to say that a literary statement can only refer to the whole body of other statements. This evident fact is meaningful only because every text demonstrates in this way the distance between itself and its object, in the process of once more traversing that distance. The object at which it is directed can never be embodied in any text; yet what emerges from this confrontation is not an endless dizzy round of texts, but the absence that inhabits them all. This is the absence of the work summing up all other texts, and cancelling them out by occupying the space of the written text, which has no difference, which is unique, which recovers the unity of the past and renders all further effort vain. This body of the letter is distilled from the text only to return to it in the representation of the nature and elements of writing. (And if there is a whole literature exploiting the artifices of representation, punctuation, layout and the addition of non-written signs, is it not precisely in order to displace one kind of unsaid and replace it by another? If one wishes to serve the text, one must first ask oneself in what service the text is supposed to be acting. To whom does the text speak? Who speaks through the text?) This is proof, if proof were needed, that the process of literature is not to become the stigmata of the relation between writing and representation, but to establish the relation between two systems of representation, writing's system of representation being unable to take any other way than that of the representation of the non-represented in representation.

There is much to be said about this operation of the non-represented: this book is an attempt to say something about it. But it should be clear that it is in the *absence of representation* that this operation is carried out and not in a deliverance from representation. The way in which certain literary 'integrists' make use of Freud's writings does not always reveal a clear understanding of them. If one wishes to refer to a 'trace', rather than to a signifier/signified opposition, how can the trace obstruct every relation with representation – even in the diastem, the spacing and the difference that call it into being? The confusion between the unrepresentable and the non-represented seems to be the source of errors of interpretation. Not that the two are unrelated. The non-represented refers us back to the sense of lack that obtrudes in the 'too full' of any representation; in its plenitude, this representation tries to block the outlet, because it is itself the result of the pressure of this lack, which can still be traced in it. The fact that this lack is at the origin of the unrepresentability of the process of writing refers back all the more inevitably to the non-representable, because it is blocked, of the non-represented. The trace maintains itself between the threat of being worn away – so causing the collapse of the whole signifying system – and its own persistence, which is revelatory of its nature, if only through reference back to all the other traces of the thing that it reveals or rather distorts as it unveils. This revelation is not continuous with its own nature, but is caught up in another web, in another texture. 'In its implications the distortion of a text resembles a murder: the difficulty is not perpetrating the deed, but getting rid of its traces' *(S.E.,* xxiii,

43). The great virtue of the concept of 'trace' is that it provides an opposition to the notion of language as a presence in itself: for it points to an absence in language. It is this absence inhabiting language that is revealing; without being confused with a materialization of the lack, absence conveys the lack in its effect and makes it possible to sustain a discourse on this absence and not to cement the identity of absence and non-existence.[11]

Yet, despite the many attempts to eliminate it from discourse, one still finds representation elsewhere, for instance in ideology, short-circuiting the individual signified. The desire to prevent creative subjectivity from being a fetish and to merge writing into the impersonality of the revolutionary movement is praiseworthy enough in its modesty. It shows us above all that 'readability' is easier when, overleaping several mediations, it is dissolved in the social body. If psycho-analysis, in centring its attention on the signified, has overleapt the mediations of the literary, we have now to say that literary 'integrism', forced by its own process to challenge a literally repressed signified, conceives no mediation between literature and ideology. Despite its overt professions, this 'integrism' reduces the value of the passion of writing, of reading and of the power of repetition to engender both the process and the challenge to it. It falls into the same willed search for 'lucidity' that it condemns elsewhere. It thus cancels itself out, in the sense that it is its own debtor. What I deprecate in this approach is not, therefore, that it neglects the signified, but that it adopts too readily the thesis of an elusive signified. The unsaid is the absence of the signified, not its ungraspability. The effect of this absence is the condition of the investment produced by what the counter-investment keeps separate. In this respect, literary exchange is, like all exchange, an exchange of desire, with a view to a deferred, postponed *jouissance*.

The originality of the literary signified can only reside, therefore, at our level of exploration, in the literalness of the unsaid of the signified. This unsaid, whose effects are displaced on the occasion of the conjoint reading–writing of the literary product (since all writing is a reading and vice versa), will be established by a study of the relation between the manifest signified and the difference between the literary signifier and the ordinary signifier. This difference has the function of introducing the effect of deception by which the web of the latent signified is attracted, caught and held in its network. But this attempt never manages to make the two planes coincide and, at each reading–writing, the project fails and the difference is unveiled in the substitution in which something else is revealed. It is the constantly renewed and never successful attempt which replicates the difference between the ordinary signifier and the literary signifier (a difference that is supposed to imprison what refuses to be named in the manifest) through the genre, construction and organization of the work. Repetition hollows out the bed in which this disparity must be filled and, by rendering it more perceptible, apprehends it. Theatrical representation multiplies this difference between the ordinary signifier and the literary signifier by stressing all the non-literary signifiers, the physical means at the disposal of the actor: prosody, phrasing, use of the body, which are here not only seen but exploited – one can see how it is, in fact, almost as much a duplication of difference as an increase of it. It is this time-lag in the oppositions between the signifiers of language (ordinary and literary) and the non-linguistic signifiers that serve, as it were, as a transmission belt for another duplication, that of the opposition between the spoken words of the play and its staging in scenes, acts, and so on.

The other side of the Oedipus complex

My approach, then, has led me to place the Oedipus complex in the forefront of my psycho-analytic reading of tragedy, in the signifier/signified relation or the analysis of the trace, since in the last resort every text springs from a murder (of the father), carried out with the intention of obtaining pleasure, sexual possession (of the mother). This is the radical, some would say imperialist, conclusion to which I am led.

The Oedipus complex is generally known in the form of the positive Oedipus complex of the boy: rivalry with the father leading to parricidal wishes and to a desire for the mother to the point of its incestuous fulfilment – extreme forms whose expression is represented only in the unconscious. But, from 1923 onwards, Freud showed the existence in each individual of a double Oedipus complex, both positive and negative (the second being the reverse of the first). These two terms each occupy one end of the chain, of which only traces, which have survived repression, remain. The girl is subjected to the same structure as the boy. As a result, the human being of either sex carries within, by the very fact of human bisexuality, a double identification, masculine and feminine: the seal of Oedipus. It follows, therefore, that the Oedipus complex is at least quadruple – positive and negative, masculine and feminine – for each individual.

Where the application of psycho-analysis to works of art usually concerns the positive Oedipus complex in the boy, that is to say, the situation of rivalry with the father and love for the mother, the three chapters of this book take as their focus of study the relation of hostility between son and mother, husband and wife, father and daughter. I have chosen three examples: the *Oresteia* of Aeschylus, the only trilogy in the full sense that has come down to us from ancient Greece, Shakespeare's *Othello* and Racine's *Iphigénie en Aulide.*

Each of these three chapers was written individually, independently of the others, yet together they form a whole whose parts are interdependent. On the one hand, the subject matter of these essays was taken from the tragic stock of western civilization (ancient tragedy, Elizabethan tragedy, classical tragedy). On the other hand, the themes of which these works speak all relate to one aspect or another of the Oedipus complex.

The *Choephori* in Aeschylus' *Oresteia* and the two *Electras* by Sophocles and Euripides make us witnesses of the murder of the mother by the son. Shakespeare's *Othello* shows us the murder of the wife by the husband, Racine's *Iphigénie en Aulide* the murder of the daughter by the father.

These thematic relations are modified, of course, by the differences inherent in the three texts, for they are separated by varying periods of time, and their tragic forms are set in contexts quite dissimilar from the sociological, historical and aesthetic point of view. But we know that these works extend well beyond these particular determinations and still concern us today.

I have tried not to force the works into a prefabricated mould. In each case, I have allowed myself to be guided by the context. Thus Aeschylus' *Oresteia* has dictated the comparison between the three ancient tragedians – especially as it gives us a unique opportunity, given what has come down to us of ancient tragedy, of comparing the treatment of the same theme by Aeschylus, Sophocles and Euripides. This led me to compare the tragic myths of Oedipus and Orestes and to study their relations.

In the case of *Othello*, on the other hand, I have confined myself to an intrinsic study, without going beyond the frontiers of the tragedy. I have concentrated on the internal arrangement of its parts and examined the node of forces represented by its characters, studied the distribution of the feelings of love and hate in the relations between Ares and Eros, between Eros and the death drive.

Lastly, *Iphigénie en Aulide* suggested a double study. While the *Oresteia* led me to an approach that might, roughly speaking, be called synchronic, *Iphigénie* offered a diachronic comparison between ancient tragedy and classical tragedy, between Euripides and Racine – especially since Euripides wrote in one year his last two plays, *Iphigenia in Aulis* and *The Bacchae*, which mark the end of ancient tragedy. The murder of a daughter by a father in the name of human sacrifice is balanced by the murder of a son by his mother

– Pentheus killed by Agaüe in the course of a Dionysiac orgy. Ancient tragedy ends with the myths of its origins. The matricide with which we began brings us, at the end of the course, to maternal infanticide. The circle is thus closed.

The eye too many

This prologue is longer than it should have been, but it has, I believe, its own necessity. It was not the place for an exposition of the psycho-analytic conception of the work of art, of the bases of psycho-analytic criticism on which my psycho-analytic reading of the tragedies is based. I could not avoid discussion of certain tendencies in the work of literary theoreticians, who zealously guard the special character of the literary, while denying the role of desire in the production and consumption of literature. And yet the task of the psycho-analyst is not to convince: he would succumb to the illusions of the conscious if he pretended not to understand the role of the obstacles that are set up to the admission of the unconscious into the conscious. This is hardly important. What we find it difficult to forgive King Oedipus, the neurotic, the artist and, for that matter, the psycho-analyst – and what they cannot forgive each other – is having *one eye too many*.

I

Orestes and Oedipus
from the oracle to the law[1]

> But that they make their processions and sing their phallic
> hymns in honour of Dionysus, they would be committing the
> gravest sacrilege. He who rules Hades and Dionysus are one
> god, who afflicts them with frenzy and for whom they celebrate
> the festival of the wine harvest.
>
> Heraclitus

Psycho-analytic hermeneutics and tragedy

Who is qualified to write about tragedy? We have the Hellenist or
the philologist, concerned with literal accuracy, mistrustful of any
interpretation that sacrifices accuracy in an attempt to re-establish a
full meaning, which even today remains obscure: we have the tragic
actor concerned in his interpretation to convey the tragic emotion to
his audience without passing through the labyrinth of sterilizing
criticism. Is there, between these two, a place for a psycho-analytic
commentator, sharing with the other two the common ground of
hermeneutics – a hermeneutics that would neglect neither of these
poles to the exclusive benefit of the other? The psycho-analyst would
strive, then, to rediscover that letter and that flesh of tragedy reunited within his own truth. Was not this what Freud was aiming at?
On 15 October 1897, he wrote to Wilhelm Fliess, a witness of his
self-analysis:

I have found love of the mother and jealousy of the father in my own case
too, and now believe it to be a general phenomenon of early childhood...
If that is the case, the gripping power of *Oedipus Rex*, in spite of all the
rational objections to the inexorable fate that the story presupposes, becomes intelligible...Every member of the audience was once a budding
Oedipus in phantasy, and this dream-fulfilment played out in reality
causes everyone to recoil in horror, with the full measure of repression
which separates his infantile from his present state.   (Freud, 1954, 223–4)

If psycho-analysis owes a huge debt to tragedy, it is by virtue of
this bequest. It may even feel it was founded in order to attempt to
unveil, to those who feel themselves implicated in the effects of the
tragic feeling, the ways and means by which this feeling operates.
This investigation, then, might well set off not by the ways of
analysis of the spectator, but by those of the semantic articulations of
tragedy.

It will become clear that the point of view I have adopted is not that of the study of a literary genre – though I intend to return to the consequences of this passage from epic narrative to tragic representation. Nor will it concern the relations between an author and his work – there is no credit in resisting this particular temptation, given the paucity of the information. And however fruitful it might be to consider the function of tragedy in the social context from which it emerged, or the study of its relations with the birth of democracy, or its relations with the sequelae of the Orphic religion or the Eleusinian mysteries, I shall adopt none of these approaches. However illuminating those approaches may be that try to restore in the collective reality the movements of a society becoming conscious of itself through its own achievements, and creating its institutions in order to achieve that consciousness, they leave on one side both the deeper meaning of these movements and the specificity of the tragic phenomenon in its relation to the subject.

Is not the main problem that of knowing precisely how tragedy converted myth into spectacle?

Psycho-analysis has felt more drawn to Greek civilization than to any other, and this is understandable. This period seems to move into and occupy a gap, the Judeo-Christian interval, and perhaps illuminates this interval retrospectively. And at no other period in history have men thrown more light, through their projected divinities, on to the concrete issues of desire: struggles to the death for possession of a woman, betrayal of a lover's oaths, the grief and wounds of lost love, ruthless struggle to the death against a respected adversary, the conflict between the indissolubility of alliances in common sacrifice and envy at the moment of sharing brilliant conquests, the quest for power and the desire for its recognition as shown in the wearing of its insignia, the challenge to the foundations of divine and human law, courageous lucidity at the point of death, the opposition between the duties of the heart and of the law, the overreaching drive that sends the hero on his quest – constantly baffled – for the truth, or for some illumination that either recedes or devastates...In all this proliferation of myths, tragedy is one way of decanting them: it leaves them to settle and fixes them in a particular form. It is not by approaching the problem frontally, in general terms, that I shall reach the answer that the means at my disposal permit. But by putting these means into practice, I shall show that the discovery to which they lead is revelatory of that truth, because it too uses these means, both to express itself and to conceal itself from us.

Underneath this proliferation of themes, tragedy forces us to choose and to recognize in the ones that have constellated into tragedy those that have formative value. For the psycho-analyst, the

cycles of Argos and Thebes are the models to start from. There seems
to be nothing in the tragic writers themselves to sanction this choice.
Yet the work of Aeschylus, Sophocles and Euripides, creative as it
was, did not escape the *méconnaissance*[2] that marks every subject in
respect of the signifier he utters.

So I suppose I must justify this choice if I am not to be thought
arbitrary. It is not to say that other situations have less interest, or
are valuable only as pale reflections of these primal themes, or simply
that the *Oedipodeia* and the *Oresteia* constitute essential, fundamental models in which the problematic of all tragedy – and perhaps
of all human endeavour – is situated. The other tragic situations are
certainly as moving and effective, and this emotion and effectiveness
are bound up with the way in which the problems they refer to are
treated – and they are treated with the greatest possible coherence.
But, in the last resort, analysis would show that beyond the particular
case they represent, they are joined to the common trunk of those
tragic primal situations. Does not Aristotle in his *Poetics* regard the
family as the tragic milieu *par excellence*? Are not kinship relations
those in which the emotions of the spectator are mobilized to produce
the strongest effects through the violence of the contrast between love
and hate? Is it not logical, then, to consider that among all the tragic
situations those of the *Oresteia* and the *Oedipodeia* have a special
paradigmatic value, since their principal theme is centred on the
relations between progenitors, or relations between progenitors and
their offspring? (When sociology sets out to explain the foundations
of creative forms, it is bound to come up against its own limits.
So when J.-P. Vernant traces the origins of Greek thought through
the various social structures of Greek history, and accounts for the
birth of philosophy at this or that particular stage, he is necessarily
brought finally to the concept of power, its material and moral expressions, its symbolism even – or rather, above all – for the most
primitive and fundamental forms of social structure. How, then, can
we avoid, in all the various forms in which power is embodied –
tribal, clan, or democratic – the question of family structure and the
function of the father?)

The psycho-analyst feels on his own ground here. To ask oneself
whether kinship relations constitute the tragic or whether the tragic
elucidates these kinship relations may be meaningless, formulated in
that way. Let us say rather that they reveal something essential about
the subjectivity that is inseparable from the tragic, by uncovering
the relation of the subject to his progenitors, or that the study of these
relations may be fully conceived only in the context of the tragic, so
revealing its role as constituent of subjectivity. I shall attempt to
show this.

The thematics of the *Oedipodeia* and of the *Oresteia*

> He [Oedipus], who had the power to unlock the riddle of the
> Sphinx, and he too who trusted with childlike confidence
> [Orestes], are, therefore, both sent to destruction by what the
> god reveals to them.
>
> Hegel, 740

Just because the *Oedipodeia* and the *Oresteia* both deal with questions of kinship, there would be no reason, *a priori*, to set up between them coherent relations of opposition, other than on the basis of their thematic differences.

Oedipus commits parricide and incest, Orestes commits matricide and champions the cause of his father. In the *Oresteia*, the mother does not commit incest, but is the agent of the parricide. In short, both situations focus on the study of triangular relationships, of the subject's relation to his progenitors. So it is hardly surprising that studying this comparison reveals an opposition so deep that it is more properly to be considered as a 'complementarity'.

In fact, everything seems to set up Oedipus and Orestes in an opposition, beyond themselves, which reflects the different fates accorded to the Labdacides and the Atrides. The race of Atreus not only reaps misfortune through the operation of fate; it actually provokes it and brings it upon itself. At Argus they dream of nothing but vengeance, expiation, murder and sacrilege. Agamemnon is the king who utterly destroys Troy, taking arrogant pride in the annihilation of the conquered city and the destruction of its gods. Clytemnestra is drunk with hate, even in her dreams; Electra is possessed of an inextinguishable thirst for vengeance; Orestes can perform his duty only by shedding blood for blood. If he allows the crime of the murder of his father to go unpunished, he will be prey to the most terrible evils. When Clytemnestra has murdered her husband, she expresses no feelings of repentance:

> This is my husband, Agamemnon, now stone dead;
> His death the work of my right hand, whose craftsmanship
> Justice acknowledges   (Aeschylus, *Agamemnon*, 91)

Orestes has only one moment of hesitation before he plunges the dagger into his mother's breast. And when the impending victim realizes that persuasion cannot save her, she threatens her son with pitiless retaliation. Cruel feelings are not always put into the mouths of particularly black characters. They are the language of exchanges with no half-measures, of exorbitant demand, all-consuming and never satisfied.

Oedipus and his ancestors, on the other hand, deflect evil away

UNIVERSITY OF WINNIPEG
LIBRARY
515 Portage Avenue
Winnipeg, Manitoba, R3B 2E9

from them. By sending the accursed son far away, the parents hope
to prevent the oracle from being fulfilled. Oedipus himself leaves
Corinth, his adopted country, because he has been warned by the
gods of the threat that lies in wait for him and which he believes
hangs over his supposed parents, Polybus and Merope. So he takes
the direction opposite to the one in which, he thinks, misfortune
awaits him; but in doing so he meets his destiny. When the presump-
tion of the crime begins to become clear, he goes straight to the truth
and pursues his investigation even when the accusing finger seems to
point at himself, without despairing of freeing the city of which he is
king from the sufferings that beset it. Oedipus struggles against the
traps, the double meanings, the false evidence, the guilt attributed to
others for the crime of which he is unwittingly guilty, and is not
deceived by Jocasta's soothing assurances.

The *Oedipodeia* is a centrifugal myth. Just as misfortune must be
diverted by exile from the home in which it is threatened, so, once
the misfortune has occurred, the truth that must bring deliverance
from it is sought elsewhere, outside its territory: at Delphi, the seat
of Apollo; at Corinth, where Oedipus has spent his youth and where
the first suspicions concerning his true descent are aroused; at
Cithaeron, the presumed place of his death. Only after these de-
partures from the centre, on which he is accompanied part of the
way by the fellow-travellers, Creon, the messenger from Corinth, and
the shepherd who took him from the hands of his parents, is the truth
finally brought back to its nodal point: that of the double sin, produced by a birth that should never have taken place.

The *Oresteia* is a centripetal myth: everything takes place at the
centre, in the home. Agamemnon and Orestes return to their native
city from war or exile. The first is assassinated in his palace, the
second vows himself to vengeance over the dead man's funeral pyre
and fulfils the vow by committing matricide in the same place as the
regicide and as expiation of it. There is no intermediary here between
the protagonists, and no disguising of the truth. Only cunning is
needed to execute the crimes once planned.

These two images suggest two types of movement in the unconscious. In the first, the repressed undergoes constant displacements that
remove the expression of its content ever further away in its distortions and disguises. In the second, on the other hand, the unconscious
is presented with unusual transparency, as the bearer of an excess of
signification; so what is ordinarily veiled or minimized is expressed
with a crudity that suggests some defect in its symbolization.

These differences are to be found in the situation of the two heroes.
Orestes acts in full consciousness, under pressure from Apollo whose
instrument he wishes to be, carrying out his murder in all lucidity.

Oedipus, on the other hand, is the plaything of *méconnaissance* and is unaware of the implications of his acts, both when he commits the parricide at the crossing of the Thebes and Daulis roads and when he commits incest in the royal bed. At the end of its course, the tragic action reserves very different fates for each of the heroes when the mission of the first and the investigation of the second are completed. Orestes imposes on himself the sight of images of terror: he is hallucinated and persecuted by the 'bitches', the Erinnyes set on him by his mother. Oedipus pierces his own eyes, inflicting blindness on himself. Thus the dénouement is carried out in opposite ways. Orestes is acquitted by the court of Athens, after Athene has admitted that she is too unsure of her divine judgement and calls on the opinion of the wise men of the city to settle the conflict between son and mother. This acquittal has the value, it has been shown, of a rebirth. Oedipus, on the other hand, after expiating beyond all due measure the pollution he brought with him, finds peace in his death; for the gods call it down upon him in the wood sacred to those same Erinnyes who had been persuaded by Athene, after the case that they lost against Orestes, to transform themselves into the Eumenides, beneficent goddesses who protect the city.

Nothing sums up these different problematics so well as the confrontation of two key characters, mediators between men and gods, used to dealing with the gods and capable of conveying their will: Cassandra and Teiresias. Cassandra, made captive by the leader of the Atrides, is weighed down by the love she dared to refuse Apollo. She was given the gift of foresight and prophecy, but punished in this very gift, since her prophecies were doomed to go unheeded, which makes a sterile woman of her. What Apollo punishes in Cassandra is the desire that she will cease to inspire, that is, the desire to know. No prophecy is acceptable for him who does not expect a fortunate outcome from belief in the power of the Other. All that remains to the prophetess – she who went back on a promise of love – is to accept the sacrifice from the hands of another woman, Clytemnestra, who also breaks the oath that binds her to her husband, but carries her refusal of the man to the point of crime.

Teiresias, whose blindness prefigures the blindness that Oedipus will later inflict upon himself, is a magus honoured in the city, living in the shadow of power, guarded in the counsel he offers. He dispenses sparingly and hesitantly the truth he holds in his hand. He knows and is silent. He ponders 'both that which can be taught, and that which is forbidden to human lips', but he is well aware that 'when wisdom brings no profit, / To be wise is to suffer' (Sophocles, *King Oedipus*, 34). And when he does speak, it is only to become the target of Oedipus' accusations; his utterance produces an image of

Oedipus in which the latter wishes only to see a stranger, in which he refuses to recognize himself. The seer says to him:

> You are pleased to mock my blindness. Have you eyes,
> And do not see your own damnation? (Sophocles, *King Oedipus*, 37)

That is to say, you criticize the instinct that guides me, when you cannot see that which is in your own heart, and yet you blame me.

For Orestes, as for Oedipus, the seer belongs to an older generation. Cassandra is his father's companion, she will announce at the moment of her death the future return of Orestes seeking revenge. Teiresias, challenged by Oedipus, will denounce the power of the tyrant by appealing to his own parents' recognition of his merits. The message of truth that proceeds from their lips comes to light after following a very different route. Cassandra speaks unbidden and confirms the authenticity of her power – 'Do I miss? Or has my arrow found a mark you know?' (Aeschylus, *Agamemnon*, 84) – a power that tears away the veil of consciousness in a prophetic trance of which it may be said that she lays bare the future only to throw herself ineluctably into death. It is particularly striking that Cassandra should deliver the substance of her prophecy in a lyrical passage in which she converses with the chorus in a sort of chant. When the lyrical episode comes to an end, the scene starts again 'from scratch', in a spoken interchange, as if nothing had been said, and as if, for the tenor of her prophecy at least to be understood if not accepted, it was necessary to go over once again all the allusions, the gropings and the complications necessary to a true account.

Teiresias is sent for, praised, questioned, ordered to dispel the mystery of the past for the good of all. He declines to speak, he is evasive, he speaks allusively, brushes aside the threats and attacks, and delivers up the truth only under the immunity he enjoys from the god's protection.

There is a double face of prophecy here, a double image of the unconscious. The first is its ruptures, its fragmentations, its spontaneous upsurge, its total unveiling and annihilation, the penalty for betraying an oath to the god. The second is its retreat from the place where its mysteries and its silences, its false trails, its situation in the wake of the god must emerge. This diptych closes upon itself, and one cannot say what is hidden behind these masks. It is revealed to us only through them. But it is as if a deeper cohesion unites each of these expressions with the messages they utter, as if the code of the secret can only be negated or rejected; negated by its own abrupt unveiling, so that the subject who sees or hears what is offered to him may stand aside when he has heard what he came to hear – those who listen to Cassandra behave as if they had neither eyes nor ears;

rejected precisely because of its uncertainties, its obscurities, its
incoherences. From the logical point of view, all Oedipus' reasons
have more substance than Teiresias' absurd prophecy. How could the
blind man know more than him who can see? That he does is
revealed in one question, which the prophet is bound to ask, though
not in so many words: 'Who is speaking?' What he actually asks is:
'Do you simply know whose son you are?'

It is as if a prophecy, however shrewd it may be, which falls short
of any desire, any demand, is inevitably diverted to the annihilation
of the content of the message, of the speaker or of the receiver.
And the man who questions or seeks awaits the answer to the
question asked, but can only, on receiving it, reject it when it proves
contrary to his desire. This double dilemma reminds us of the un-
knowability of the unconscious and the necessity of apprehending it
by the very modes through which it expresses the secret of its utterance.

It is surely no coincidence that the truth should come in the
Oresteia from the lips of a woman and in the *Oedipodeia* from the
lips of a man. We are bound to note the respective roles played by
the two sexes in the two cycles.

The *Oedipodeia* is a tragic cycle in which men play the more
important part. Apart from the episode of the Sphinx and the incest,
which is presented, as has been pointed out, as a consequence of the
parricide, it is the relations between the men that matter most.
The primal sin was committed by Laius who received an oracle from
Apollo. Oedipus was saved by the shepherd. The question addressed
to the supposed son of Polybus concerning his origins comes from a
man who has drunk too much. The parricide is committed in the
course of a brawl. At the investigation only male witnesses are called
upon and, during this investigation, we see a new conflict reproduced
between Oedipus and Creon. Oedipus' life is saved only because he is
protected by Theseus, a hero like himself, who receives him and
defends him against his own sons. The final episode of Oedipus' life
sets him in conflict with them; the father curses his male descendants.
His line will die out in a fratricidal struggle.[3]

In the *Oresteia*, everything proceeds from the women. It was
Helen's infidelity that was the first cause of the disastrous process of
retribution; as a result, a terrible power is conferred on female
seductiveness. It is a goddess, Artemis, reproaching the Achaeans for
wishing to exterminate a city that she compares to a pregnant doe
pursued by bloodthirsty eagles, who holds the fleet at Aulis and
demands a virgin in sacrifice if the expedition is to go on and succeed.
The rancour left by the memory of this daughter sacrificed to
paternal ambition, and the jealousy aroused by the concubine who

serves his royal pleasure excite the hate of the mother and wife. Clytemnestra is, undoubtedly, the central figure of the trilogy, the only character present in each of its three parts. Although Orestes is the executioner in the murder that deprives her of life, it is Electra who puts the weapon in his hand, the daughter's aversion for her mother being greater than the son's. The persecutory divinities who pursue Orestes are female divinities, worshipped only by women. Lastly, at the trial, it is a woman, the favourite daughter of Zeus, who settles the debate and acquits the guilty man.

The *Oedipodeia* rises gradually towards the light; the *Oresteia* is imbued with the power of darkness, as Clémence Ramnoux has shown:

Night also lives in the human imagination between an archaic phantasy of the mother in her splendour, regal, endowed with magical powers, and a theological notion as sophisticated as the secret of the ineffable...There is some uncertainty as to her rank in the sacred texts: was she originally the first or the second? Is she the universal mother of those men or the mother of a generation apart? In a later, much more refined intellectual register, night comes to designate the unapprehensible thing, the thing that forms no longer manifest and which names can no longer express.

Ramnoux, 23; see especially the chapter devoted to the
Orestia, 109–54

So there are a number of arguments in favour of the view that this confrontation is a fruitful one, that these two tragic myths may be seen not side by side, but face to face, in a mirror relation. A more rigorous analysis must derive from this framework of generalities. In order to examine the problems of the duality or unity of these two tragic myths – of their identity and their difference – I shall now leave the comparison between the two cycles and analyse in greater detail the structure of the one that has received less attention from psycho-analysts. In this way, we may be better able to avoid preconceived ideas. What stands out as odd in the work may well have a more familiar resonance to our psycho-analytic ears.

The function of the dream in the *Oresteia*

Till Zeus the Pleader came to trial
And crowned Persuasion with success.   (Aeschylus, *Eumenides*, 179)

I

The *Oresteia* falls into three main movements: the murder of Agamemnon, Orestes' revenge through matricide, the verdict of the Athenian court. Now, although the *Oresteia* as a complete trilogy is the work of Aeschylus alone, its central movement was treated by all three tragic writers. Aeschylus' *The Choephori*, and the two *Electras* by Sophocles and Euripides form, therefore, a new synchronic trilogy, a grouping specially apt for a comparison of the thought of the three authors and for an analysis of the treatment of a tragic theme. This case is as remarkable as it is unique: there is no other instance of such a situation. I shall not make a comparative analysis of the three plays: this would be beyond my competence and has already been done by a number of Hellenists. But I must not miss the opportunity to make a structural study of a theme of particular concern to the psycho-analyst, that of matricide, especially since it is introduced in a way that is of particular concern to us.

The sign that warns the protagonists and the spectators that the threads of the central movement are being woven together is the account of Clytemnestra's dream. We have two versions of this dream, that of Aeschylus and that of Sophocles. Significantly Euripides, reshaping the development of the action, ignores it: and this absence is itself an element of comparison whose importance will emerge from the comparison between the dreams as imagined by Aeschylus and Sophocles.

Let us look at the dream in Aeschylus. We learn of it through a series of questions and answers between Orestes and the chorus, female slaves from the palace in which Clytemnestra reigns, who bring libations of wine to offer at the tomb:

> ORESTES: Did you ask what the dream was? Can you describe it clearly?
> CHORUS: She told us herself. She dreamt that she gave birth to a snake.
> ORESTES: What followed? Or was that all? Tell me the point of it.
> CHORUS: She wrapped it in shawls and lulled it to rest like a little child.
> ORESTES: Surely this new-born monster needed food – what food?
> CHORUS: She herself, in her dream, gave it her breast to suck.
> ORESTES: Her nipple surely was wounded by its loathsome fang?
> CHORUS: Yes; with her milk the creature drew forth clots of blood.
> ORESTES: This dream was sent. It came from her husband, Agamemnon.
> CHORUS: She screamed out in her sleep, and woke in a fit of trembling;
> And through the palace many lamps, that the dark had dimmed,
> Flared up to reassure her. Immediately she sends
> Libations, hoping to purge this poison at its source.
> ORESTES: I pray, then, to this earth that holds my father's bones,
> That the dream's meaning may be thus fulfilled in me.
> As I interpret, point by point it fits. Listen:

> First, if this snake came forth from the same place as I,
> And, as though human, was then wrapped in infant clothes,
> Its gaping mouth clutching the breast that once fed me;
> If it then mingled the sweet milk with curds of blood,
> And made her shriek with terror – why, it means that she
> Who nursed this obscene beast must die by violence;
> *I* must transmute my nature, be viperous in heart and act!
> The dream commands it: I am her destined murderer.
>
> (Aeschylus, *Choephori*, 122–3)

If we turn to the corresponding passage in Sophocles, here Electra's sister Chrysothemis tells of her mother's dream:

> I was told she saw our father returned to life,
> Standing beside her; and he took the sceptre
> That once was his, which now Aegisthus carries,
> And planted it near the altar, where it sprouted
> Into a leafy bough, casting a shadow
> Over all Mycenae. This much I was told
> By someone who heard her telling the Sun her dream.
>
> (Sophocles, *Electra*, 81)

At first sight, the differences between the two versions seem quite marked. In Aeschylus, everything takes place in the dream between the mother and the symbol that represents the son, the snake, in a striking relation in which one can at once note:

1. the circular, closed space of this relation: the child emerges from the womb only to take the breast and destroy both breast and womb;

2. the limitation of the sphere represented in the maternal body: womb–breast;

3. the absence of any allusion to the father;

4. the absence of any allusion to kingship, to the city;

5. the termination of the dream by the mortal wound in the union;

6. the direct, raw aspect of the events represented symbolically.

Sophocles relates the same event in a very different way; the overt contents are opposed at every point:

1. the airy space of the relation: the open place of the stage;

2. the disengagement from any corporal attachment;

3. the presence of the father and the allusion to his rival, Aegisthus;

4. the manifestation of the father in the insignia of kingship;

5. the termination of the dream by the evocation of a birth and of the development of a power that concerns the city;

6. the indirect and veiled character of the events represented symbolically.

Finally, we note that the Aeschylean dream is constructed piece by piece in the crossfire of questions and answers, and that its signification, deciphered by the two antagonists, is immediately perceived. But the Sophoclean dream interposes an intermediary narrative and witnesses, and these are successive links at the end of which it takes form as text.

This confrontation shows us, if it were necessary, that oppositions cannot be attributed solely to differences of tragic temperament between the two authors. They are the sign of a change of values in the meaning supported by the dream-signifiers in the two tragic actions.

II

One observation stands out if one compares the tragic myths of Oedipus and Orestes. In the first, the dream plays no role. (We can ignore Jocasta's attempt to shrug off guilt by saying:

> Nor need this mother-marrying frighten you;
> Many a man has dreamt as much. Such things
> Must be forgotten, if life is to be endured.

> (Sophocles, *King Oedipus*, 52)

This dream is subject to a double negation. First, it signifies nothing; second, when the plot reveals that incest has taken place, it is the result not of an unconscious desire that has found expression despite the subject's precautions, but of a misunderstanding. Note the ambiguity of the line, 'Nor need this mother-marrying frighten you', which may mean either that Oedipus is protected from punishment by his innocence or that he can continue with impunity.) The density of the action is concentrated around a search that is remarkable for the way in which the evidence is obtained and cross-checked. The crime from the past that Thebes is expiating through the plague epidemic is relegated to the confines of a repressed truth, as distant as the truths glimpsed in dreams. But it is through the bringing to light, the re-establishment of a past, lost meaning, reconstituted by the backward-looking investigation, that our interest in the hero and our compassion for him are sustained.

In the *Oresteia*, on the other hand, the reality of the dream is constantly attested, at least in Aeschylus. The text makes frequent reference to it. (There are, in order, the monologue of the watcher; the first dialogue between Clytemnestra and the chorus, in which the chorus imputes the news of the sacking of Troy to one of the queen's dreams; the scene of the return of Agamemnon, in which Clytemnestra recounts the dreams that have haunted her nights in her husband's absence, describing at length the misfortunes she believed he was suffering; lastly, the dream that we are now examining. Two 'equivalents' may be added to this list: Cassandra's inspired trances, which are very different from Teiresias' clear, precise predictions; and the beginning of *The Eumenides*, in which the apparition of Clytemnestra's ghost spurring on the Erinnyes represents in a fairly obvious way the projection on to the stage of Orestes' phantasy world.) It will be argued that nothing is more natural, given that Aeschylus is more interested in dreams than Euripides or Sophocles.[4]

But if the world of the dream finds its place most naturally in the work of Aeschylus, if it is best served by him as a native of Eleusis, the most mystical of tragic writers, it is also because he is as much at one with the myth of Orestes as Sophocles was later with the myth of Oedipus. Aeschylus' language, imbued as it is with the powers of darkness, finds in its very fibre the web in which the matricide is woven. The wish-fulfilment unfolds before our eyes, through the medium of an almost erotic style, in a language that seems to spring from the gut, and forces us to experience the whole *Oresteia* as a long nightmare. We participate in it at a sympathetic level as the movement of the tragic theme unfolds, as the meaning of the undertaking takes shape.

It seems that the *Oedipodeia* unfolds like an attempt to interpret a forgotten dream, in which each stage by which it is elucidated helps us also to recall it. The *Oresteia*, on the other hand, unfolds in the dimension of the dream itself, as the action actually takes place; when the dream itself is brought to the fore, what occurs is something like the commentary on what is being acted out on the other scene that the dreamer himself sometimes provides extemporaneously within the dream.

The moment of greatest tension in Aeschylus' *Oresteia*, the moment around which the rest of the trilogy is ordered, occurs when, throwing down their masks, Orestes and Clytemnestra speak their final dialogue. But the tragic emotion is not born only out of the horror of the crime that follows, the abomination that makes one shudder. It also has its source in the effect of resurgence, of renewal, found in the scene that has already taken place in the dream. The last words of the mother, who has bared her breast, not so much to arouse pity as to fascinate by arousing the most deeply buried impressions, is an exact replica of the image of the dream: 'Here is the snake I bore and fed' (Aeschylus, *Choephori*, 137). During this exchange, the partners let fly deeply wounding arrows at one another, as if the true martyrdom were not so much the death that is about to take place as the opportunity it affords the two participants of tearing each other to pieces. In this confusion, identities merge and images serve to convey the alternate desires of father, son and lover.

> CLYTEMNESTRA: My own child, see this breast:
> Here often your head lay, in sleep, while your soft mouth
> Sucked from me the good milk that gave you life and strength...
> ORESTES: Come on;
> I mean to kill you close beside him. While he lived
> You preferred him to my father. Sleep with him in death;
> For you love him, and hate the man you should have loved.
>
> (Aeschylus, *Choephori*, 136)

The image of the mother here provides only the support in which the objects of his desire serve to complete it. They are interchangeable figures: one of the terms of a relation in which the phallic character occupies the place of the other term.

But this dream is a dream of original bonds. In the crucial scene, Clytemnestra is identified by her son with the bad breast, with the breast that is refused or which is at the exclusive disposal of the other, at any rate with the breast which does not feel the lack of a child, for which the child is not the sign of the mother's lack. For his part, Orestes, in his own interpretation of the dream, recognizes himself as the bad object of the mother, that which reminds him of his castration. But, if we apply to him Melanie Klein's model of the division into good and bad objects, the split ego has attributed to it the same dichotomy and Orestes sees himself represented in the primal union that must bind him to the mother by the bad part of his ego, that which dissociates and destroys.

So Clytemnestra's dream and its 'simultaneous interpretation' by Orestes are welded together, as if they were parts of a shared phantasy.

This explains why a character who seems no more than a simple cog in the action – Cilissa, the nurse – is given an entire scene in which the most moving maternal feelings are expressed through her lips. She is obviously an image of healing, in contrast with the terrifying Clytemnestra. As the dispenser of the attentions that fulfil the child's most primitive needs, she moves us not only by her devotion, but because she can show that none of the activities of child-rearing can be isolated from a demand. The declarations of Clytemnestra and the nurse about Orestes' rearing contradict one another. When Clytemnestra tears open her dress in order to weaken Orestes' resolution, there can be no doubt that this is an act of seduction, in which she is seeking to arouse sexual temptations. The justification for her gesture –

My own child, see this breast:
Here often your head lay, in sleep, while your soft mouth
Sucked from me the good milk that gave you life and strength
(Aeschylus, *Choephori*, 136)

– sounds very like a lie; for Cilissa, who has no self-interest in the matter, has just said:

But my Orestes!. . .Bless his heart, he wore me out.
I reared him, took him new-born from his mother's arms.
(Aeschylus, *Choephori*, 130)

(Just possibly Clytemnestra is referring to pre-natal feeding, during pregnancy, when Orestes was still part of herself.) What must be received, if not exorcized, is the message that emanates from the object of those breasts:

Why, you understand,
A baby knows no better; you must nurse it, then,
Like a dumb animal, whatever way seems best.
A child in a cradle can't explain what troubles it;
Whether it wants to eat, to drink, or to make water,
A baby's inside takes no orders; it's too young.
Well, often I could tell; and often, too, I know,
I guessed it wrong; and then I'd have to wash his things,
For nurse and laundress both were the same pair of hands.
(Aeschylus, *Choephori*, 130–1)

Aeschylus goes straight to the point in referring – as if casually – to the constituent role of the recognition of demand and relating it to the desire of the person to whom it is addressed:

So I did double duty; yes, and I brought up
Orestes for his father.   (Aeschylus, *Choephori*, 131)

So there is no such thing as natural rearing; the child learns that he signifies, that he is not only the object of solicitude, but can also ask questions: beyond experience, he finds himself retrospectively structured as the subject for an Other. This preponderance of the Name-of-the-Father[5] grounds the subject in pre-verbal communication.

Aeschylus' *Oresteia* is thus pregnant with this dream, though it is entirely absent from the *Oedipodeia* and also from Euripides' *Electra*. How, then, are we to understand the situation of Sophocles' *Electra*, where the dream is absent from the work in spirit, but present in the letter? As we have seen, this letter is considerably altered in relation to that of Aeschylus. Although a certain mystery clouds Sophocles' *Oresteia*, it is no longer the enigmatic night-world in which the signs of the gods appear at any moment, pregnant with the past crimes and future misfortunes of the cursed family of Atreus. There is no secret here except the secret necessary and indispensable to any successful plot. The deep, hostile night of the Aeschylean world gives place to the brightness of day. This day arrives at last when the usurpers of Argos are overthrown by a conspiracy planned in all lucidity and with no particular invocation of the underworld, no attempt to obtain the protection of the dead father.

The whole of Sophocles' tragedy is constructed on a series of contrivances and surprises that contrast with the sobriety of Aeschylus' sparing use of artifice. The most curious example is the account of Orestes' death spoken by the tutor. The extreme beauty of the passage might suggest that the way the author develops the incident cannot be accounted for by mere psychological necessities: for example, in order to give greater credibility to this account by the circumstantial character of the evidence. Should we not see it, however, as an index-myth about the true nature of the character of Orestes? He becomes a perfect hero, spirited, combative, triumphing over his enemies (except for the last one, of course); in short, he is a conquering prince who will soon enter the fray to recover his lost rights, and is less preoccupied with the matricide than in recovering for Agamemnon's house the powers that are its prerogative. It is an interesting thought that the tutor, who plays an important part in the success of the plans of Agamemnon's children, may be seen as Sophocles' equivalent of Aeschylus' nurse.

These differences of atmosphere between the two works extend to the general development of the tragedy: there is a diminution of the role of the chorus, more characters, a more complicated plot, an emphasis on the psychology of the protagonists, a 'dramatization' of the tragic style, and so on: all the changes that occurred between 458 and 415 B.C., and which Nietzsche deplored in *The Birth of Tragedy*. (We know that it was Sophocles who introduced the third character. Aeschylus made use of this innovation in *The Eumenides*, but it is noticeable that in *Agamemnon* and *The Choephori*, the dialogue takes place only between two characters at a time. The third character intervenes only once, and this is no accident: at the moment when Orestes is preparing to kill his mother and is overcome with scruples, he consults Pylades, who replies by reminding him of the oath he has made to Apollo. Pylades' reply, the only words he speaks in the whole play, enable us to understand his undeniable function as Orestes' double. Obviously, this reminder expresses the voice of the gods, the voice of the paternal superego.)

The relations between the dream and the murder are more mysterious in Sophocles. It is Electra who reads into them the message that the moment for revenge is approaching, but there is nothing here comparable with the revelations that pour from Orestes' lips. Nor is there anything comparable, when the time for settling accounts finally comes, with the effect of duplication, of repetition, that we have observed in *The Choephori*.

On the contrary, the dream-symbolism situates it very much at a distance from the peripeteias that are to take place in the action. And yet the dream heralds, though it does not actually organize, those peripeteias. It is certainly no more than a sign indicating what is to come. But it is as if the dimension that it is meant to evoke is that of absence. Not because it recalls the existence of Orestes, which is also the case in Aeschylus' dream, but because the whole dream takes place in a time that is not the time of the action. Agamemnon reappears, he plants the sceptre that he once carried, before Aegisthus took it from him. (It is remarkable that Aeschylus should have introduced Agamemnon's sceptre, as he also introduced that of Darius, who was appealed to by the Persians at a time of crisis. This is because, in fact, Agamemnon never ceases to be present. Buried ignominiously, without the rites due to his rank, he cannot be appealed to for redress. If he is present, it is in the pollution to which he has been subjected, which his children hear, and which makes it impossible to invoke him other than through the silence that an appeal to him produces. But this silence may also imply some reservation on the part of the dead man about the murder to come.)

The blossoming laurel does not refer to a present reality; it is not part of present time; it is a promise beyond the enterprise foreshadowed in the dream, an image of its possible success, but above all an indication of the future. It springs from the seed of the sceptre, of which it is the product by transformation. But the seed also implies its own disappearance, so that from its burial may spring the resurrection of what has now fallen into alien hands. Notice how far we are here from the Aeschylean forms of expression, where the chain of events instantaneously becomes a succession that permits no diversion. What we have here is no longer the coalescence of the object with the desire for it, but, on the contrary, a constant resumption, reference back, disappearance, transformation and reappearance. The interweaving of different time-scales seems to refer here to the inseparability of the vicissitudes of the object and of the quest for it, which makes the object the substitute, ever open to change, for a desire that is sustained by this irreducibility to the movement that it engenders.

Notice that, in the two dreams, the snake and the sceptre symbolize the sexual potency of the father. Although the snake undoubtedly represents Orestes, in Aeschylus' dream it is clear that it is also a symbolic allusion to the penis, to Agamemnon's penis. Psycho-analytic dream symbolism leads us to give it this meaning; but also, for the Greeks, the snake was the supremely chthonian animal through which the world of the dead is able to communicate with the world of the living. There are several superimposed significations in the image of the snake emerging from the vagina:

1. the child (Orestes) emerging from his mother's womb,

2. the father (Agamemnon), returning from the world of the dead by means of his son.

Between these two representations is an intermediary form:

3. the child (Orestes) dead, in accordance with his mother's desire, but returning to life and frustrating this desire by his return home.

So Orestes' fable, which enables him to present himself at the palace as the herald of his own death, is not contingent, but neces-sary, since it corresponds to the desire of his mother, and because by this speech the dead son may become the dead father. One may indicate a further relation: that between the seizure of the breast by the child–snake and the coitus with the mother by the penis–snake. This suggests that the projected matricide, which enables Orestes to discharge in the name of his father the revenge that is due to him, also has the nature of a substitute for coitus carried out in his father's place. It is a destructive coitus, but one that enables Orestes to assume the paternal attribute and to use it in his place.

These relations go some way towards bringing the dream in Aeschylus and the dream in Sophocles closer together. Support for this is to be found in the dream as recounted in Stesichorus (see Delcourt, 1959, 22): 'She thought she saw coming towards her a snake with a bloody head, and suddenly it was Agamemnon.' The allusion to the generic power of the father in Sophocles is indicated very clearly, almost literally. The notion of destruction is banished here; rather the fertilizing role of the penis is stressed. The matricide is eliminated in favour of the posterity of Agamemnon's children.

It would seem, then, that what differentiates these two dreams is not so much their theme as the arrangement of their symbolism, their structure.

The presence of the father in the dream becomes the sign of the major absence on which desire as desire by the Other is grounded.

This remark finds an application in the manner of the action of Sophocles' *Electra*, in which we are presented with a double murder in the sense that it corresponds to a double desire. Electra and Orestes have each formed separately, without conspiring together, a plan of revenge that leads to the crime.

Thus the final test bears no resemblance to the duel in the *Oresteia*. The situation has been profoundly transformed. The mother/son couple is out of sight. The presence of Orestes is only inferred, for no tangible mark of his action is detectable. The murder is encompassed by his silence; on the other hand, Electra's *jouissance* knows no bounds. The trap of the tragic emotion is to attribute our momentary anxiety to the savage cruelty of her revealed passion; but this anxiety is really governed by what is concealed from us – the silent desire of Orestes for his mother.

The same goes for the end of Aegisthus, who repeats this triangular situation. When Orestes invites Aegisthus to identify the body he is passing off as his own, we know that it is really Clytemnestra stretched out on the ground. 'Are you so blind / You cannot tell the living from the dead?' Orestes flings at Aegisthus (Sophocles, *Electra*, 116). This ambiguity applies as much to the dead woman as to the revenger, and Orestes' desire is no doubt stimulated here by the reflection back on to himself of his own speech. He refuses to execute Aegisthus for the moment and pushes him into the palace: 'Go to the place in which you killed my father; / There you shall die' (Sophocles, *Electra*, 117).

Here, in this double Oedipus complex, the whole tragic movement is grounded on the desire of the Other, and not on its recognition in the Other, as it is in Aeschylus. In the *Oresteia*, Orestes takes the risk of presenting himself at the palace without any intermediary, as if he sought the ultimate proof of being cast out from the sphere of maternal desire, but in reference to this desire, which is perceived at the level of the subject only as a return marked by what the situation leaves open, indeterminate, problematic.

There is a place, then, for the question of the subject in his articulation with the desire of the Other: in Sophocles' *Electra*, it is outlined in the mutual exchange of feelings between brother and sister which, taken separately, reveal their incomplete character.

Euripides' tragedy entirely recasts the two earlier ones. In certain respects, it may seem like a synthesis of Aeschylus and Sophocles, but only on the level of thematic elements. In my view, it still belongs to the Oedipal framework, but to a greater degree centres the problem on femininity. It might be thought, then, that this justifies the complete disappearance of the dream, which now becomes otiose. This does not mean that nothing replaces it. What, in Aeschylus, is discourse from the maternal unconscious in the form of a dream becomes in Euripides – justified no doubt by a concern for psychological verisimilitude – a phantasy of the daughter.

The trick that Electra chooses to make her victim come to her is the story of her confinement; this requires her mother's presence and collaboration in the ceremony in which the child is given its name.

This offers a surprising parallel with the dream of Clytemnestra in
Aeschylus. Inevitably a child born in the house of Electra, however
mysteriously, represents a threat, albeit a remote one, to the life of
Clytemnestra. Here, in phantasy, Electra gives rein to her own
desire for a child that would be an instrument of death directed
against her mother, an imaginary child received from the father.
This phantasy child is Orestes himself – we are not allowed to forget
that Electra is the elder of the two children. By offering to the
infanticidal desire of the maternal unconscious the bait of a fictitious
birth, this particular phantasy fulfils them. The wealth of suggestive-
ness in the choice of this device becomes clear when one remembers
that Electra is still a virgin after marriage, humiliated by the condition of her husband, but strong in her preserved virginity.

The psychological development in Euripides' tragedy makes the
expression of the unconscious more veiled; the tracks of desire
become blurred, the significations less clear, beneath the overt
psychological pseudo-logic. In short, the tragedy intensifies in
secondary elaboration.[6] But the deep meaning reverts to its first
expression.

III

My analysis of the two dreams shows that their differences are
founded on an internal coherence; they both form the mirror in
which is reflected the whole problematic that it is the task of the
tragedy to expound and convey. What we must now consider is the
extent to which these problematics are opposed or overlapping.
I shall set these differences in relation to the Oedipal structure, to
the primal triangulation that unites the subject to his progenitors,
themselves bound together by their sexual difference.

The situation is inevitable (every human being owes his procreation to two other human beings, one of his or her own sex, the
other of the opposite sex) but at its culmination the Oedipus complex
must be understood in its developed form. Each of the two parents is
the object of feelings of affection and hostility; that is to say, in
addition to the positive Oedipus complex – it is often thought there
is no other – we must take into account the negative Oedipus complex, which, in the case of the boy, is expressed as love for the father
and hate for the mother. In most cases, the two complexes coexist,
but sometimes they can be reconstituted only from vestigial or very
fragmentary elements (Freud).

So the first question is, whether Orestes is to be taken as a
representative model of this complementary modality of the Oedipus
complex. Aeschylus' *Oresteia* embodies a situation that goes well
beyond a mere inversion of the Oedipus complex. One may try, and

it has been tried, to find here a way of exculpating Orestes for his unconscious wishes to murder his father or to make the matricide equivalent to a sadistic coitus (Ernest Jones). But, confronted with tragic situations, we scarcely need to reverse the appearances to discover the truth. The truth is already inscribed -- as in *King Oedipus* – in the very development of those situations. Freud did not add a new signification to their development, but confined himself to revealing their effect. Our task is more to bring out the articulations that give it a certain coherence, which is not registered at the emotional level, but without which the tragic pathos would remain ineffective.

The only character common to the three parts of the trilogy is Clytemnestra: she is the principal figure. The myth she bears is that of the imago of the phallic mother. Having devoured the paternal potency, she becomes the possessor of phallic power.

> And then I struck him, twice. Twice he cried out and groaned;
> And then fell limp. And as he lay I gave a third
> And final blow, my thanks for prayers fulfilled, to Zeus,
> Lord of the lower region, Saviour – of dead men!
> So falling he belched forth his life; with cough and retch
> There spurted from him bloody foam in a fierce jet,
> And spreading, spatted me with drops of crimson rain;
> While I exulted as a sown cornfield exults
> Drenched with the dew of heaven when buds burst forth in Spring!
> (Aeschylus, *Agamemnon*, 90–1)

Such an imago is an object of fascination and terror for the child, who shares in its power, while the imago threatens him with the visiting of that power upon him. In order to take his place at the level of the mother's desire, the child must pass in his quest through the father's penis incorporated in the mother, and can reach his goal only in so far as the bearer of desire stands in its place. The imaginary capture to which his desire is subordinated draws him towards the net held out to him and he rushes into it to seek the object of his mother's desire. There he is caught, confusing its frontiers with his own, paying for his achievement by the permanent inclusion within him of an irreplaceable figure that cuts him off from the ways of interhuman exchange.[7]

The father is present in this relation only through the maternal defile, or at least he is present there only as an obliterated reference. The dream that announces the reversal of Clytemnestra's situation does not at all imply the resumption of power by Agamemnon, the restitution of the throne and the end of her reign; it is the drama of a corporal return in which part of herself is detached, becomes autonomous and kills her. This part, which is precisely the part desired by herself as a phallic attribute, renders the masculine presence superfluous or anonymous and implies no reverence for its speech. Furthermore, any aproach by the mother must be preceded by a liturgy performed around the paternal grave. This is necessary not so much to obtain the father's support, since he makes no approving sign by way of answer, as to revive in each of the protagonists the memory of his power and his mutilation.

In as much as one can say that the Oedipal situation (in the Oedipus myth) is the tragedy of blindness, blindness created by the pursuit of the power and desire to reach the truth concerning the mystery of origins, the Oresteian situation (as I said above, only Aeschylus embodies it fully) is the tragedy of madness, in which the subjective position is attained only through a break with the natural bond that unites the subject to the mother. It is a necessary break, and involves murder, but it is constituent of the subject. Yet it is an impossible break here in that the separation from the maternal image is followed by its instantaneous re-embodiment and its resurgence in the psychotic delusion that restores it to its inalienable place. However, the two situations are not separated by an unbridgeable gap. In certain variants of the Oresteian myth, Orestes recovers his reason and is cured by cutting off one of his fingers (Pausanias). We see here the transition between the problematics of fragmentation (psychosis) and of castration (neurosis).

Just after murdering his mother, Orestes appears before the Choephori, in the terror of his mourning, but not yet overcome by madness. At this moment, the Choephori make the first – somewhat over-hasty – reference to his victorious emancipation:

> Right and success are with you; then why clog your tongue
> With inauspicious words? You have set Argos free,
> And all her people; the two beasts that plagued us fell
> Helpless before your sword. Why speak of ill to come?
> (Aeschylus, *Choephori*, 142)

Orestes replies to this evocation by re-establishing in delusion the mother's maternal presence, represented by the bitches which she set upon him:

> Look, women, see them, there! Like Gorgons, with grey cloaks,
> And snakes coiled swarming round their bodies! Let me go!
> (Aeschylus, *Choephori*, 142)

We are reminded of Freud's remarks about the Medusa's head, in which the myriad snakes have the function of denying castration as many times as the phallic symbols are represented. It is an image of a castration sent back to Orestes after the castration that he has just inflicted on the mother; he did not succeed in being her phallus during her lifetime, but the act of murder has opened her up to his desire.

Hellenists like Marie Delcourt, who can hardly be supposed to look kindly on psycho-analysis, have seen an erotic element in the pursuit of the Erinnyes. But even if one attributes to their ill will a tinge of sexual excitement, their quest of Orestes has the appearance of a nurse–infant relation turned inside out. Their function demands not so much that they mutilate and tear apart the victim but that they empty him by absorption of the substance with which Orestes' body is filled. This is clear enough in the orders given by Clytemnestra to her emissaries:

> Storm at him
> With hot blood-reeking blasts blown from your vapourous womb,
> Wither his hope of respite, hunt him to death!

> (Aeschylus, *Eumenides*, 151)

It also appears in the fate that they are preparing for Orestes:

> You shall, for your soul's guilt,
> Give us your blood to *drink*
> Red from the living limb. . .
> Your *withered* flesh shall sink
> In payment for her blood,
> In penance for her pain,
> Down to the world of death. . .
> A clamour of Furies
> To paralyse reason,
> A tune full of terror,
> A *drought* in the soul!

> (Aeschylus, *Eumenides*, 156 and 159; my italics)

We find here the same vampire-like relation that marks the relations between the imago of the phallic mother and the fruit of her womb. Exchanges can take place only through the total absorption of one term by the other, the passage of the very principle of the existence of one into the other. So we are not surprised to learn from the lips of Clytemnestra's ghost, urging on the drowsy Erinnyes, what is at stake in seizing Orestes: it is her own continuing life that is at stake. It is not only that the capture of Orestes would give her back the day; it is that her encounter with her son has totally dispossessed her, deprived her even of the existence of a shade, and so the Erinnyes have as their mission literally to disgorge him in order to reanimate the interrupted circulation between the two parts of the same organism.

The conjuncture described in Sophocles' *Electra* is that which corresponds to the so-called developed formula of the Oedipus complex. But instead of being a nexus of opposed tendencies in the same individual, produced by the coexistence of opposed drives, the two sides of the Oedipal relation are illustrated in all their fullness in the couple formed by Orestes and Electra. Indeed, compared with the corresponding play by Aeschylus, the transformations concern the passage from a two-term structure (Orestes–Clytemnestra) – the other two being less important – to a four-term structure (Orestes–Electra / Clytemnestra–Aegisthus), which is of the same importance. The placing of this quartet makes it possible to establish functional differentiations within it. The functional differentiation that first stands out is the aspect of rivalry in the relation between daughter and mother, which is developed in a way not found in Aeschylus. It is not confined to the outbursts that occur whenever Electra and Clytemnestra meet, but is duplicated by the antagonism between Electra and Chrysothemis. This rivalry for the father's love is manifested, for example, when Electra proposes to substitute, for the libations sent by Clytemnestra to ward off the threat coming from the dead man, the sisters' own offering, and then turns on her younger sister, reproaching her for her lukewarm attitude and for compromising herself with their father's enemies. But it is above all in the scene when Clytemnestra is murdered that the exaltation of her hate, hitherto held in check, breaks all bounds. The love for the father is embodied here in the veneration she shows for Orestes.

As for Orestes, the identity between his feelings and Electra's should not cause us to forget that his sex, being the opposite of his sister's, gives them an inverse value in the Oedipal combinatory: he does not duplicate Electra's thematic, but serves as its complement. However, these two constellations do not cancel each other out as if by the addition of a plus or minus sign. The confrontation of contraries does not have the effect of turning the contradiction round on itself, that is to say, to exhaust it in an endless rotation. The displacement on to a new figure restarts the movement and prevents it from becoming bogged down in its primal givens. It is Aegisthus' function to assist this disengagement.

This is how the emphasis given to the relations between Aegisthus and Orestes must be understood. It is not for nothing that the scene in which Orestes and Clytemnestra confront one another – and there is no hint of this in Sophocles – is replaced by that in which Orestes and Aegisthus stare at one another, each seeking in the other a single, final explanation. Moreover, it is significant that Sophocles concludes without any allusion to Orestes' madness. Thus, although Sophocles' *Electra* sets out most explicitly to show us a daughter's aversion for her mother – incidentally we are shown how supporting the father's cause serves a number of secondary purposes and underlines the heroine's claim to the phallus[8] – it goes beyond the matricide that is its culmination and gives place once more to the conflict between the son and the mother's lover. This development makes Orestes not so much a matricidal son as a prince who has set out to regain his throne, expelling the usurpers who had deprived him of it. (That is how I would explain the importance of the chariot race in which Orestes is supposed to have been killed. Arriving as the bearer of his own supposed corpse, he fulfils the image of the dream: he will be reborn from his ashes at the end of a trial, just as the laurel sprang from the buried sceptre. Similarly, the deliverance of Electra opens the gates of maternity to her. It is at this point that Euripides takes up the thematic of Electra. In the scene in which Electra calls down curses on Aegisthus' corpse, the reproaches about her degrading marriage carry much further than in the works of the other two tragic writers the expression of penis-envy in the wild virgin.) The last word, then, is given to this re-establishment of the Oedipal truth.

Sophocles' *Oresteia* is dominated by the phallic signifier as paternal signifier possessed of a power (that of kingship), a cause (that of the conqueror of Troy, the chief of the Achaeans, brought low by his fraternal enemy on his return from war) and a word that has the force of law, debated and discussed, but around which a challenge is organized. The murder of Aegisthus by Orestes takes its place in the legendary continuity of events in which the young king dethrones the old king when his hour finally comes.[9] The support found here in a memory to be rehabilitated transfigures the gesture: it changes this relation of succession from a mere transference of power into a turning-point within a continuity that needs to be preserved. This result is secured by an act of violence made more atrocious by the fact that the person executed proves to be the mother's lover. This may suggest a particular form of involvement, and leads us to ask certain questions: Who is the object of Orestes' desire? What animates it?

Does this mean that I see an absolute distinction between the two situations revealed here and that I want to eliminate the first from the Oedipal context? If, with Sophocles, I am right to speak of an 'Oedipalization' of the *Oresteia*, because I see something in it that links it to the developed formula of the Oedipus complex, this does not mean that I exclude from this complex whatever may seem connected to the situation as elucidated by Aeschylus. Let us not forget that Oedipus, too, on the road to Thebes, met the Sphinx, which is the homologue of that imago of the phallic mother that

I recognized in Aeschylus. It was her death that opened up the road towards the city to which his glory and his destiny called him. In fact, one never escapes from the Oedipal configuration, since its ternary structure is constitutive of human subjectivity.

The difficulty in settling the case of Orestes stems from the fact that his crime was committed by divine order, based on the need to punish the guilty, with a view to restoring a fallen legitimacy. What we are confronted with here is not, as in the case of Oedipus, an involuntary crime, the result of chance or misunderstanding. In the latter case, there was at least an 'objective' crime, whatever the intentions of the unfortunate defendant. And it is this that renders Orestes' guilt mysterious and difficult to understand. However, just as ignorance or the uttermost fatality of chance is enough to exculpate Oedipus in his own eyes, so the justifiable reasons for his action, or the guarantee given him by Apollo's protection, do not shield Orestes from misfortune. To see it merely as the result of a disagreement between opposed divinities would be to slip through the first loophole which offers a way out of the difficulty.

In fact, in both cases, the guilt springs from the act of transgression. The rule that is transgressed has an absolute character: parricide and incest are in no circumstances justifiable. Matricide falls under the same ban. These crimes may, when adequately expiated, be relegated to silence and oblivion. But whatever the circumstances, in no sense will it be a matter of course, once the transgression has been committed, that he who has crossed this frontier may continue to live as before. The trap tended to Orestes is of the same nature as that of the superego, which commands the subject to serve the cause of the father while forbidding him to use the means reserved to the father alone.

It is the sacred character of both rule and transgression – even, as in the case of Orestes, their inevitability – that crowns the tragic *phobos*. It is what Oedipus and Orestes have in common.

Marie Delcourt observes that matricide is part of the ancient stock of legends, but is connected with no ritual (1959, 11). The legends that have parricide as their theme are linked to two rituals of which they are a transposition and between which, it is believed, though it cannot be proved, there is a continuity.

The first ritual, agrarian in type – of which the legend of Osiris is the perfect example – tells of an annual marriage between Mother Earth and a young man who, after fertilizing her, is sacrificed, dismembered and the pieces of his corpse scattered through the fields. The second, both agrarian and political in character, turns the annual husband into a king whose strength is a guarantee of the fertility of the soil and of the fruitfulness of the community. As he grows old, his power declines under the attacks of the most vigorous members of the group.

This observation is of great importance. There is a certain undeniable resonance between the agrarian ritual and the analysis I have just made of the mother/child relation between Clytemnestra and Orestes (annihilating union, fragmentation of the subject, absorption into the maternal body, and so on); but is it not the lesson of the ritual here that it fixes clearly the limit between the natural and the human? In the first case, there is no transgression, and death is simply the consequence of the act of fertilization. In the second, it is the result of the challenge directed at the capital power, which is no longer the power of the king alone, but of the group. As soon as the mother is individualized as a human person, matricide can be understood only under the aspect of the agrarian and political rite and as such must pass through the reference to the transgression against the power of the king. We see here how telling is this absence of a ritual proper to matricide. The mediating place of the mother appears in broken outlines, as it were, as does the identification of human ritual with political and phallic power. The business of matricide cannot be confined to the relationship, however direct and exclusive it may seem, between a son and his mother. The voice of the father cannot be eliminated, simply because each of the two terms of the couple has his or her reasons, the one for speaking in the father's name in so far as he identifies his cause with his own, the other for having reduced him to silence for all the wrongs he has committed. Although the trinity seems to be constituted here by the two terms of the dual relation and the unity of the body that they form together, this fragile totality is constantly destroyed by the emergence of a third party who speaks for the 'real'. It is easy to see that this was the function of Pylades. (Cassandra and Apollo are to fulfil the same function: the former when Agamemnon is about to fall into the net in which he will perish, the latter when the Erinnyes are about to overtake Orestes. Taken up again at the highest level, this situation is to be found in the intervention of Athene and the judges between Apollo and the Erinnyes.) The fact that this voice authorizes him to carry out the murder is less important than the reminder of his promise under oath.

On the other hand, within a necessarily triangular constellation, matricide must occupy a place apart. According to the legends, it always results in madness. The problematic thus opened up is that of the birth of the subject who must emerge from his alienating relation with the mother through the mediation of the rule of which the father is the symbol. In a second stage, not so much genetic as dialectical, the constituted trinity will open up the ways of *méconnaissance.* The subject may then cancel out his own presence in the phantasy of the union of the other two or, recognizing himself in it as a witness, or even as a participant, eliminate the significance of desire: or yet again, affirming it, no longer recognize in it the original partners. Such is the power of this dimension of absence, which can project the subject outside himself, into his race across the world. Because he has lost none of his primal attraction towards transgression, he will become absorbed in the business of the spectacle.

IV

A dream is interpreted, we know, only with the help of associations provided by the dreamer, which enable us to pass from the manifest content to the latent content, which alone is endowed with true meaning, in so far as it links the desire of the dream with the desire of the dreamer. Our investigation has shown that for a created work, it is the whole content of that work that performs the associative function. In this case, meaning is born, not from a study of the psychology of the dreamer, but from an analysis of the tragic style, the writing and the architecture; of the relations of the hero or heroes with the other characters and with one another; of the arrangement of the events and sequences that makes it possible to elicit what the dream does not say in its bare text. The dream is detached from the totality of the discourse of the tragic spectacle and takes up a marginal position, adopting a different tone, as a kind of indication of the meaning that runs parallel with what we are shown by the development of the action, which the dream is disclosing to us, although this revelation is not communicated to us. In the context of the Oedipal problematic, this approach has led me to situate Aeschylus' dream in the relations between the child and the phallic mother, and Sophocles' dream in the double aspect of the developed formula of the Oedipus complex.

I go on to make some remarks on the situation of the dream from a more general semantic standpoint: between oracular speech and human speech. The nature of the dream is ambiguous in ancient tragedy. It goes beyond the intellectual individuality of the dreamer, since it is received as the emanation of a divine message, a signal warning mortals and reminding them of some truth that the gods have predicted and announced in more official terms. The message requires interpretation. The dreamer is sometimes perplexed about the meaning he should give it, but does not doubt that he must receive his share of missing truth through the same channels as those of oracular interpretation. But this interpretation concerns him in his personal destiny, all the more so as he is himself the source of the enigma. Now the oracle, the supreme expression of the god's mind, is a source of misunderstanding, even a cause of catastrophe. Hegel was to remark, mockingly: 'He [Oedipus], who had the power to unlock the riddle of the Sphinx, and he too who trusted with child-like confidence [Orestes], are, therefore, both sent to destruction by what the god reveals to them' (Hegel, 740).

We come here to the question of the meaning of tragedy, which pure Hellenists (Bonnard and Ramnoux), sociologizing Hellenists (Thomson, Lacarrière) and philosophers have tried to resolve in various ways. The idea of an evil god (Ricœur) – a principle of good counsel and a power for leading astray – whose struggle with the hero creates the tragic situation and of which the spectacle makes us free, might be subjected to a psycho-analytic interpretation.

The exceptional and still undiminished power of ancient tragedy shows us that the gods play a necessary role in it, and that one cannot see their influence as the result of an arrangement both cruel and fortuitous. Without them, tragedy can survive, as in the later forms of Shakespeare or Racine. In these forms, it becomes the upshot of an impossible situation, a hopeless passion, or events which transcend the capacities of the individual. But it will lack the essential constitutive element of Greek tragedy, and perhaps of all tragedy. If the role of the gods were to represent absolute fatality or the totally arbitrary, there would be no sense in the guilt that still afflicts the hero, for all the purity of his intentions. We have to have the strange combination of a certain responsibility on the part of man, yet also his innocence, within a play of events that he does not control, but which he submits to. The particular character of this responsibility is not easy to understand, for it does not spring from a clearly understood acceptance of the task assigned to the hero in the circumstances in which he is placed. He is always in the position of an emissary, a delegate, speaking for some higher power, though his action can never be reduced to that of a mere pawn. This ambiguous situation cannot be clarified except by accepting that, before any tragic situation can arise, what is originally at issue is a demand that the god should endorse one's actions. In other words, it is because there is some desire in the tragic hero, expressed as a demand that must be sanctioned by the god's agreement; and the tragic situation is created by the final withdrawal of that sanction. But, conversely, it is because this desire is always apprehended as involving some not-understood transgression that this agreement of the god is necessary and its unexpected outcome tragic. The duplicity of oracular speech enables us to remove the illusory mask from desire and from the demand that sustains it. It marks the failure of any attempt to cir-cumscribe and imprison the knowledge of a truth in the locus of the

Other.[10] The spectacle presents – and this is its primary instructive-
ness, the rest being merely a secondary bonus – the search for an
agreement between a human desire formulated as a demand, and the
divine answering speech which needs to convey its consonance with
the desire of him who formulates the demand.

The dream is situated at the juncture of these two perspectives.
It is something which comes to the dreamer and so is a form and
narrative that concerns him; but it is that which is given by the god,
and so is a communication of his will. The dream is half-way
between the oracle communicated by signs, to which it is related by
the fleeting nature of its figures, the ambiguity of the forms and
their aleatory definition, and the oracle communicated by words, to
which a verbal interpretation would correspond. But this interpretation must be, like the answer expected from the oracle, an apprehension of the symbolic. Tragedy reveals this trap.

The role of the dream, on the other hand, its effectiveness, is to be
found in the relation between the manifest content as it is given to
us and the complexities of the tragic questions that it touches on
(and not by the immediate interpretation it is given). This juncture
is established only through the mediation of the linking elements
that interact with one another in order to bring us to understanding.
Hence its truth lies in the indirect pathway that opens up between
us and this new relation. As such, the dream is a signifier of tragedy
and tragedy a relation of this signifier.

The obliquity of Apollonian speech elucidates the relation of
subject to signifier (Lacan). Here, the lesson of Aeschylus' *Oresteia*
is paradigmatic. That the way that leads to the truth is inseparable
from the approach that links the subject to the signifier is proved by
inversion in the allegory which Cassandra personifies. She has the
power to receive and recognize signs, to know and divulge this truth,
but by another fiat of Apollo, punishing a broken vow of love, she
cannot be believed.

Apollonian speech, which finally prevails in the *Oresteia*, does not
triumph by an absolutist proclamation of power, for all the
privileged place Apollo enjoys in the counsels of the gods. It requires
the deliberative channel of forensic debate – and before a human
court – as if this stage were necessary to its fulfilment.

This ending shows that the meaning of the *Oresteia* cannot be
reduced merely to an expression of the paternal right prevailing over
maternal right. This classic thesis was proposed by Bachofen. In any
case, it is now doubtful whether matricide really was included in the
framework of the Delphic ethic, which was once thought to have
demanded it (in the sole case, admittedly, of vengeance for a father's

murder). Certainly, we are reminded that Apollo speaks for Zeus, although, according to Marie Delcourt, the choice of this divinity to support Orestes has more to do with the likeness of their two fates: before becoming god of Counsel and Speech, Apollo, like Orestes, killed the Python, the chthonian and maternal monster, and had to be cleansed of this crime. His ending for the *Oresteia*, that is, the recourse to the human court of the city, is a master stroke of Aeschylus' genius.

When he has won the case, Apollo disappears without signalling his victory. Orestes himself scarcely behaves like a plaintiff who has received justice, but rather as a grateful suppliant; for, as Mazon points out, the verdict is not an absolution.

In the case of Apollo and Orestes, matricide signifies liberation from maternal power and the promise of a second birth, rendering the subject liable to the power of the father – for this is what the purification of Orestes amounts to. But by a compensating action, the recognition of the signs of which the phallus is the bearer implies that no one can lay claim to it absolutely.

Athene has opted for the father, giving the casting vote when each of the adversaries had an equal number of votes; but, by deciding in his favour, the benefit of her verdict puts the party to which she gave her support under a strict obligation to her and to the means by which the case is decided. The legal institution to which she gives a sacred force at this moment must share its nature both with the authority of which the father is the depository and with the principle of exchange by which he holds this power. This exchange is expressed not only through the antagonism between the parties, but through the expression of contrary opinions within the court. This division provides the basis for a reassertion of authority through the acceptance of a decision by majority vote. We see that Athene, most virile of goddesses, vindicates the lost Clytemnestra by recovering her own position as authority after having surrendered it, and by virtue of that very action.

So the relation consecrated by the exchange is ratified by a sign that goes beyond the equivalence of the terms exchanged, but can be shown only in that framework in which it is first given away in exchange.

*Trans*mission is set against *con*fusion. The Erinnyes demand reciprocal absorption, and a return to the undifferentiated mingling of internal, maternal foetal bloods in a lethal relation. Orestes sets up against this, in his purification, the proof afforded by contacts between unrelated bloods; and this shows that his defilement is at an end, since his encounters have been followed by no ill effect. But he must wait for the judgement of the court before this authorization to practise exchange is proclaimed. In a sense, the experiment of the exchange must be carried out in the court, through the opinions of the two parties and the divided vote which precedes the declaration of a verdict.

Self-submission to the working of institutionalized regulation will imply, over and above the constitution of parties in opposition to each other and the division of the suffrage, the exercise of interpretation. Each of the two parties only identifies itself with the phallus, under whose aegis it would like to be placed, in order to cause the transcendent authority to declare itself. It places paternal power in a position of symbolic opening. On the one hand, because the expression of its legitimacy, inseparable from its interpretation as such, is fragmented, so to speak, in this custom that copes with a whole realm of possibility, which is left in silence and shadow. On the other hand, because in declaring itself in this way this power lays bare its conjectural character, as if the challenge addressed to the phallic power – a challenge implied in its obligation to affirm itself – cannot but reveal its inability to show a major truth and be forced to refer the question elsewhere. One grasps the difference from the procedure of the oracle, which first asks for the sanction of the god in order, on behalf of that sanction, to act in the direction of transgression. With the setting up of the court, transgression is the occasion by which transcendent authority is forced to define itself and, by the very process in which it gives proof of its unchallengeable qualification, it indicates the limitation of its power, which must be accepted by whoever is brought before it.

Judgement is no longer, therefore, the apotheosis of a legislating father, but the unveiling of a discourse that must be sustained by its uncertainties and limitations. The body of the judgement is a mutilated body: it reveals in its mutilation the meaning of the transgression that initiated the trial without succeeding in giving voice to the phallic omnipotence left outside it, without having been able to hear it speak.

Hegel was to elucidate part of this contradiction, but concluded in a way that was more compatible with a hope for the advent of absolute knowledge:

If, then, the ethical substance by its very principle broke up, as regards its content, into two powers – which were defined as divine and human law, law of the nether world and law of the upper world, the one the family, the other state sovereignty, the first bearing the impress and character of woman, the other that of man – in the same way, the previously multiform circle of gods, with its wavering and unsteady characteristics, confines itself to these powers, which owing to this feature are brought closer to individuality proper.   (Hegel, 739)

The opposition between masculine and feminine becomes, in the Oedipus complex, a true individuality in its two elements (the condition of the exercise of a full use of speech): the establishment of the relation of the subject to the signifier in the ambiguity of the signifier. The exercise of speech confronts one at once with this dialectic of exchange. The refraction of the signifier upon the speaker, the astonishment he experiences at what he says, the way the discourse eludes him, the gap between the signified intention and the signifying discourse, between the expected and the heard, reveal that the speaking quality of the subject is constitutive of his alienation in discourse, in the dream and in its interpretation.

If tragedy and the tragic spectacle operate as an introjection of the stage, so that each spectator rediscovers in himself the obliquity of speech, psycho-analytic treatment is essentially the same. The relation to the analyst has no other outcome. Sometimes the analyst is identified with the Pythoness who must communicate the word of the god, the supposed possessor of a truth; sometimes he is situated in the place of the consultant himself as when the patient exclaims at certain moments of distress 'What do you want of me?', when he does not know how far he must go into himself, or to what expiation his silence is delivering him. The encounter with castration marks this investigation: a failure of the major signifier, the inability to discover it, the repeated return of demand by the lack that affects every answer and which drives one to extend the investigation postponed until death.

From his very division, man will derive his only good fortune, that of having to seek himself in this tension that tears him apart: 'dissonance become a human creature, but what is man if not that?' (Nietzsche).

The function of tragedy: desire and its representation

> Spirit does not appear in its dissociated multiplicity on the plane of this onlooking consciousness [the chorus], the indifferent ground, as it were, on which the presentation takes place; it comes on the scene in a simple diremption of the notion.
>
> (Hegel, 738)

I

What we have found at the end of our investigation shows us to what extent a sociological interpretation of tragedy falls short of the essence of the tragic phenomenon. In this respect, the *Oresteia* is the most revealing example. Yet repeated attempts have been made, in this tragedy even more than in others, to find echoes of political preoccupations such as the suppression of the Areopagus. Beyond such incidental concerns, the role of Aeschylean juridicism, apparent in all the works of the great tragic writer, has often been stressed. Aeschylus, the true founder of the genre, and passionately concerned with justice, is thought to have written the tragedy with a revolutionary intention.[11] If this interpretation were correct, it would raise more problems than it solves.

Jean-Pierre Vernant has shown how the development of the city goes hand in hand with the differentiation of functions originally performed by a single individual, and later fused in the crucible of the power of the *basileus*. But this separation is not a mere fragmentation. Not at all: the division of power into its elements brings them into opposition, in a dialectical relation. The initial power is originally the province of gods with no intermediaries with men, and of men invested with a quasi-divine power who assume all its aspects, creating between these two worlds relations of an absurd, incoherent, unpredictable logic. With the differentiation between juridical and religious powers, a new relation is established. The public task of drawing up laws falls to the *polis*. *Laws* take the place of *the law*. The law was the emanation of the will of a single individual; laws are the expression of a public will, the transactional processes of the exchange on which power is based, instead of the arbitrary fiat that held sway before. In this situation, religious initiation comes to play a different part, aiming at 'transforming the individual independently of the social order, to be realized in him like a new birth that snatches him from the common statute and enables him to accede to a different level of life' (Vernant, 1962, 48). This evolution of power is closely bound up with the technical inventions of warfare or with an increase in wealth, but it also shows that these two are constantly transcended by their signification, in that they lead to reflection about the essence of potency.

However, if justice is a fundamental, dominant theme in Aeschylus' drama, Hellenists have also constantly insisted on the religious element in his thought, without discerning the contradiction that that conjunction might reveal, but simply attributing this disparity to the mysteries of a complex personality. One has to choose, it would seem, between a message addressed to man as citizen of the *polis* and a fable concerning a subject called to a truth of a more timeless order, concerned above all with individual salvation. We have either to reconcile the terms of this bipolarity, or to transcend the contradiction.

In accounting for the paradoxes in Aeschylus' jurisprudence, Mazon explains that for Aeschylus right is never immutably arrogated to one of the antagonistic parties, but that the sequences of their actions cause right constantly to shift. In other words, it is not so much a question of right as of desire. So it is as if – between desire experienced and desire fulfilled with right on its side – the very experience that constitutes it, by transmuting it from the state of project to that of realization, had the power of instantaneously diverting the subject and defining a void that distracts him from his aim. This creates a kind of fall that supersedes the intention as soon as its satisfaction comes into sight and, in the last resort, challenges its legitimacy. This movement out of orbit, this constantly repeated disparity between intentions and deeds, is the source of disjunction between the cause, the past of this desire, whose legitimacy had been recognized, and the fulfilment of this desire, which is suddenly corrupted in relation to the thing it was supposed to fulfil. This shows the essentially conflictual and ambiguous nature of desire, which is conceivable only as desire of the desire of the Other. Hegel, who understood tragedy so profoundly, wrote:

The act itself is this inversion of what is known into its opposite, into objective existence, turns round what is right from the point of view of character and knowledge into the right of the very opposite with which the former is bound up in the essential nature of the substance – turns it into the 'Furies' who embody the right of the other power and character awakened into hostility. (Hegel, 741)

The fulfilment of the act sustained by desire reveals the indissolubility of the link between the desirer and the object of his desire. Its realization reveals the thing which, in the sphere of the object, completes what is lacking in the subject's desire. The subject is unaware that the part subtracted from his desire of the object is returned to him by the latter as a reflection that he himself perceives through having, unknown to himself, come to be reflected in it. Orestes knows only the violence of his mother and apparently desires only the reparation that delivers him from shame, as Apollo commands. What he is subjected to in the terrifying vision of the Erinnyes is his own violence and his own desire, of which he himself is unaware, turned back upon him after the murder as a reflection of what was apparently absent in his desire and only to be perceived as an attribute of maternal desire.

The relocation of right is made necessary by this exteriorization in the act that reveals the hidden part of the intention or of the cause of the desire. But if we wish to see the relations between the concerns of the tragic writers and the problems posed by this right in process of being constituted we realize how partial, in both senses, it would be not to stress the extent to which that which is shown from the stage is precisely what right cannot be expected to know, what belongs to the law of desire, whose transformations form the linking thread of the tragedy.

The interpretation of tragedy as the product of an evolution in religious life sounds more like an approximation with which we must be satisfied than an understanding that goes to the heart of the phenomenon. Confronted by the striking originality of the birth of tragedy, one is bound to think that we cannot help reducing it to forms familiar to the human consciousness. Just as we saw that the element in tragedy capable of being related to right was the very thing that eluded that right, so what appears to relate tragedy to the religious life is the very thing that later got it condemned as a godless spectacle, for all the tribute that it pays to the gods. In the last section, I pointed out the link between desire and oracular speech – the first seeking in the second endorsement of an implicit transgression. At his highest, the tragic writer becomes a theologian: he creates a religion rather than observes one. So Marie Delcourt points out that the oracle of Apollo ordering Orestes to commit matricide is not part of any Delphic tradition (1959, ch. VI).

II

In insisting on the value of the spectacle, I would stress the role played in it by *representation*. By representation, I mean the process, bound up with the theatre itself, which consists in performing an action constructed around a fable or story. It is not enough just to tell it or to hear it; it must be put into the mouths of characters given life in order to sustain their own discourse, so that the events recounted by the story or fable are given a fresh vitality and are not simply narrated. The theatre is this resurrection that makes stories come to life again, the unfolding of the spectacle.

But by representation I also mean that activity of the mind that usually designates the internal figuration or reproduction of some situation or previously perceived object that is thus brought back to consciousness. In this sense, the representation of the fable or story demands its reproduction in the spectator. But in the Freudian sense representation has wider connotations. Representation is that delegation by which the activity of the drives is manifested so that it assumes a form through which it becomes known. Evidently this second meaning forms a more important part of symbolization, since representation is seen here as half of a reality whose other half is hidden. In defining tragedy, I want to stress this second meaning: for I see in it the process by which, through the world of the drives that is its hidden reality, desire is given its representatives. Without reference to the drive, it becomes difficult to understand the emotional reactions tragedy arouses in the spectator. If we extend this concept of representation to apply to a whole series of discourses that existed before tragedy, we come to understand tragedy as the product of transformations whose representative types have produced various realizations: myth, cult, hymn, epic.[12] The modes of representation that they constitute are not at all directed at mastery of the external world: they have little effect on it and are incapable of transforming it. Yet they have a collective function that is no less important: in various ways, they assuage painful, unpleasant tensions, compensate for the lack of satisfaction of human desires, protect against internal dangers, as Freud pointed out in 'The Claims of Psycho-Analysis to Scientific Interest' (*S.E.*, XIII, 185–7) and, of course, in 'Totem and Taboo' (in the same volume). Each mode in its own way is representative by virtue of its function of delegation. Each, too, is related to the individual system of representation with which it resonates in the subject who receives it either as listener, spectator or participant.

The more elaborate the representation becomes, the more its primary function of becoming the delegate of the activity of the drives is reshaped, complicated or distorted, to the point where its original purpose may be totally disguised. So tragedy may reverse its original aim and make suffering a source of *jouissance* through the spectator's masochistic identification with the hero. This is the price paid for the representation of the spectator's megalomaniac phantasies. And it must be observed that to turn suffering into a source of *jouissance* is the greatest possible triumph of the pleasure principle. Similarly, the dream, although a realization of desire, nevertheless produces dreams involving punishment. In them desire and its punishment are both realized.

However, the remarkable thing about the evolution that culminates in tragedy is that it leads to this representation of representation. In other words, representative discourse is no longer content to suggest, to evoke or to narrate representation, but itself represents it in the space of the theatre.

How is the *Oresteia* subject to the treatment of these various representative discourses? The entire series is not available, since no ritual involving matricide is known to us. But three types of representations are at our disposal: that of epic narration through the Homeric poems (to which must be added other narratives); that of pictorial representation on pottery; and that of theatrical representation in tragedy.

I have pointed to an evolution from Aeschylus to Euripides that I have called the Oedipalization of the *Oresteia*. It would be over-simple to see this modification of the thematic as a progression similar to the evolution from the pre-Oedipal to the Oedipal, for this evolution is peculiar to the taking up of the myth at the theatrical level. Another evolution, in the opposite direction, may be found in the oldest representative discourses, that is to say, from the Homeric poems to Aeschylus' trilogy. This evolution shows the transformation of an Oedipal situation (the reconquest of a usurped throne, the elimination of the old king by a younger prince, and so on) into a pre-Oedipal situation (the imago of the phallic mother, destructive of the paternal penis, the dominance of the mother–son relation, and so on).

Two cycles may be defined: from the Homeric poems to Aeschylus, then from Aeschylus to Euripides.

Marie Delcourt has examined, in the works of the poets and vase-painters before tragedy, the various versions to which the myth gave rise. So, in Homer, there is no mention of the character of Clytemnestra in the cantos in which the *Oresteia* is mentioned (*Odyssey*, IV, 514; III, 194; I, 30–47; III, 309); she is mentioned only in the later cantos of the poem (XI, 411; XXIV, 199).[13] It is Aegisthus who murders Agamemnon, and Orestes' revenge is a deed that is certainly inscribed in the Oedipal context; this act kills two birds with one stone, since it revenges the father and at the same time puts the son on the throne in his place. No mention is made of the punishment of Clytemnestra, just as her share in Agamemnon's murder, odious as it may be, is, after all, only indirect. She does no more than aid Aegisthus in his act.

In other accounts, by Stesichorus, Pherecydes and Nicolaus Damascenus, a new theme appears, that of Orestes persecuted by his mother, either directly or indirectly through Aegisthus. This introduces an element of psychological verisimilitude: Orestes by killing his mother revenges himself and responds to her hostility.

The vase-painters show an actively murderous Clytemnestra. They do not go so far, it should be noted, as to show the son raising his sword against his mother. He is busy executing Aegisthus – his rival – who lies, pierced by the sword, pouring out his blood and his entrails. Clytemnestra emerges from behind, axe in hand, ready to kill her son. The next stage, which is not shown, would give the reversal of this situation, on the ground of legitimate self-defence.

In all these representations, therefore, whether verbal narrative or pictorial image, the stress is laid on the rivalry between the men (Agamemnon/Aegisthus, then Orestes/Aegisthus), and the confrontation between mother and child is avoided. When the mother is introduced it is as Aegisthus' accomplice in Agamemnon's murder, or as Aegisthus' ally when Orestes commits his act of revenge.

Moreover, a motive is provided by way of a psychological explanation for the matricide. It should be noted how audacious, how
unique, Aeschylus' version is: how structurally true it is. It ignores
the relation of rivalry between Aegisthus and Agamemnon, since it
makes Clytemnestra alone responsible for the crime. This has
nothing to do with misogyny, which is subordinated to the structural
truth of the whole. Aeschylus also ignores the relation of rivalry
between Aegisthus and Orestes. He provides no psychological motive
for the matricide. He does not avoid the moment of truth in the
myth, which is the confrontation between mother and son, the
moment that gives this legend its specificity.

The matricide is taken as belonging to the system of kinship
relations; it is the consequence of the oracle of Apollo through which
the voice of the father, destroyed by the mother, is expressed; and
its punishment before the acquittal is persecution by the nocturnal
representatives of the mother, in the delusion that pursues Orestes.

So I would say of Aeschylus' version that it is the pivot of the
myth, the only one to respect its problematic specificity, the only one
to reflect its essence. It is interesting to wonder what the personality
of Aeschylus owes to the fact of having attained this truth. It would
be no less interesting to ask what tragedy as representative of
representation has contributed to it.

III

In what sense, then, does the specific problematic of Aeschylus'
Oresteia particularly concern the question of representation? In
'Moses and Monotheism', Freud recognizes in the *Oresteia*, according to Bachofen's classic interpretation, the transition from the
matriarchal social order to the patriarchal social order:

Under the influence of external factors into which we need not enter here
and which are also in part insufficiently known, it came about that the
matriarchal social order was succeeded by the patriarchal one – which, of
course, involved a revolution in the juridical conditions that had so far
prevailed. An echo of this revolution seems still to be audible in the
Oresteia of Aeschylus.   (*S.E.*, XXIII, 113–14)

Freud draws an important conclusion from this:

But this turning from the mother to the father points in addition to a
victory of intellectuality over sensuality – that is, an advance in civilization,
since maternity is proved by the evidence of the senses while paternity is a
hypothesis, based on an inference and a premiss. Taking sides in this way
with a thought process in preference to a sense perception has proved to be
a momentous step.   (*S.E.*, XXIII, 114)

During the trial, in which the father's side represented by Apollo and the mother's side represented by the Erinnyes confront one another, the son of Zeus tosses this argument into the discussion: the mother is merely the receptacle of the child, the nurse of the father's seed; the true procreator is the father who can even create without the help of the mother. This strange view, so contrary to the lessons of nature, is based on an example: that of Athene, who, as we know, owed her birth to Zeus alone. One is bound to wonder why Aeschylus thought he could win the day by citing this argument. So perhaps we should see the story as a parable. This miraculous birth, the effect of a displacement upwards, takes place, as we can hardly forget, in the head; and Athene is worshipped as goddess of Reason, Wisdom and Inventiveness. The purport of Apollo's argument seems to be, therefore, that creation cannot be the realm of women, for it is the mind of man that creates, man alone is creator of psychical activity. This brings us back to Freud's opposition between maternity, which is attested by the evidence of the senses, and paternity, which must be deduced. This gives precedence to intellectuality, which is in turn the product of its creation.

For Freud, intellectuality is to be understood in the broad sense of psychical activity as opposed to sensory activity (especially sight). In the traditional opposition between the intelligible and the sensible, Freud includes under the same term the most wide-ranging intellectual processes: 'The new realm of intellectuality was opened up, in which ideas, memories and inference became decisive in contrast to the lower psychical activity which had direct perceptions by the sense-organs as its content' (*S.E.*, XXIII, 113). To declare that paternity is more important is to declare that the son bears the name of the father and becomes his heir. When Freud seeks for the cause of this evolution he stumbles on a difficulty: what authority imposes this criterion? 'In this case it cannot be the father since he is raised to this authority by progress itself.' So we must link psychical activity and paternal dominance to a common root that will account for both. We shall find this common root in the dimension of absence.

What place does representation occupy in the intellectuality of which Freud speaks? It is the response to the absence of the object. The movement of desire that awaits satisfaction when the object is lacking gives place to representation by means of the phantasy of wish-fulfilment. Representation stands in an intermediary situation between that sensory-perceptive activity that requires the presence of the object and that activity of thought that accounts for the existence of this object, despite its absence in the external world, by means of deductions and inferences (see Freud, 'Negation', *S.E.*, XIX, 235–6). The representation that implements only the identity of the perceptions obeys the logic of the primary process under the domination of the pleasure principle. Psychical activity, which rests on the identity of thoughts, is subjected to the logic of the secondary processes, obeying the reality principle. Reality testing becomes established only when the objects that once brought satisfaction are lost.

In the *Oresteia*, representation plays a double role. The conclusion of the trilogy which sees the father's cause triumphing over that of the mother implicitly favours the process of thought over representation. Hence the importance accorded to language in the debate. The cause that wins the trial is that of speech: 'Zeus, the Pleader... crowned Persuasion with success,' says Athene. By the same token, this decision frees Orestes from the terrifying representations of his mother's representatives.

The *Oresteia* is, therefore, the theatre of a number of overlapping oppositions:

1. Erinnyes   against Apollo
2. night   against sun
3. feminine   against masculine
4. maternity   against paternity
5. family   against city
6. blood   against pact
7. representation   against speech
8. the sentient   against the intelligible

In fact, this opposition overlaps that of the imaginary and symbolic, as set out by Lacan, who also links symbolization, language and the Name-of-the-Father.

But it is by means of theatrical representation, the representation of representation, that this truth is stated. This is why tragedy is not a dissertation or a reflective or religious discourse, but above all a means of reaching the unconscious through representation, which has much greater power of conviction and effect than a philosophical or moral message.

Here the dimension of absence is reversed: representation is born from the absence of the object; the representation of representation gives the object more life, embodies it and gives it a new existence. One must distinguish between the object of representation, the object through which the represented fable speaks and representation understood in its turn as an object that poses the question 'What type of object is concerned in tragedy?'

Freud believes that the process of affirmation is part of the activity of Eros, whereas negation is part of the death drive. What, then, is the reality of tragedy: does it or does it not exist? This question is as pertinent for the myth that it represents as for the status of theatrical representation itself. Faced with this alternative, we can only adjudicate by considering the case of those peculiar objects that both are and are not what they represent.

Tragedy has a function as memory and representation, but its discourse can be expressed only through the mediation of the actor. As Hegel observed: 'This universal individualization descends again, as will be remembered, to the immediate reality of existence proper' (738–9). The case of the tragic actor is like that of the colossus, to which Jean-Pierre Vernant has devoted a fine study.[14] Both help to effect the passage between the world of the living and the world of the dead, each has a right to existence only in the space by which he is bounded, or in the duration of its manifestation. Actor and colossus both belong to this category of the double to which Vernant proposes to add the dream, the shade and the supernatural apparition. A psycho-analist would see both as expressions of the transitional object described by Winnicott. By 'transitional object', Winnicott designates the first possessions that do not belong to the body itself: bits of rag to which the child becomes attached, the corner of a blanket or, later, a teddy-bear or doll, which are absolutely necessary to the child, especially at the moment when it is going to sleep. Winnicott relates these objects to the mother's breast, of which they are the first equivalent. It is equally important that these objects should be and should not be what they represent. This is a manifestation of that division of the subject, operant in fetishism, first described by Freud and developed by Lacan.

Now, if the function of the actor may be set in the same framework, tragedy as a whole, as the realm of this transitional object, assumes this function for the spectator.

Thus theatrical representation is at the crossroads of this opposition between the sensible and the intelligible, between the existent and the non-existent, the real and the unreal, yet belongs to neither.

IV

Following Hegel, Ricœur has expressed surprise at this Greek ethic of 'inactive compassion', produced by sympathy but also by powerlessness. This is perhaps to underrate the power of identification in the spectacle. Nietzsche seems to have understood its effects: 'The gaps between man and man give way to an overwhelming feeling of oneness, which leads back to the heart of nature' (Nietzsche, 60). (With the intuition of genius, Nietzsche speaks of the 'maternal bosom' in speaking of the chorus. The chorus, deriving from the dithyramb, involving that fusional identification with primal being, the expression of the maternal bosom, may therefore be contrasted with the protagonist, the hero of the spoken action, the expression, according to Nietzsche, of the Apollonian world of appearance and, according to Freud, of the primitive father. Aeschylean tragedy oscillates according to the unstable equilibrium of chorus and dialogue, an equilibrium broken by the later tragic writers in favour of dialogue, of Apollonian speech, of the Name-of-the-Father.)

Let us not dwell on this undifferentiating fusion, but observe the process of visualization that makes the tragic universe a universe of the gaze, and the world of the heroes a world of observers: 'to see one's self transformed before one's self, and then to act as if one had really entered into another body, into another character' (Nietzsche, 67). It is this otherness that is essential. The performance of the spectacle allows the representation to operate and to detach itself from participation in the act. It is not only a distancing, it is, in the very operation in which it is realized, the appearance of the subject as Other.

By the duplication of representation (myth is representation, tragedy is representation of that representation), by this enactment that gives a second life to the fable (just as the dream brings to life the thoughts that it represents), the myth which, in the epic, was a discourse offered for representation, is transformed in tragedy into a discourse imposed by representation. It becomes discourse of the Other.

Myth is no longer merely suggested to its recipient with an invitation to enter into it, but is returned back to him, projected. The projection implies the return to the subject of that which, once suppressed, is externalized – and which, in fact, he cannot escape. The subject encounters the Other by this detour, which he experiences as a return. The tragic hero, says Hegel, externalizes the internal essence. This brings us, perhaps, to the very foundations of representation. Given the endorsement of this otherness, representation may follow the ways of meaning, since this meaning will be represented as the concern of the Other where the subject has nothing to do except feel sympathy. On the other hand, since it is in the eyes of the subject attributed to the Other, the subject can no longer rid himself from the representation and must see himself as among those who are playing in his place. Only by counting on an obligatory spectator – caught up in the web woven for the Other – can representation perform its function.

The author of the spectacle, therefore, is at once the individual who wrote it, produced it and acted it, and he who finds himself anonymously forced to witness it. In Antiquity, attendance at the tragic festivals and competitions was a duty. This participation required that the spectator should cut himself off from the ways of action, of motility, and immobilize himself in the spectacle, just as the dream is born of the powerlessness to act associated with sleep, and the refusal to allow free rein to the nothingness of absolute primary narcissism. But, as in tragedy, the scenario of the dream demands our participation in the spectacle, however much we wish to be free of it. This helps to explain the importance I have attached to the dream as an expression, to use Freud's words, of what takes place in 'the other scene', or in 'the scene of the Other', as Lacan would say. Tragedy appears to be the representation on behalf of the Other of what cannot be represented before the eyes of the subject. It follows then, that representation is inseparable – as re-presentation – from interpretation.[15] The origin of tragedy, therefore, is the most complete expression of the representation of desire in so far as it is inseparable from the interpretation of a secret or lost meaning.

The many acceptations of the word 'logos' are well known: speech, discourse, theory, which last primarily signifies the witnessing of a procession, or spectacle. In this respect, I would give particular importance to this primary, truly fundamental value of the forms of narrative, in order to bring out the transformation operated by tragedy.

In introducing the second character, Aeschylus broke his earlier bonds and inaugurated a new discourse. Sophocles created the third character, an innovation that Aeschylus was to use in the *Oresteia*. It would be right to say that, for all that he was a lawyer or theologian or philosopher, Aeschylus was a poet and a dramatist above all else. But poetic and dramatic invention proved inseparable here from the conceptual universe that weighed on the tragic poet, even if he was unconscious of it. It has been said of Aeschylus that he was as much a Pythagorean as a poet. The discourse of the *Oresteia* – an early form of three-cornered dialectic – is still linked to dual relations, which include certain of the kinship relations referred to above. It opens with the fully assumed ternary discourse of the *Oedipodeia*. Tragedy has illustrated these types of discourse, these representations of desire, in situations involving kinship relations.

If the symbol is narrative (of some basic story), and if this narrative is inseparable from an interpretation, just as the interpretation requires the narrative which it is its function to interpret and which is itself the result of an interpretation, we can understand that the meaning is inseparable from this interrogatory embodied in the story and from its projection. Now, I have maintained that this story is about kinship relations. What the Hellenists (Ramnoux, Vernant) show us is that the initial knowledge concerns generation myths and kingship myths which the cosmogonies express and which implicitly pose the problem of power. 'Myth does not ask itself how an ordered world emerged from chaos; it answers the questions "Who is the sovereign god? Who has succeeded in reigning _(anassein, basilein)_ over the universe?" ' (Vernant, 1962, 108).

The dependence of the subject on the Other, which we cannot escape because of human prematurity at birth, establishes the Other as the possessor of power and as the locus of the truth of the subject.

By relation to the Other I mean a kinship relation, the presence or absence of the Other defining ways in which the subject himself signifies or, more exactly, is signified by the Other. I would say, then, that this kinship relation, which refers back to the fundamental story, must follow the ways of representation if it is to embody itself – not because representation is a mould into which it pours itself in order to take shape, but because representation is its very manifestation. In so far as the kinship relation is constitutive of the subject, its representation is manifested either in the absence of the parent who retroactively structures the subject as the subject of desire, or in the absence of the subject representing to himself the parental interchange. In short, it is because the question of the relation to the Other is presented as representation that representation in turn is presented as representation of the relation to the Other. Thus to represent the kinship relation and while representing it to embody this kinship relation is one and the same phenomenon. Representation and interpretation as givens of subjectivity appear here as inseparable not only because any representation presupposes interpretation, but also because to link representation with the relation between the subject and the Other necessarily involves interpretation as a result of this interrogation, the Other revealing itself as a mystery, an opacity, a secret meaning to be discovered. This is the signification of the conception of desire as desire of the Other. It should be added that this opacity and this mystery are not only those of the unknown or the indeterminate, but a property, an appropriation of the Other, which hypothetically possesses it.

v

The tragedy of Oedipus derives from the movement against the current that forces him, if he is to find a solution to the future of Thebes, to reconstitute a past that is alien to him but of which he turns out to be the unsuspected inheritor. In this recognition after the event we begin to see ourselves in him and we suffer with him when, at the end of the investigation, he is forced to call himself, against his will and by the order of the god, a committer of parricide and incest. But the situation of Orestes is quite different.

Here there is no enigma to unravel, but a story that is all too clear, which everyone knows. There is no apparent ambiguity in this situation, only a cause that demands justice. Orestes scarcely hesitates before committing his act of revenge – just time enough to hear the confirmation of his ineluctable duty. He is reminded of the imperative task – if he is to live among men, even though only in opprobrium and defilement – of having to write his history, which his mother has effaced. For a father twice dead – once by murder and a second time by the failure to perform the rites that should have accompanied his burial – cannot be inscribed in a genealogy. 'The children of a hero save his name from death,' says Agamemnon's son. Orestes' individual fate can only take off from this void that challenges his right of citizenship. In fact, he is the son of nobody, for what guarantees the individual his place in the world of human beings is not his physical presence, but the signifiers by which he is recognized in life as in death. So, in the murder of his mother, the motive of his crime is by no means his animosity towards her, if it exists: it is part of the necessary passage that he must cross in order to call himself the son of Agamemnon. In order to set down a past that he knows only through the marked, but not signified place of his father's grave, in order to clear the way for the Trojan epic that will be the glory of his line and which remains inaccessible, unavailable to him, he must restore life to Agamemnon, for it is on this re-habilitation that the endorsement of his father's existence as a whole depends. By this gesture, he has access at last, at any cost, to an identity that has so far eluded him.

To deprive Clytemnestra of life is first of all to fulfil this pro-gramme, which lifts the silence from around his father's name, and opens up to Orestes the status of subject. Orestes scarcely has a choice. He is threatened by lepers 'whose rabid teeth / Eat the flesh till human shape is gone' (Aeschylus, *Choephori*, 113) if he leaves his father's death unpunished. Yet he is condemned to find his own punishment in the remedy, since if he does his duty, he falls into the grip of the Erinnyes. It is not destiny that turns against him here in an unexpected reversal; a situation with no way out awaits him, whatever solution he adopts. This brings us to the heart of this problematic of night. As Ramnoux reminds us, whatever is chthonian is infernal, but night is still more terrible.

So here he meets this unexpected dilemma; how is he to acquire his filial right, and add his name to his father's in a continuing lineage, yet also destroy the means by which he came to life? He is guilty of a cardinal sin not only because in eliminating his female parent he dries up his own source of life, but also because he destroys, in acceding to sonhood, that which grounds paternity. By dissolving the bond that unites mother to father, he commits a crime as grave as parricide, even though he perpetrates it at the command of the father. Such is the absurdity of the dilemma that

brings about his doom, whichever alternative he chooses. That this
discourse is exhausted in duality is shown beyond any psychological
explanation by his ethic. Orestes' 'Let me kill her and let me die'
also finds its illustration in the words of the chorus:

> Let word pay word, let hatred get
> Hatred in turn, let murderous blow
> Meet blow that murdered.   (Aeschylus, *Choephori*, 115)

This is an expression of the symbiotic exchanges characteristic of
psychotic discourse. In contrast with this discourse of retaliatory
subjectivity, the discourse is one of *méconnaissance*.

Oedipus – those who challenge psycho-analysis have said it often
enough – *did not know*. He did not know, when he opened the
investigation, that his father was already dead; so set out, in his own
prophetic words, to defend the memory of the assassinated King of
Thebes, 'as if he were my father'. He did not know that this queen,
the reward of victory, like booty handed out indiscriminately, was his
own mother. Nor did he know where he was born, as Teiresias
reminds him. Because Oedipus knew none of this he was able to
decipher the riddles, to which he owed his life. And so throughout
his life he was able to seek that father whose death opened up the
way to the maternal bed – only to find himself at last in the situation
of a man who, acceding himself to the paternal condition, becomes
the source and locus of questions in the discourse concerning his
ancestry.

The mark of the sinner set upon him leads him, despite himself,
against himself, in his heart of hearts; it leads him where he had to
come, to his castration encountered at last, where it is no longer a
question for him of power or knowledge, where he can only question
the signs that come from himself, master what comes from within,
delivered up to the desire of men who will dispute his inheritance
before he is even dead. It is not certain that he has succeeded in his
last mission, whatever he says to the contrary. His behaviour up to
the last hour has nothing serene about it and his ambiguous end is
as much an apocalypse as an apotheosis.

So form of expression and tenor of discourse are closely bound up
in this conception of the symbol as narrative. On the other hand, the
narrative of this fundamental story resists any attempt to reduce it to
a single discourse, since it may be transmitted and formulated
according to such different codes that its message alters considerably.
The scope that it offers for such different structural combinations
testifies to the powerful resistance offered by the Oedipus complex,
as constitutive of subjectivity, to allowing itself to be grasped as a
fixed, closed totality. I have been able to show how these variants, a

dual relation in the simple or complex triangularity of the double Oedipus complex, positive and negative, set its single form at the level of a fundamental myth that is never approached except at its limit.

Although representation plays the basic role in the relation to the Other, as I have recognized, it belongs nevertheless to the imaginative order. Representation belongs to the symbolic order by its structure, that is to say, by the mapping and arrangement of the elements that constitute it, as much in the relations it forges between the principal characters as in the system that links together the elements that compose it. It is the major function of the Oedipus complex to lend itself to these diverse combinatories.

There certainly is, then, a fundamental story, but it is in so far as it does not involve a secret form that the quest for its lost meaning originates various discourses that engender one another.

The final stages of my commentary may have given the impression that I have moved very far from the ground of my undertaking: psycho-analytic investigation. The richness of Freud's *œuvre* gives it a polysemic character which, as experience and theory show, allows an open use. I have chosen the least direct, but perhaps also the most conjectural approach. (The teaching of Lacan has been a most valuable guide in my work.) My investigation into tragedy becomes meaningful only in relation to the problem posed by Freud concerning the relations between the drive and its *Vorstellungsrepräsentanz*[16] and, therefore, concerning desire and its representation. Conversely, I have situated representation in the wake of desire, of the relation to the Other.

I have found an agreement between the expressions of these successive forms of the logos and the levels that emerge in Freudian theory: that of the drive, of its *Vorstellungsrepräsentanz* and that of language.

Tragedy seems to me to be a privileged example of that conjunction of the representation of desire and the effects of discourse, an expression of a modality of speech in which speech is at one with its mode of appearance, where the visual and auditory perception of the spectacle are its manifestation. But it would be wrong to see tragedy as a threshold, a limit of speech. Heraclitus, philosopher of fire, said as much of the soul 'whose limits one will never find, however far one explores its ways, so deep is the logos in it'.

After writing this chapter, I came across a number of texts that were relevant to my subject. I should like to mention two of these. There is Melanie Klein's 'Some Reflections on the *Oresteia*', which is in-

cluded in the posthumous collection *Our Adult World and Other
Essays.* I reviewed this book in *Revue française de psychanalyse,*
xxviii (1964), 816. A version of this review follows in the appendix
to this chapter. I should also mention Jean-Pierre Vernant's fine
study of Sophocles' *Electra,* 'Hestia–Hermès', which is to be found
in his *Mythe et pensée chez les Grecs.*

APPENDIX

Some reflections on the *Oresteia*

Those who do not have an aversion for the work of Melanie Klein,
but regard it with interest and sympathy, will not be surprised to see
that the posthumous work published by her executors includes a long
study of the *Oresteia.* One may not be much interested in this
legendary projection and in the Aeschylean trilogy, but it is still easy
to imagine how this work calls for an interpretation according to the
Kleinian system. The only surprise is that Melanie Klein should have
waited so long before doing it. This study should prove a worthy
addition to a valuable body of work that was regarded by its creator
as a continuation of Freud's. The attention that I have myself given
to the *Oresteia* and the comparison of my conclusions with hers have
led me to examine this work again.

After giving a brief summary of the trilogy in Gilbert Murray's
translation, Melanie Klein, as in many of her articles, presents a
summary of her theses. One notes her most recent discoveries concerning envy. She places at the verge of development, beside the
mechanisms of introjection, projection, splitting, fragmentation and
negation, the envy that underlies relations between the child and the
mother, which are dominated by the duality of the erotic or destructive drives. The child's envy of the mother is an envy of her creative
power as a provider of food, and is a desire to appropriate this power
and to destroy it. This desire to destroy is directed at the object of its
dependence, the mother's breast, desire for which merely increases
the hate and envy. (One might note in passing the convergence of
this concept of envy with Lacan's concept of desire.) This concept of
envy as the basis of the destructive drives leads, when the depressive
phase is reached, with the threat that it represents for the child of
the total loss of the object, to the corollary concept of reparation.

Melanie Klein sees a confirmation of her theses in Greek thought.
Hubris (excess) is followed by Dike (justice) as a punishment for
having infringed Moira (fate). Similarly, envy, under the influence of
the superego, gives way to reparation.

We know that Aeschylus' work, and the theme of the *Oresteia* in particular, lends itself very well to an illustration of this Greek morality. This view of right, so personal to Aeschylus, has been stressed repeatedly. Right does not inhere integrally and permanently on the side of one of the parties to the conflict; it seems that as the action develops, desire is manifested behind the cause, at the point of origin, but proves forbidden, and so culminates in a reversal of that right into the right of the antagonist. The exchanges between the characters, unyielding, cruel, lacking in any delicacy or subtlety, confront us with a form of justice very close to retaliation. One can see that there are many things here that lend themselves to the Kleinian phantasmagoria.

But Melanie Klein goes further: she interprets the characters of the heroes according to her well-known dialectic of the schizoid–paranoid position and the depressive position. It is fascinating to observe the extent to which her conclusions run counter to my own. Having taken the Oresteian situation as a typically psychotic one, in comparison with the Oedipal situation, which is typically neurotic, I saw in Orestes a mythological model of the psychotic. For Melanie Klein, on the other hand, Orestes is something less than a psychotic, in so far as it can be said that neurosis exists in a system like hers, which seems entirely constructed to account for the modalities of the psychotic universe. At least she establishes a distinction between the paranoid–schizoid position to be found at the base of serious (schizophrenic) disorders and the depressive position underlying less serious (melancholic) disorders, if only because they are critical and intermittent. For Melanie Klein, the fact that a subject is capable of a reaction of mourning is evidence that the depressive phase has been reached. The absence of mourning, therefore, would appear to be the sign of a fixation at the paranoid–schizoid phase – a very serious sign. Now, Orestes, she tells us, has just such a reaction after murdering his mother.

It is hardly reasonable to discuss the nosographical diagnosis of a tragic hero. Such controversies are even more sterile than those concerning the cases of individual patients. Still, I cannot see how Melanie Klein presents a mental state that she finds characteristic of a transition between the paranoid–schizoid stage and the depressive stage, 'a stage when guilt is essentially experienced as persecution' (Klein, 37). It seems to me, on the contrary, that Orestes shows the characteristics of a persecution psychosis. I fail to see how such a psychosis could not be based upon guilt. Melanie Klein thinks that there is almost an incompatibility between the paranoid–schizoid phase and guilt, since guilt presupposes the notion of a total object with regard to which one feels guilty, whereas the anxiety of the paranoid–schizoid is that of a reversion into retaliation. In fact, there is no true guilt in Orestes; for him, there is punishment, which is known, foreseen, and expected, for murdering his mother; just as he would also have incurred terrible punishment had he not revenged his father's death. So what we have here, without any doubt, is a system of retaliation. But Melanie Klein bases her theory on Orestes' desire for reparation. The question is, whether he wants to rid himself of a defilement that sets him apart from other human beings and to take his place once more among them as Agamemnon's son, or to show his repentance with regard to the maternal object. Klein, it is true, might well have said that Orestes' sentence was a sign of the destruction of the introjected good objects and the free rein left to persecution anxieties by the bad objects. . .

Let me note in passing that Melanie Klein places no value on the fact that the matricide is carried out in a crude and direct way. (Unlike its expression in a disguised form as the triumph of Oedipus over the Sphinx, which brings about the death of the latter.) In so far as these phantasies are her main concern, there is nothing surprising here. Klein sees in this no more than a sign of the negativity of Orestes' Oedipus complex. The total, that is to say, double Oedipal constellation is manifested in various ways in the trilogy. Electra reveals a positive Oedipus complex, and the rivalry between Clytemnestra and Cassandra (the latter being a filial substitute) is an index of the presence of this positive complex. On the other hand, Apollo, who encourages and supports Orestes, indicates a negative Oedipus complex. Athene, Zeus' favourite daughter, whose influence finally wins the day, is a sign of the positive Oedipus complex. This might be expressed as follows:

	Oedipus +	Oedipus −
Parents' generation	Aegisthus	Clytemnestra
Children's generation	Cassandra	Orestes
	Electra	
Gods	Athene	Apollo

Agamemnon's place cannot be shown here, for he is a sign sometimes of the positive Oedipus complex (Cassandra, Electra), sometimes of the negative Oedipus complex (Clytemnestra, Orestes). That is why, in my view, he rightly acquires particular status. Melanie Klein sees him merely as the agent of excess (the sacrifice of Iphigenia, the sin of pride before the gods).

My principal argument against the Kleinian system – an argument that is also directed against a number of systems which, without actually claiming allegiance to her, are inspired by her, though not in their lack of rigour – is the disappearance of the paternal reference. By this I do not mean the disappearance of the father. The figure of the father is certainly present at several points in Melanie Klein's work and the strictly Oedipal reference is less absent in her work than is often believed. But the father is present as the double of the mother. He is a secondary object because he appears later – an opinion that corresponds here with that of the geneticist psycho-analysts who, nevertheless, criticize her so much – and because he functions practically as if he were a secondary maternal object. This is not to say that Melanie Klein does not recognize the specific characteristics of the father. The father is certainly a man, who normally attracts the favours of his daughter, but (and the conception of the mother with the penis emphasizes this shift) he is nowhere given his position as reference. That is to say, he is not the object of the mother's desire, he is not the representative of the third position – that excluded/non-excluded middle, which gives an added dimension to the psycho-analytic conception of paternity. He is not the sign by which the phallus enters the child's world through the discovery of its absence at the level of the mother.

In other words, the Oedipus complex as a circuit of exchanges is *senseless*, without *sense*, that is to say, it does not give a direction to the traffic of the objects, values and investments. Although Melanie Klein represents one of the most daring currents in post-Freudian thought, Jacques Lacan, by a diametrically opposed orientation, tips the scales towards the other pole, that of the re-establishment of paternal primacy.

We find this Kleinian levelling down again in her conception of the superego. She lists several of its representatives in the *Oresteia*. The Erinnyes provide an image of its most archaic forms, oral-sadistic and anal-sadistic in nature; Agamemnon, the most evolved aspect (that of the tenderly loved father); Cassandra, prophetess of misfortune, reflects that part of the unconscious that has become conscious but denied; Apollo, the destructive desires of Orestes projected on to a superego image and – last but not least – Zeus, Father of the gods.

In this syncretic ensemble, the gods are treated in exactly the same way as the men. What we find here, in a different context, is something for which Melanie Klein has often been criticized: a lack of distinction between real and phantasized objects. What I was saying about the father is to be found here in the composite figures of this superego in mosaic. Zeus no longer reigns over the Pantheon of the gods: he is placed on the same level as his children. There is no authority in paganism for such a levelling down.

But this general lack of differentiation deprives our examination of its pivot, its axis, a code that makes a coherent reading possible. The Oedipus complex is first of all the human condition in its generality before it is the particular language of this or that human condition (psychosis or neurosis). To say this is, then, to re-establish the gap of signification between, in all their difference, the role of the father and of the mother.

However, this valuable work contains many highly illuminating observations concerning phantasies of non-birth – babies who in the child's phantasies are killed in the mother's womb, who cannot be born, but remain as dead internalized objects, nevertheless active as good or bad objects. The mother's food sustains not only the life of the living creature but also the dead, internalized object it carries within it. Much becomes clearer in the light of this illuminating interpretation.

The conceptions of the symbol that Melanie Klein provides here give pause for reflection. The author attributes to symbols a role in the fixation of the *phantasy*. Thus phantasies 'attach' themselves to objects and 'congeal', transmitting the activity produced by the energy of the drive from a continuous, fluid, permanent, expanding mode to a bound, limited, discontinuous form. Objects, both phantasy objects and real objects, acquire a symbolic status. One is reminded of the words of Maurice Merleau-Ponty: 'Being *is that which requires creation of us* so that we may experience it.' But this creation, Melanie Klein says, is so urgent only because the most loving of mothers cannot satisfy the powerful emotional needs of the child. Thus the symbol is a piece of flesh over its gap. How, then, can we fail to take Melanie Klein's words further and say, beyond what she says, what she has not said, but says all the same – namely, that the internalized image of the dead father, the creator of the dead children that we bear within us, is creation, a manifestation of the symbolic.

2

Othello
A tragedy of conversion
Black magic and white magic

For the use of Alain Cuny

...e che da me le Donne Italiane imparino, di non si accompagnare con huomo, cui la Natura, e il Cielo, e il modo della vita disgiunge da noi.

> Giraldi Cinthio, quoted by Bradley

For when the flames of love arise,
Then Self, the gloomy tyrant, dies.

> Muhammad ibn Muhammad (Jalal el Din),
> quoted by Freud (*S.E.*, XII, 65)

The psycho-analyst and *Othello*

What is a psycho-analytic reading? Let us not play the innocent and dodge the difficulty by replying: it is a reading by a psycho-analyst. The psycho-analyst reads Shakespeare for two reasons. First, because Shakespeare is a literary genius, whose creation is a rich source of knowledge about man. The enormous impact of his work, in which almost every man feels concerned, indicates that this knowledge is of a fundamental kind. Second, because Shakespeare is an investigator of the human characteristics that throw a bridge between that humanity of which all men are part and the humanity that belongs to the proper field of the psycho-analyst: that of neurosis and psychosis. Just as there is an alienation common to all men and an alienation that affects only some of them, Othello belongs, by good or ill chance, to both registers. Every man feels inevitably involved in jealousy, since he is born of two parents one of whom was the object of his desire and the other an obstacle to the fulfilment of his desire; some men experience insane jealousy, though the clinician observes a whole range of intermediary states between the most ordinary structures, those closest to the common condition of men, and the most mysterious structures, those furthest removed from communicable experience.

So the psycho-analyst approaches *Othello* with curiosity and sympathy. What does he hope to find? Before answering this question, let me deal with some of the possible objections to his approach. The analyst does not arrive before the text in a virginal state. He is pregnant with his knowledge, that is to say, burdened, bound by his prejudice. He cannot attain the emptiness that he must practise whenever he undertakes the analysis of a patient, listening with his 'third ear' to the new sounds of the analytic speech. He cannot do this, because the text that is submitted to him is not the text of a psycho-analytic session. That is a form of speech that is both free in that it has let go its rational moorings, and constrained by the analytic pact to say everything. So, on the one hand, we have an analyst with an analytic theory – that of Freud on jealousy – and, on the other, a text communicated through written speech, which is no more analysable than its author would be through it. So is not the whole undertaking doomed to failure, especially if the analyst desires to hear only the text and not the author? There is a false dilemma here. If the analysis is true, then the analyst derives true knowledge about man from it. He may set out to verify it, even when the technical conditions of analysis are not fulfilled, as if he were confronted simply by one of the various modes of disguise that he encounters in his practice. It is a frozen disguise, and therefore not accessible to an interrogation capable of providing an answer, even a veiled one. But it is a fixed disguise, that is to say, apprehensible, open to as many readings as are necessary to form an opinion. Meaning is veiled but also unveiled by that very veiling, since the veil clings so closely to what it hides that it reveals its contours exactly.

Did not Freud think that psycho-analytic therapy was itself merely one of the aspects of applied psycho-analysis, psycho-analysis claiming above all to be a theory and method that would lead to general conclusions that went well beyond those derived from the treatment of the neuroses? Through what language can the encounter between a subject (psycho-analyst) and an object (*Othello*, the Shakespearean tragedy) take place? Through language written to be represented. *Othello* is a play written to be performed, to be represented. It implies the existence, therefore, not so much of a reader as of a spectator–listener who has to be involved. The psycho-analyst's reading will therefore be a double reading: a reading of the text and a reading of the representation, that is to say, a search in the organization of the signifiers for whatever it is that affects the spectator–listener through its representation in the representation. In short, the question is, why was the Elizabethan spectator, and why are we ourselves, interested in the spectacle?

This first double reading will, therefore, be confronted by another double reading, that of the Freudian theory of jealousy with that of the phenomenology of the experience of jealousy. It might be thought that one could establish a relation between, on the one hand, the representation and the phenomenological experience of jealousy, both grouped under the banner of the conscious, and, on the other hand, the organization of the signifiers that support the representation by acting on the spectator–listener and the Freudian theory, the last two being placed at the level of their effects on the subject in the register of the unconscious.

Freud deconstructs the conscious experience of jealousy. He proposes its 'construction' at the level of the unconscious. Shakespeare, who describes an insane jealousy in order to make his public share it, succeeds in this, because he set in operation, unknown to himself, a homologous construction.

I STRUCTURE, SUBJECT, TRIAL

Synchronic difference and diachronic difference

Of Shakespeare's four major tragedies, *Hamlet, Macbeth, Lear* and *Othello*, the last is the only one with a contemporary setting. Based on a story by Giraldi Cinthio, *Othello* dates from 1604, three years after *Hamlet*, a year before *King Lear*, two years before *Macbeth*. (A comparison between Cinthio's and Shakespeare's plots, interesting as it may be, only brings out Shakespeare's genius in pruning, simplifying, tightening up – for the whole interest of *Othello* derives from the articulation between the elements of action, character and language. Two differences are perhaps worth mentioning. In Cinthio's version, Iago is in love with Desdemona and his villainy is motivated by the fact that his love is not reciprocated. Moreover, the crime is committed jointly by Iago and Othello, who simulate an accident.)

The *Hecatommithi* (published in 1565), from which *Othello* is taken, is a collection of stories recounted by passengers during a sea voyage from Rome to Marseilles in 1527. Shakespeare found the material for a tragedy in an anecdotal narrative, similar to the interludes that are interspersed among the adventures of *Don Quixote* to entertain the reader. This was not the first or the last time that Shakespeare was to use a contemporary plot, but *Othello* is the only tragedy in which he did so.

It is as if the distance that tragedy always requires – a distance that gives the hero his special aura and which is usually produced by setting the scene in the past – was created here by the myth of a distant origin. Certain critics, among them Oscar Campbell, have noted a certain 'far away and long ago' quality in the character of Othello himself. The last descendant of a race of giants, he is too large-scale a figure for this small world. The play is called *Othello, the Moor of Venice*, thus marking the distance between the hero's native country and the city of the Doges.[1] But this substitution for the diachronic effect of a synchronic effect proves a source of ambiguity.

In my view, there is a very close correspondence between the contemporaneity of the action and the foreign origin of the hero, that ultimate foreignness that complete blackness would represent for a Renaissance world in the process of discovering strange new lands.[2] These links enable us to understand that there is, from the very beginning of the play, a context of alienation – the sociological aspect reflects it – whose aim is to establish a difference (which Othello would like to reduce by his admission to Venetian citizenship).[3] The essence of this alienation is original here, and dependent on place of birth, where in the ancient tragic forms it was usually established by the evocation of a mythical time or the exceptional circumstances surrounding the hero's birth.

The two worlds and their representatives

There are in *Othello* two worlds: that of men and that of the gods. The human world is divided into three classes.

First, there is the 'class of power', that of the state of Venice, administered by the Doges. This class is jealous of its power and of its wealth. It serves as a framework to the tragedy, appearing at the beginning and at the end. But this class, which sits in council and represents 'the bloody book of law', subtly betrays it to safeguard its own interests. As often in Shakespeare, the class of power is one not quite on the point of collapse, but which has lost its self-confidence and is under reprieve. The Turks are defeated, not by the Republic of Venice, but by the storm. But Venice has already revealed its weaknesses in the failure of old Brabantio to get a father's word respected. For if Desdemona's consent is enough to declare her marriage valid, why defend Cyprus and prevent it from being seduced by the Turks?

Then there is the 'class of pleasure', to which Desdemona belongs, the class of love and gallantry, of the flower of Venetian youth. Desdemona in no way surrenders this world, whatever she says, as is clear in the scene of her arrival in Cyprus. No doubt she wishes to be associated with Othello's military exploits, but is it not obvious that she goes on enjoying the pleasures of the girl she still is, judging by the sport and mirth of the second act, while her husband is still at sea, perhaps even in danger? Othello and Iago do not belong to this class. Desdemona – despite her desire to share Othello's life as a soldier – does not renounce the advantages of her sex, and Cassio, though a soldier, does not forget that there are times when a handsome officer is also a gallant. Cassio, too, belongs to the class of pleasure. Not that he is entirely part of it: he is there as a mediator.

The third class is that which communicates between the first two. It is the 'class of war', between the power that it serves and the pleasure that it despises. It is the class of heroes and of men. Othello's tragic situation stems from the fact that by his marriage he stands between power and pleasure and is incapable of bringing together these two extremes which, for him, are as far apart as heaven and earth.

Opposite this speaking world there is the silent world of the gods, who work away unheard and unseen by men. There is an opposition between the Moorish god , who work through magic and sorcery, and the Christian God, a God of love, of fidelity, but also a subtle, crafty God, whose servants bear on their faces a thousand contradictory and mysterious expressions that are a source of deception. Once the transgression has been committed with the marriage of Desdemona and Othello, made possible by Othello's conversion, this conversion itself turns against him the Moorish gods of his birth, whom he has abandoned, and also turns away from him the Christian God, who wishes to have nothing to do with him. Together they make him pay for this conversion with his life.

No individual figure emerges to represent the class of power. The agents of the law, the Doge in particular, are, quite rightly, a mere expression of the government, as also are the senators, apart from the sorry figure of Brabantio. They display neither strength, virtue, nor courage. They react to the Turkish threat rapidly and efficiently, but they do not refer to a heritage in danger, or to a threat to some part of the national territory. Cyprus is a warehouse to be defended, a key position on the trade route to the East. It would seem that Shakespeare intended to contrast the magnificent monstrosity of the Moor, who arouses pity, with the timid mediocrity of the Doge's ambassadors as represented by Lodovico and Gratiano. In the last act, when Roderigo, Cassio and Iago are killing one another and cries for help echo unanswered in the night, Lodovico is concerned more for his own safety than with rising to the situation:

> Two or three groan. It is a heavy night.
> These may be counterfeits: let's think't unsafe
> To come in to the cry without more help.   (v, 1)

It is the same Lodovico who brings the tragedy to an end, as the ambassador of power:

> Myself will straight abroad and to the State
> This heavy act with heavy heart relate. (v, 2)

The last word is for the Republic of Venice, its governors and its God.

It is not difficult to establish a relation between the characters of the first act and the 'messengers of Venice' of the last act, passing judgement on Othello's crime. It might be said that Lodovico is to the Doge what Gratiano is to Brabantio. The first two are the representatives of the interests of the state, the second two of the rights of the family. The Doge and Lodovico lay down the law and issue orders, but they do not persuade us of the authenticity of their idea of justice or authority. Brabantio and Gratiano are pitiful figures who would have been quite incapable of preventing either the elopement (in Brabantio's case) or the murder (in Gratiano's). Here, as often in Shakespeare, power is suspended. The fact that this situation recurs so frequently shows that the Shakespearean universe does not so much stigmatize power for its mistakes as bind it indissolubly to its decline. Moreover, Shakespeare shows how impossible it is for any power to maintain itself at the level at which it is expected to operate. Political power is linked with paternal power under the emblem of the phallic signifier. It is to this that Othello must come, in this tragedy; it is here that he must prove himself before Eros by acceding to the situation of a husband, that is to say, by taking in Desdemona's eyes the place of the father from whom he took her. And Desdemona, with her own lips, before the entire Senate, has declared in his favour. He wanted the father's place: he has it. This is as much as to say that he puts himself in a position to lose it.

The class of soldiers is represented by two major figures: the valiant Moor and his ensign Iago. Othello, called to plead his cause before the senators, describes himself thus:

> Rude am I in my speech,
> And little blest with the soft phrase of peace. (i, 3)

For Othello, peace is the time of love. It is not so much that he lacks eloquence, since it was precisely his eloquence that seduced Desdemona, but it is a soldier's eloquence and it was through the accounts of his adventures that he won his bride:

> And little of this great world can I speak,
> More than pertains to feats of broil and battle. (i, 3)

Many commentators have pointed out there is nothing 'rude'

about Othello's style, with its hyperbole and high-flown figures of speech, spiced with evocations of his African condition that verge on bombast. His powerlessness when confronted with the experience of jealousy lies in his use of the traditional language of love. When he questions himself for the first time about the possible causes of Desdemona's infidelity (III, 3), he cites his age ('for I am declined / Into the vale of years'), his colour ('Haply, for I am black') and his manners ('And have not those soft parts of conversation / That chamberers have'). His vacillation in love corresponds to a failing in his language.

Iago's misogyny is striking and has been noted by everyone. It is easy enough to interpret it as stemming from the homosexuality that unites the members of what Freud called that 'artificial crowd', the army. For the moment, let us just examine his attitude to women; the first scene of the second act gives him an opportunity of expressing this in the play of apologies in which Desdemona invites him to participate for her amusement. Iago emerges as the soldier for whom all women are tarts, 'Players in your housewifery, and housewives in your beds'. The important point for us is to note the signification of this attitude for Iago himself. For it obeys an imperative: narcissistic mastery in the omnipotent exercise of the means at his disposal in the service of self-interest. This is his false scent; this return of desire, which is expressed only through its negation, will not prevent it from being linked with his unconscious desire, of which I shall say more later. The malignity that has been analysed, though seldom accounted for – critics have been right to say that it is without foundation – is not enough to dispel the mystery of the character and cannot be taken as the ultimate motive of his action.

Cassio is the third element of this triad. We have already placed him, as Desdemona's companion, in the class of pleasure. But he is also a soldier, the Moor's lieutenant, having overtaken Iago, his senior, in obtaining this promotion. He differs profoundly from the other two in manners and upbringing: ''tis my breeding / That gives me this bold show of courtesy' (II, 1). He has neither the rough manners nor the crude speech of a soldier. Iago calls him 'a great arithmetician', and a 'bookish theoric' (I, 1). He is a wit rather than a hardened soldier, a man who knows how to talk to the ladies, a master of all the gallantries that win their hearts. 'Very good; well kiss'd! an excellent courtesy!' remarks Iago, observing him and biding his time. He is the Moor's exact negation and provides an image very close to one of those patrician's sons who were rivals for Desdemona's hand in Venice and to whom she preferred Othello.

Othello, Iago and Cassio constitute the three points of the male triangle, a triangle imposed on the female triangle formed by Desdemona, Emilia and Bianca. Although Desdemona is the central figure in this triangle – as Othello is for the class of soldiers – she assumes her full value only when associated with Emilia, who serves as her lady's companion, and is contrasted with Bianca, the prostitute, with whom Othello identifies her at the end of the tragedy. Thus three images of woman are drawn. Desdemona is the young bride, the young beloved, hardly yet a woman, still close to the masculine part of herself in phallic identification with her husband. Emilia is the married woman, who has lost the early illusions of marriage, the object of the sarcastic remarks of her husband, whom she serves with submission, but to whom she is not bound by fidelity. We do not know whether to believe Iago when he accuses her of having been the mistress of both Othello and Cassio. It may be that this, like others of his remarks, is a calumny – but she herself, at the end of the tragedy, when Desdemona asks her whether she would be unfaithful to her husband, replies unambiguously: 'In troth, I think I should; and undo't when I had done' (iv, 3). What, then, distinguishes Emilia from Bianca, the soldier's girl, a prostitute, perhaps, but a good-hearted girl for all that, who is sincerely in love with Cassio? The fact that she gets money out of it? Emilia, an honest woman, who is not without generosity, since she is to sacrifice her life to vindicate the truth, says: 'who would not make her husband a cuckold to make him a monarch?' (iv, 3).

Desdemona, at the very beginning of her married life, seems to be confronted here with other types of femininity and, at this point, she has not yet opted decisively for any one of them. She contains within herself the ambiguity of several possible ways.

The subject between two trials

Who is, where is, the subject in Othello? The title seems to provide an answer: Othello is the hero as subject. This is obvious enough but it does not take us far and leaves the real questions unanswered. Is the subject, then, the subject as the subject of the tragedy, jealousy? There is a middle way: these two aspects may be brought together to reveal the subject as jealous hero. But this is to settle the matter rather prematurely, for it is to use words pregnant with meaning that seem rather too self-explanatory. Why is it necessary to dwell on the topic of jealousy at all? Is it not so widespread an experience that anyone may identify with it directly enough to understand on the normal scale what Othello experiences in an exaggerated form?

Let us suspend judgement on jealousy and its signification. Let us note simply that the subject in the structural sense is the trial, the trial as process of the tragedy, as the nodal point of the forces interlinked in the spectacle. It is the spectacular trial of the destruction after its conquest, or by its conquest, of the love-object whose loss involves the loss of the ego. It is as if this misfortune were a terrible penalty, a punishment laid down by some invisible authority.

If we think back to the four great tragedies, we note that the tragic element in *Hamlet* derives from circumstances that take place before the action of the play, and which confront the hero with obligations that he feels incapable of carrying out – the revenge of his father's murder. In *Macbeth*, the ambition that brings the hero to his downfall is primarily punished for crimes that it did not baulk at. As for *King Lear*, it is a defect of judgement that is expiated so dearly by the old king. There is nothing comparable in *Othello*. Here, everything is as it should be. Othello is a victorious captain whose marriage was also a sort of victorious battle sanctioned by a treaty – the approval of the Doge – and who suddenly falls as by some purely internal mechanism, which can be attributed only to insane passion. The subject, therefore, is the trial of insane jealousy.

But we must take things quite literally. For it is certainly a trial that is involved here. Indeed, the whole play is stretched between two trials: the trial of Desdemona's elopement with which the tragedy opens and the trial of her murder that brings it to an end, with the suicide of the jealous husband. *Othello* is the trial between two trials.

This final slaughter, in which only the deaths of the husband and wife concern us, forces us to seek the reason for this fatality. There is a suggestion here of the fulfilment of an oracle as in Greek tragedy. One sets out in quest of some equivalent that takes its place, like the appearance of the ghost in *Hamlet*, the strident predictions of the witches in *Macbeth*, or some riddling remark thrown out by the Fool in *Lear*. We must be content with less here: with a single sentence, in which Desdemona's father gives full vent to his sorrow and disappointment. His words serve as a curse that is to hang over Othello for the rest of his days.

The transgression, the necessary correlative of the punishment, is here (as always) paternal transgression. The elopement fully justifies the father's anger and ensuing curse. The law has been violated. The law here is respect for the father's trust in admitting the foreigner into his house: 'Her father loved me; oft invited me' (I, 3). But is this law simply the human law of hospitality? Does not such a series of misfortunes indicate an angry God? (Both Charlton and Swinburne mention the comparison with ancient tragedy.) Who would the gods be if they were present? Is it the Christian God from whom Othello forces Desdemona to ask pardon before her death? And who is Othello's God? Is it the God of his conversion? Is it some pagan god of war to whom Othello sacrifices everything? Would it not rather be the gods of Mauritania, whom he never mentions, but who are those of his birth? But who are the Moorish gods, what do they want? We have no means of knowing at first. Let us question the trial, which will tell us. Essentially, this trial will be a witches' trial; the Mauritanian god is a sorcerer's god.

The two trials

The elopement trial and the murder trial have the same object, the same cause, Desdemona. These two trials are won by Othello in somewhat different circumstances. In the elopement trial, he gets the sentence reversed and the secret marriage accepted. In the murder trial, he snatches victory as if from old Brabantio, who would hand him over to the courts, by inflicting his punishment on himself. His suicide, like that of any criminal, baffles justice. Othello gives himself death as he gave himself Desdemona. He was the author of the elopement and the author of the murder: he will be the author of the punishment. He does everything himself, preparing the way to the grave as he prepares the way to the bridal bed, as if all this was of concern only to him. The crime and the suicide are inextricably linked: a part of himself conquered by himself is destroyed to prove that it is conquered, bringing with this conquest the destruction of the conqueror who eternally proves that he is inseparable from his conquest.

The law of Venice recognized Othello's right to elope with Desdemona and to make her his. The law might take her back from him. The law did no more than approve his cause, a necessary approval for whoever wishes to live among his fellow men. But, in preference to life among men, Othello chooses his own law and his own desire, for which he needs no other approval than his own. To accept that the punishment should come from Venice is to accept a third authority between himself and Desdemona; it is to find himself once more face to face with something he wished to tear himself away from. To die for Venice, for Desdemona, yes. To die at the hands of Venice, Venice having taken Desdemona back from him, is to be for ever separated from the love-object. For Othello, the law and desire are one.

Sorcery and oracle

If we began at the end, with the outcome of this second trial, in the presence of the representatives of Venice – Lodovico and Montano, and more particularly Gratiano, the brother of Brabantio, Desdemona's dead father, who is thus represented by his brother – it is because the end often throws light on the beginning. Thus it is by means of a cunning trick – a hidden dagger – that the disarmed and guarded Moor succeeds in killing himself before the eyes of his judges. The effect of deception that is the keynote of the tragedy is even more striking if one remembers that the suicide by stabbing re-enacts Othello's account of how he once punished a Turk, 'a circumcisèd dog', for having beaten a Venetian and insulted the state. In doing so, Othello, despite the allegiance he has shown to his new masters and to his new God, kills himself by identifying himself with the victim closest to him in race and origin. Also, in the very movement in which he affirms his loyalty to Venice, by carrying out justice on himself, he subtracts himself from its law. The simulacrum here becomes truth.

Deception has once again been effective – again, for it was through deception that he seduced Desdemona. Travellers have leave to lie, but there is nothing to show that Othello lied in the fantastic accounts he tells of his own history. His deception lies elsewhere. While speaking to the father, he sought the ear of his daughter, who was attending to household duties.

> This to hear
> Would Desdemona seriously incline:
> But still the house-affairs would draw her thence;
> Which ever as she could with haste dispatch,
> She'd come again, and with a greedy ear
> Devour up my discourse: which I observing,
> Took once a pliant hour; and found good means
> To draw from her a prayer of earnest heart
> That I would all my pilgrimage dilate,
> Whereof by parcels she had something heard,
> But not intentively. (1, 3)

Brabantio's supervision was deceived only because Othello could not be suspected of courting his daughter: he had devoted his life to soldiering and, unlike Desdemona's usual suitors, whom she had rejected, Othello was no longer a young man. This is why the old man cannot see in this marriage, as do his peers the Doges, a natural consequence of a very ordinary situation. He needs other reasons: the Moor has some power, the Moor uses sorcery. Yet he has had a presentiment of the outcome in his dreams: 'This accident is not unlike my dream' (1, 1), he remarks when he learns of Desdemona's elopement.

Nevertheless, he goes on to speak of

> charms
> By which the property of youth and maidenhood
> May be abused.

'Thou hast enchanted her,' he tells the Moor:

> Judge me the world, if 'tis not gross in sense
> That thou has practised on her with foul charms;
> Abused her delicate youth with drugs or minerals
> That waken motion. (I, 2)

For the nature of this virgin, brought up in the Christian religion, a patrician's daughter, could not be deceived without sorcery, without ˙some mixtures powerful o'er the blood'.

The whole action of the tragedy is enveloped in the mystery of unleashed acts of violence that constantly surprise: the sudden attack of the Turks, the sudden rising of the storm, the dispersal and almost miraculous shipwreck of the enemy, the survival of the Venetians, sailing through the storm unscathed. Over all these events hovers the shadow of the supernatural. Othello possesses a particular charisma since the deeds of valour associated with his 'star' may indeed be imputed to some extra-terrestrial power. At the very beginning of the play, Iago links Othello with demoniacal imagery. He wakens old Brabantio by yelling up at his windows:

> An old black ram
> Is tupping your white ewe. (I, 1)

In this metaphor the erotic and satanic elements remain indeterminate, while two lines later, the latter completely obscures the former and retroactively tips the scales of meaning in one direction:

> Arise, arise!
> Awake the snorting citizens with the bell,
> Or else the Devil will make a grandsire of you (I, 1)

Othello is mentioned even before he appears in that space of phantasy that we do not enter. We seek him in the darkness of the scene that centres around the father's sorrow, as he himself will seek the handkerchief given to Desdemona to seal their union:

> there's magic in the web of it.
> A sibyl, that had number'd in the world
> The Sun to course two hundred compasses,
> In her prophetic fury sew'd the work;
> The worms were hallow'd that did breed the silk;
> And it was dyed in mummy which the skilful
> Conserved of maidens' hearts. (III, 4)

We may see in this two-hundred-year-old seamstress the phallic mother who combines in her creation the composition of silk and mortuary dust to make Desdemona's wedding veil – a veil held up between Othello and Desdemona because above all it is evidence of the Moor's desire for his mother. For it was she who gave it to him. On this point Shakespeare assigns a double origin to the precious material. According to the first version (III, 4), an 'Egyptian charmer' gave it to Othello's mother, while according to another passage in the last scene of the play the Moor declares that the handkerchief was given to his mother by his father. In so far as Shakespeare provides no justification for it, the mystery of this double origin must contradict any simplistic explanation such as, for example, that the Moor made it all up in order to frighten Desdemona. The mystery can only be cleared up by elucidating the phantasy that underlies the story. That is why it seems to me to be preferable to leave things as they are and to see in the coexistence of the two versions an invitation to articulate them one upon the other.

Is not the apparent contradiction like a double inscription of Othello's desire? The two versions are separated by Desdemona's death. Alive, she must be possessed of the attributes of a charm that she herself cannot inspire, but which is conferred on her by the handkerchief. She joins the line of women: the sibyl, the 'Egyptian charmer', the mother, all surrounded by a halo of omnipotence conferred on them by a gift such as that possessed by the Egyptian woman who 'could almost read / The thoughts of people', an omnipotence that goes with the handkerchief, its possession being a guarantee of the desire inspired by the love-object. Othello says of this talisman:

> while she [the mother] kept it,
> 'Twould make her amiable and subdue my father
> Entirely to her love; but, if she lost it,
> Or made a gift of it, my father's eye
> Should hold her loathèd, and his spirits should hunt
> After new fancies. (III, 4)

The father's eye is also the eye that Othello deceives in seducing Desdemona. When Desdemona is dead, Othello appears before the Venetian authorities sitting as an improvised court. It is the father who reappears on this occasion so that Othello may designate him as the one who gave the handkerchief to his mother, in recognition of her desire of the phallus.

The attribution to women of the power to charm, to which Othello is the first to refer, is contrasted later with the fact that it is her husband's wish that Desdemona should radiate beauty and charm. Each of Desdemona's attractions is later transformed, under the effects of jealousy, into a magic power: 'Death and damnation!'

(III, 3). There is a devil in Desdemona. One may well wonder whether Othello is not evoking in the language of his new religion the powers of his ancestral faith. And in declaiming that Desdemona is a witch, is he doing any more than re-establishing her, after this loss of the handkerchief, in the series of maternal figures of primitive omnipotence, all-powerful in evil as they were in good? What was excluded from the phallic power reappears at the end of the tragedy only after Desdemona's death, in reference to the paternal speech that was betrayed by conversion to the Christian God. Othello's Name-of-the-Father (Lacan) having been defaced by this renunciation, it falls to another ridiculed father, Desdemona's, at the beginning of the tragedy, to invoke a punishment, however purely moral and ineffective it may be, following the elopement in which Othello is linked without mediator to Desdemona. But this paternal speech will be swamped in the illusory triumph over authority that the Doge's endorsement has made legal by recognizing the validity of the marriage.

For Othello will emerge absolved from the witch trial. In fact, Othello never doubted that he would. He never feared the justice of the Doge, and when he presents himself before the Senate, assembled as a court, he listens quietly to the Doge's promise to Brabantio:

> The bloody book of law
> You shall yourself read in the bitter letter
> After your own sense; yea, though our proper son
> Stood in your action. (1, 3)

This cannot touch him: he is the pillar of the state, the guarantor of the power of Venice. Iago has already said as much to the spectator:

> For, I do know, the State –
> However this may gall him with some check –
> Cannot with safety cast him. (1, 1)

Othello confirms this when he defies Desdemona's father:

> Let him do his spite:
> My services which I have done the signiory
> Shall out-tongue his complaints. (1, 2)

In Jacques Lacan's terminology, I should say of Othello that at the moment of the tragedy he *is* the phallus. Or, as Lacan shows, *having* it implies that one ceases to sustain the belief that one *is* it. And all Othello's misfortunes stem from the fact that *being* a great captain, he will have to pass to the state in which he *has* a wife. The problematic of having her will reappear in everything affected by the question of 'having' or 'not having' the handkerchief.

This power attributed by Brabantio to Othello, this black magic, is simply the phallic power, the effect of Othello's seduction of Desdemona. The identification of the young Venetian woman with the triumphant hero of a thousand perils is thus expressly designated by Shakespeare:

> She wish'd
> That Heaven had made her such a man. (I, 3)[4]

And Othello says confidently and no doubt truthfully:

> This only is the witchcraft I have used.

Brabantio is thunderstruck by his daughter's betrayal. In time, it kills him. Henceforth, all that remains for him is to struggle against the black magic with white magic. His God has betrayed and abandoned him. His peers are concerned more to preserve their wealth than their honour. Having lost, he asks, with cruel irony, that they should move on to the only matter that is of concern to the Doges at that moment: 'on to the State-affairs.' Nevertheless, he throws out a warning that serves as a kind of fate for his victor:

> Look to her, Moor, if thou hast eyes to see:
> She has deceived her father, and may thee. (I, 3)

The eye of the betrayed father becomes the evil eye of the challenge, which will bring about the ruin of the wife who loses possession of the talisman. This is the equivalent in *Othello* of the oracle. And, as often in situations in which the oracle speaks, the hero replies with the quiet assurance of a favourable present. Thus the presumptuous Othello replies confidently and trenchantly:

> My life upon her faith. (I, 3)

He will pay for this reply with two lives rather than one, and will lose his faith.

II DESIRE

The object of desire: between Desdemona and Othello

It is usual to develop analyses of *Othello* around the trio formed by the object of jealousy, Desdemona, its inducing agent, Iago, and the induced subject, Othello. When one limits oneself to this perspective, one is caught between tautology (jealousy is jealousy, it is inexplicable, it is without foundation) and lack of verisimilitude (*Othello* is a mere melodrama, totally divorced from reality). In the second case, one has no need to explain how a brilliant captain praised for his intelligence loses his head so easily when confronted with so crude a piece of scheming. One swings constantly between two theses, the first that makes Iago the diabolical constructor of the effective machinery in which Othello is caught like a fly in a spider's web, the second in which Othello, predisposed to jealousy, seizes upon the bait offered him by Iago to feed the green-eyed monster that inhabits him. In all these analyses one is struck by the exclusion of one term and the silence on one question. The discussion eliminates the character of Cassio, who is regarded as negligible, hardly more important than Roderigo or Montano, and not a moment's pause is given to the question of the possible foundation of Othello's jealousy: is it conceivable that Desdemona might love Cassio? In this case, the handkerchief plays the role of the decoy or lure, though this is not its only effect. Since Cassio possesses Desdemona's handkerchief only by accident or by someone else's design, and since Desdemona did not give it to him, the love attributed to them by Othello is pure imagination. But this exclusion and this silence are highly suspect. To begin with, one forgets that the play opens with an event that concerns Cassio: his recent promotion, which does not follow the normal course of events, to the rank of the general's lieutenant (*lieu-tenant,* one who takes the place of and replaces, when necessary). This promotion is presented to us solely from the point of view of the jealousy it arouses in the man who has most to lose from it, the ensign Iago, who is Cassio's senior. But the promotion is also evidence of another fact: Othello's predilection for Cassio; and we have no reason to reject the hypothesis of a possible favouritism on the part of the Moor. Indeed, by his behaviour, Cassio appears in no way to conform to the image that one has of the Moor's lieutenant, the man who must replace him on all occasions. On the contrary, he proves to be rather weak, irresolute, naïve, effeminate. Certainly this Phoebus is attractive: young, handsome, well-bred, educated, a good talker, gallant, one who wins the hearts of young women by the attentions he pays them. It seems that Othello is hard put to justify this passing over when Iago's emissaries demand an explanation for the appointment. It is said that Othello

> Evades them, with a bombast circumstance
> Horribly stuff'd with epithets of war. (i, i)

In the scene in which Iago casts suspicion on Cassio, Othello says that he 'went between us very oft'. That is Cassio's precise situation: he is between Desdemona and Othello. This means that he offers the young Venetian woman all that an education as a gallant has taught a young officer about the courtship of the fair sex and that he offers Othello his professional life as a soldier by way of gaining his affection. When Iago accuses Cassio and Desdemona of having an illicit love affair, we react in protest, indignant at such calumnious treachery. But it would be naïve to see this as no more than pure invention. Iago does not invent this hypothesis simply to serve his own ends: he is convinced of it. Or rather, he anticipates it with discreet signs, but he does not create it out of nothing. Cassio, before the Moor, welcomes Desdemona to Cyprus; he does so in such a way that it is difficult to draw the line between admiration felt for the general's wife and a new kind of emotion. 'Divine Desdemona' is hailed like a queen:

> O, behold,
> The riches of the ship is come on shore!
> Ye men of Cyprus, let her have your knees.
> Hail to thee, lady! (II, 1)

And, in Othello's absence, Iago makes the following commentary on their conversation:

He takes her by the palm: ay, well said, whisper: with as little a web as this will I ensnare as great a fly as Cassio. Ay, smile upon her, do; I will gyve thee in thine own courtship. You say true; 'tis so, indeed: if such tricks as these strip you out of your lieutenantry, it had been better you had not kiss'd your three fingers so oft, which now again you are most apt to play the sir in. Very good; well kiss'd! An excellent courtesy! 'tis so, indeed. Yet again your fingers to your lips? Would they were clyster-pipes for your sake! (II, 1)

Before we accuse him of vulgarity for this last remark, we should rather recognize at this point the mark of homosexuality in Iago's jealousy. The analysis of Desdemona's feelings that Iago gives Roderigo bears the mark of his subjective position, of course. But it is not entirely disqualified on that account. It may also contain a grain of truth – and when he declares, 'Desdemona is directly in love with him [Cassio]', he expands and therefore necessarily distorts what is visible of a courtship that at this stage is no more than light-hearted in its aims and traditional in its methods. Nevertheless, we should examine its development attentively. Will Desdemona's love of Othello last? Would this love at first sight, as Iago experiences it, prove to be no more than a flash in the pan? 'When the blood is made dull with the act of sport, there should be – again to inflame it, and to give satiety a fresh appetite – loveliness in favour, sympathy in years, manners, and beauties; all which the Moor is defective in' (II, 1). Now, Cassio has all these things: everything that the Moor is defective in. The probable is not always true and the true not always probable. But is not the scene in which Desdemona should have shown more anxiety for her husband, who was still at sea in the midst of a storm that had not yet calmed, and in which she seems to have been very glad of Cassio's company, a sign of things to come? 'Didst thou not see her paddle with the palm of his hand? didst not mark that?', Iago asks. 'Yes, that I did; but that was courtesy', Roderigo protests. 'Lechery, by this hand...They met so near with their lips, that their breaths embraced together' (II, 1), Iago swears an oath with Roderigo, the spurned suitor, now tricked by his supposed friend, by offering him his hand as a sign of his sincerity. But as he does so his outstretched hand becomes in his phantasy first that of the courteous lieutenant, offered to Desdemona, then Desdemona's fingers penetrating Cassio from behind. Under sarcasm and mockery Iago masks the anticipated pleasure aroused in him by the play of interpenetrating breaths. We should remember Freud's observation about the desire of the jealous man who tears away the veil of the unconscious in order to make himself receptive to the secret of the signs of female seduction, which have been robbed of their significa-tion by social usage. This extra-lucidity concerning the recognition of their erotogenic value, which has been eroded by social practice to such an extent that those who exchange them have lost any sense of their original function, is paid for in full by the *méconnaissance* of the part played in this game by the jealous man who deciphers these signs and interprets them. This prevents him from being the recipient of these acts of homage so that he is assured all the more of finding himself in a space outside his own view, brilliantly occupy-ing the place too discreetly held by the female source of these messages. But we should not see this solely as the effect of projection. Projection also comes into play when he begins to interest us in the spectacle. In any case, there is, for the moment, nothing improbable in Iago's analysis. His description of Cassio – 'a knave very voluble; no further conscionable than in putting on the mere form of civil and humane seeming, for the better compassing of his salt and most hidden-loose affection...a slipper and subtle knave; a finder-out of occasions...the knave is handsome, young, and has all those requi-sites in him that folly and green minds look after' (II, 1) – is perhaps exaggerated, in order to revive Roderigo's tottering faith. But it sins not so much by its falseness as by the illusion of insight to which it lays claim. Moreover, when he is alone, Iago shows that his appraisal of the situation is more moderate and that this appraisal is not simply pretence:

> That Cassio loves her, I do well believe it;
> That she loves him, 'tis apt, and of great credit.　　　　　(II, 1)

What follows is to show that Desdemona's 'inviting eye' has not failed to have its effect on Cassio, who has aroused Desdemona's affection. The two young people meet in secret, unknown to the general. Desdemona promises to plead Cassio's cause, that is to say, to question Othello's decision as if it were more important to her to save Cassio, whose guilt is acknowledged, than to respect her husband's judgement in an affair that hardly calls for intercessors:

> my lord shall never rest;
> I'll watch him tame, and talk him out of patience;
> His bed shall seem a school, his board a shrift;
> I'll intermingle every thing he does
> With Cassio's suit: therefore be merry, Cassio;
> For thy solicitor shall rather die
> Than give thy cause away. (III, 3)

It would seem that the critics and commentators have never read or heard those lines in which Othello's wife, the day after her wedding night, swears to her husband's second-in-command to regard his defence as being more important than any other matter, to use every opportunity, including that of conjugal intimacy, to obtain from her husband the rehabilitation of a man whom he has punished. And this is precisely what she does for the 'thrice-gentle Cassio', incurring Othello's displeasure in doing so. Realizing this, she nevertheless makes her situation worse by seeking help from a third party who has power over Othello (Lodovico) in order to make him change his mind. It is, of course, clear enough that the feelings involved here are not conscious or clearly defined in Desdemona. It is a love ignorant of itself, which grows unknown to her who feels it only because it is lived in innocence and purity. It is also a love in which all sexual desire is for the present banished. The desire is there, as desire of the Other, as Iago guesses. And no doubt Desdemona, at the moment of truth, would have perceived it. For how are we to understand, without falling into the platitudes of an explanation by blind self-sacrifice the lines she speaks shortly before her death:

> 'Tis meet I should be used so, very meet.
> How have I been behaved, that he might stick
> The small'st opinion on my great'st abuse? (IV, 2)

Later, at the moment of her death, she defends herself, less perhaps to save her life than to convince Othello of her fidelity. What is in question is not so much an infidelity in act as a desire that hits the target by corresponding with Othello's sexual desire at the moment when he encounters his lack, which everything about Cassio reminds him of. To Emilia, who finds her dying, and presses her to reveal the author of her death, Desdemona replies: 'Nobody; I myself.' These words have been interpreted as proof of her unconditional and absolute love for Othello. This is certainly the case.

But the time of this final avowal coincides perhaps with her first avowal. On her last night, Desdemona confides to Emilia, who is preparing her for bed, her true feelings for the Moor:

> my love does so approve him,
> That even his stubbornness, his checks, his frowns, –
> Pr'ythee, unpin me, – have grace and favour in them.   (IV, 3)

As she undresses, she recalls the anger of her father, who refused his blessing to this marriage. She finds pleasure in her husband's abuse. Meeting the truth, she recognizes in Othello's desire the place she has come to occupy, the place of the woman who betrays the husband after betraying the father, who now pays with her husband's hand what she once made her father pay.

My hypothesis of Desdemona's love for Cassio as part of the kernel of truth is not complete, however. It must have as its complement another aspect of things, the aspect which is much more difficult to perceive and is totally obliterated from the spectator's view. Silent, but effective, the whole mainspring of the tragedy lies here: Othello's desire for Cassio. I have already noted that the tragedy begins with Cassio's promotion to the lieutenancy given by Othello himself, which suggests a particular favour on the part of the general. We have seen that all Iago's plotting must be bent to Cassio's cashiering, which lays the foundation of the jealousy, because it causes Desdemona to reveal her desire in defending the disgraced lieutenant. It has not been sufficiently noted how necessary this episode is. It is as if, for the jealousy to work, the object of desire which Cassio represents for Othello should weaken and disappoint. Cassio's devaluation precedes or coincides with Desdemona's devaluation.

It is a strange night, which was to have been a night of celebration for all. A wedding night that the elopement, the trial and the expedition had delayed, a night in which desire should blossom, all obstacles removed. The cause has been heard without the trial taking place, victory achieved without a battle. The night of Cyprus is full of promise:

> Come, my dear love,
> The purchase made, the fruits are to ensue;
> That profit's yet to come 'tween me and you. –
> Good night.   (II, 3)

The soldiers' drunkenness and the brawl that follows are set before us, mingling the din of drinking and singing with the clash of swords, while behind the scenes the encounter of the two bodies of Othello and Desdemona is taking place. And it is this night that the general's favourite chooses to disturb. Cassio permits the worst of crimes –

apart from desertion – for a soldier: drunkenness and brawling while
on guard. He arouses for Othello the spectre of weakness at the
moment when he himself must make love his principal desire. When
the lieutenant groans, 'Reputation, reputation, reputation! O, I
have lost my reputation! I have lost the immortal part of myself,
and what remains is bestial' (II, 3), we must see that these words do
not concern him alone. In losing not only his reputation but the
Moor's love, he also sullies Othello's reputation by thus revealing
that Othello's choice of lieutenant was motivated less perhaps by
honour than by partiality.

> Cassio, I love thee;
> But never more be officer of mine. (II, 3)

Of that love, nothing is left that can sustain the esteem of his men.
In demoting Cassio, Othello, throws doubt on his own judgement in
promoting him so rapidly. By interrupting Othello's revels, Cassio
suggests the soldier's most unpredictable failing. The demotion of
the lieutenant is reflected on to the object who now occupies first
place; it passes from Cassio, his second, to Desdemona his half.
But as a result of Cassio's demotion, the term that represents Othello
as the impeccable, incorruptible general is cancelled out in the
opposition between love for his men and the love he has just felt for
his wife. This is the message that is brought back to him from the
citadel he commands, which should have been sleeping in rediscovered peace and assuaged anxiety. This devaluation of the object
of unconscious desire must bring him down so that, dislodged from
the pedestal on which he stood, he might rekindle the slumbering
feeling he inspired, in now finding himself the object of the compassion and solicitude of the Other. This Other that is his half will
be his intercessor. What Desdemona does not know is that she will
die for having revived the unbearable desire that Othello felt for
Cassio. Iago's machination will have the same result. Henceforth,
everything surrounding this unconscious, rejected love is caught up
in a struggle to the death: either Othello will triumph and Cassio
will disappear from his desire, or Othello will succumb and Cassio
will triumph. Of the various possible endings, including the one in
which the lieutenant might have been engulfed in the final slaughter,
Shakespeare chooses the triumph of Cassio. Othello asks him for
forgiveness and Lodovico pronounces the transfer of power:

> Your power and your command is taken off,
> And Cassio rules in Cyprus. (V, 2)

This is more than a rehabilitation; it is a crowning that marks the
assumption of the object and the defeat of the ego.

Othello's desire: between Eros and the death drive

Although commentators realize clearly enough that *Othello* is a tragedy of jealousy, they have done little to situate the precise context of the birth of this jealousy. It has been found surprising that Othello, at the moment of death, should so unexpectedly say of himself that he was 'one not easily jealous'. This is seen as a monstrous lack of self-knowledge. And yet there is a grain of truth in the judgement. What we are witnessing is not simply the contemporaneity of love and jealousy, but rather the contemporaneity of marriage and jealousy. As long as the love-object is free, it is not suspected, but as soon as the institutional bond is established, the bond that re-establishes the knot that unites the father and the mother, then the persecution-delusion of jealousy is triggered off. Moreover, we are not surprised that it is during the wedding night that the drama erupts. The noise of the young couple is muffled by the noise of the brawl in the citadel and the spectator is himself distracted by the carousing from the other orgy that is taking place behind the scene, in the nuptial chamber hidden from sight, where the love-object falls from the altar of idealization, at the moment when flesh is bound to flesh.

Too little has been said about this conjunction that unites the condition of soldier and the condition of jealous man in Othello's character. By separating the external framework from the action, one behaves as if the former were contingent and one fails to take account of the relations that unite the situation of the hero dedicated to a soldier's life with that of his entry into the sphere of love. Everything shows us that Othello is gifted in the art of war, that he is successful at it and that he has won glory in its practice; there is nothing to show us that he might have the same talent in love and reap the same success. Indeed, there are indications that this warrior, so bound up with his companions in arms, has considerable difficulty in accepting love and especially in being loved. In the first instance, Desdemona was a fortified place to be captured. Then she is subjected to his will, tamed. He cannot reconcile himself to seeing Desdemona as no more than a woman, his wife; she becomes the woman who will deprive him of being his wife, of no longer having to be conquered. When he sets foot in Cyprus, he goes straight to her, exclaiming: 'O my fair warrior!' This is no doubt the response to her desire, expressed ever since they were married in Venice, to share Othello's military life. On this point, a certain complicity unites them. But whereas Desdemona can play on the two aspects of her desire – the masculine aspect, which makes her a warrior's companion, and the feminine aspect, which assures her that she will receive once again from Cassio the homage due to her as a young patrician of Venice – Othello finds it much more difficult to move from the field of battle to the infinitely more perilous one of the marriage-bed.

Who can say what took place during their wedding night? And one may well wonder what Othello means when, weeping over Desdemona's corpse, he remarks:

> Cold, cold, my girl!
> Even like thy chastity.   (v, 2)

If the Moor thinks that he did not succeed in moving Desdemona, as a result of his own inability to allow himself to be invaded by love, how much more plausible the basis of the jealousy then appears. Some other, for whom this conquest was still to come, would certainly succeed where he had failed. This other, who has 'all which the Moor is defective in', is Cassio. The handkerchief testifies to this *jouissance* that Cassio has been able to give Desdemona:

> And she did gratify his amorous works
> With that recognizance and pledge of love
> Which I first gave her; I saw it in his hand.   (v, 2)

Let us not forget the precise signification attached to this magic handkerchief, whose power is to assure the efficacity of desire.

The fact that once Desdemona has lost the handkerchief she loses all value in the eyes of Othello reveals, for me, its value as a fetish. Deprived of her phallic emblem she is no more than a castrated woman – to be avoided in order to avoid any contact with castration. But that Othello himself should have lost possession of the handkerchief by giving it to her was already a great risk – a risk that she might transmit it to someone who had everything that he lacked. This narcissistic quality[5] in Othello's love, which is so marked at every point by the mapping of the signs of the phallus, is attested in certain famous lines. When Othello is finally convinced of Desdemona's infidelity, we learn what he has lost with her:

> O, now, for ever
> Farewell the tranquil mind! farewell content!
> Farewell the plumèd troop, and the big wars,
> That make ambition virtue! O, farewell!
> Farewell the neighing steed, and the shrill trump,
> The spirit-stirring drum, th'ear-piercing fife,
> The royal banner, and all quality,
> Pride, pomp, and circumstance of glorious war!
> And, O you mortal engines, whose rude throats
> Th'immortal Jove's dread clamours counterfeit,
> Farewell! Othello's occupation's gone!   (iii, 3)

What he has lost with the love-object is neither the happiness he experiences in Desdemona's arms, nor sexual pleasure, nor *jouissance*, nor the happiness of being loved, nor the possibility of himself loving. What he has lost is the glory of Eros confused with Mars under the appearances of Jupiter. Othello is made for death. The love for which he deserted death will throw him back into its arms and push him back to that death-dominated space from which he came and which tempts him still. Was this not what he expected at Cyprus, a battle in which he would be able to perish or enhance his glory, or both at once? And how are we to interpret that mysterious storm that engulfs the Turkish fleet and spares the ships of Venice[6] other than as a sign from the gods that his hour has come, and that they are withdrawing from the victorious general the sign of their favour? It will not be given to the valiant Moor to die on the field of honour, but to succumb beneath Cupid's darts on the field of dishonour. He chose love and in doing so betrayed death; love betrayed him, making him choose death.

Halfway between that Other that inhabits the strange land of love through which Othello travels with neither map nor weapons, delivered over to Desdemona's spell, and this Same, in which Othello looks at himself as in a mirror in his warrior's armour, there stands the noble, elegant shape of the young Cassio. It is by moving back that we find him here on the path that leads from the female genital object to the narcissistic love that the subject has for himself. Let us examine this for a moment. Is this not how Cassio is presented? We have only to remember the portrait that Iago gives of him, in which his subtleness, his finesse, his manners and his looks are criticized or praised, but in any case envied. But are these not the same qualities that Desdemona possesses? Moreover, Cassio is a soldier. He is no hardened old trooper, of course, but he possesses – at least until his disgrace – all the qualities of a true soldier. He is an accomplished man, possessing all the qualities necessary to please, a virility that has achieved refinement. This is, indeed, everything the Moor longs to possess, since it is precisely this that he has been unable to attain, despite his own eminent qualities. And if narcissism is Othello's most impregnable quality, it is understandable that Cassio should attract love as his chief would like to do. This would also explain the appointment, which cannot be suspected of irregularity, but which certainly springs from favouritism. In short, Cassio, while possessing the same charms as Desdemona, preserves the attributes of the soldier in which Othello would like to recognize himself. And being loved by such a figure must be delightful. Hence the identification with the love-object in jealousy, where Othello feels, almost as if he had managed to be its beneficiary, the admiration that Cassio is able to arouse. In this light, Othello's exclamation as he sets eyes on Desdemona in Cyprus – 'O my fair warrior!' – takes on new meaning. As does also the fact that his love for Desdemona has passed through the medium of Desdemona's desire to be herself a man like Othello. This brings together the narcissistic love, in which Othello's desire takes root and his object-love with which Othello finds it so difficult to accommodate himself when it concerns a female, castrated being.

No trace of this love for Cassio, which the psycho-analyst infers, is to be found in Othello's words; but is further proof of its plausibility required? It might be noted that, as soon as the jealousy is triggered off, Cassio assumes much more importance than Othello, since Othello sacrifices his love-object to him. Commentators have found it very surprising that Iago should be so much more easily believed than Desdemona, and have failed to understand how Othello blinds himself so easily to the truth. In the logic of consciousness, this is indeed very surprising. But if one accepts my hypothesis, the tragedy is to be interpreted otherwise. Othello is not so much furious at Desdemona's betrayal, as cruelly wounded by Cassio's. Cassio's infidelity – his drunkenness on guard was an indication of it – is more important to him than Desdemona's. And when Othello is consumed with anger as he witnesses, off-stage, as it were, a scene which he is not supposed to observe, in which Iago tries to provide proof of Cassio's guilt, Shakespeare chooses to arrange things in such a way that this scene takes place between two men, Cassio and Iago. Othello hastens to see Cassio miming the gestures of a woman whom he presumes to be his own wife, yet Othello also sees Cassio lavish these gestures upon the person of Iago; and when Iago tries to win Othello over to his interpretation of events, he invents a story for the Moor's benefit. He recounts to Othello how he overheard certain things that Cassio had said in his sleep:

>   I lay with Cassio lately;
> And, being troubled with a raging tooth,
> I could not sleep. There are a kind of men
> So loose of soul, that in their sleeps will mutter
> Of their affairs: one of this kind is Cassio.
> In sleep I heard him say, *Sweet Desdemona,*
> *Let us be wary, let us hide our loves;*
> And then, sir, would he gripe and wring my hand,
> Cry *O sweet creature!* and then kiss me hard,
> As if he pluck'd up kisses by the roots
> That grew upon my lips: then laid his leg
> Over my thigh, and sigh'd and kiss'd; and then
> Cried *Cursèd fate that gave thee to the Moor!*   (III, 3)

Usually, one simply admires Iago's perversity and one forgets to pay homage to Shakespeare's extraordinary insight. Nowhere is the efficacity of the decoy better shown. In his scheming, Iago has provided Othello with the phantasy before which he recoils. Using the alibi of representing infidelity, it is in fact a homosexual relation that he forces us, with Othello, to see. What the ensign sets before our eyes is a spectacle that serves as a bait of identification, in which Othello can see himself in Iago's place, madly embraced and kissed by Cassio. The wedding night disturbed by the brawling soldiers then takes on a retrospective significance. 'Just like that night...', Othello might think, shifting his gaze on to what he has been able to learn only through a third party. The thing that eludes this movement of the gaze requires that Othello, at this precise moment, should be looked at in turn by the scene that seizes his attention, more especially as Iago has given the status of impossible verification to his desire for proof:

It is impossible you should see this,
Were they as prime as goats, as hot as monkeys,
As salt as wolves in pride, and fools as gross
As ignorance made drunk. (III, 3)

This argument convinces him more than any other. Better than any other, it will hit the target.

OTHELLO: O monstrous! monstrous!
IAGO: Nay, this was but his dream.
OTHELLO: But this denoted a foregone conclusion:
           'Tis a shrewd doubt, though it be but a dream. (III, 3)

So much so that when, some scenes later, Iago invites him to hide himself in order to overhear his conversation with Cassio, in which Cassio mimics Bianca's assaults, he offers Othello a means of repeating the phantasy, so that the truth of the desire can emerge, by dramatizing, as in the account of the pseudo-dream, two men in illicit intercourse. Cassio even enacts once more with Iago the embrace that he was supposed to have given him while dreaming. This effectiveness of the phantasy rests on projection – no doubt because the dream and the phantasy are projective work. Projection operates here in its purest, essential state, that is to say, it brings back to the subject, through the medium of the outside – here the scenes of the dialogue between Iago and Cassio – what is abolished inside.

Abolished or, as Lacan would say, foreclosed. This foreclosure is different from other forms of repression; it shows more precisely than Freud himself did that all the representations of desire are so radically barred from the functioning of the subject that the subject receives signs from outside as if they were primary, as if nothing had preceded them in the subject's experience, as if they echoed some effaced, long-inoperative trace and asserted themselves with a quite original self-evidence. This is a subversion of symbolization, which is itself repudiated here, since it declares that the two halves it unites – that which is presented and that which it echoes – are alien to one another. It is as if that moment when the subject was set in motion once more by the signifiers it engenders were also a moment of the emergence of the Other as locus of discourse, of the Other as possessor of the integrality of meaning. It is as if the accumulation of the signifiers had never until that moment signified anything, covered over as it was by a shadow that is dissipated with the brutality of revelation – only to designate the unrepresentable, the unthinkable. And so the subject is crushed, dismantled, its fragments serving the meshing of gears required to constitute the meaning of the Other.

Certainly, in psycho-analysis, the discourse of the jealous man reveals an obsessive concern with the rival bordering on homosexuality. Shakespeare sets this mechanism in operation without being too explicit, without revealing too much. He is content to proceed indirectly, with a resulting gain in effectiveness. These 'pieces of the jigsaw' in the functioning of the plot bring us, in the darkness of invisible interpretation, very close to the truth.

At the end of the tragedy, only a moment before Othello's suicide, the ultimate reconciliation takes place:

> CASSIO: Dear general, I never gave you cause.
> OTHELLO: I do believe it, and I ask your pardon.   (v, 2)

These two lines sound very like refound love.

These words of reconciliation are spoken between two deaths: between Desdemona's murder and Othello's suicide, as if death had to win the day. They are words that define Cassio's precise situation between Othello's genital love for Desdemona and Othello's narcissistic love for himself, which leads him to kill himself in order to find his love again. His love! It is an ambiguous formulation that designates both the love-object and the state of being in love, one that enables Othello, through the narcissistic nature of his object-choice, to find himself again in hoping to rejoin Desdemona. (Othello kills Desdemona only when he is convinced that Cassio has been killed by Iago.)

Desdemona can be loved only when dead. Othello never spoke more passionately of Desdemona than at the moment of death, as if death were a condition of love. After embracing her, he says to the sleeping Desdemona:

> Oh balmy breath that does almost persuade
> Justice to break her sword! One more, one more:
> Be thus when thou art dead, and I will kill thee,
> And love thee after. (v, 2)

The fact that to die after her, with her, is the realization of their reciprocal attachment is clearly shown in Othello's last words:

> I kiss'd thee ere I kill'd thee; no way but this,
> Killing myself, to die upon a kiss. (v, 2)

This perfect, point-by-point duplication suggests the relation of the subject to his mirror-image. It is an absolute correspondence, a communicating reciprocity in which death may at last reunite what life has separated. It is not saying much to say that Desdemona is now truly his, since no one can take her from him; it should be added, however, that she is reintegrated in him as a missing half. Desdemona is Othello's and Othello Desdemona's: their relations belong neither to having nor to being, but to something that is common to them and which Freud called the narcissistic investment (cathexis) of the object.

That is why Othello's suicide is the logical act, the reflection on to himself of Desdemona's murder. When, alone with Desdemona's corpse, he has to reply to Emilia, who asks to see him, he says:

> What's best to do?
> If she come in, she'll sure speak to my wife:
> My wife! my wife! what wife? I have no wife. (v, 2)

Bound to her by mutual possession, he could not accept her alive. He cannot accept her dead, deprived of her as of a part of himself snatched away from him. Alive, she was dead in him as soon as she was acquired. Dead, she lives still, and he must constantly throw her off. This shows – a feature very common among those who commit murder out of jealousy, or suicide – that Othello, like them, has no consciousness of death, either of the death he is about to give or of the death he is to give himself. In killing Desdemona, he renews the moment when he snatched her from the condition in which she was not yet his wife. It would be false to think that Othello's suicide is a consequence of the revelation of Desdemona's innocence. It is the surety for Desdemona's murder. But a difference has emerged here that must be emphasized. When Othello wonders how to kill the object of his love, he rejects the dagger:

> Yet I'll not shed her blood;
> Nor scar that whiter skin of hers than snow,
> And smooth as monumental alabaster.   (v, 2)

Othello wants her in death preserved whole and entire. She died because she lacked the handkerchief, the sign of her castration; it is this same castration that must be denied with death. Only the breath will be taken from her. It is Othello who holds power over this breath:

> Put out the light, – and then put out thy light. –
> If I quench thee, thou flaming minister,
> I can again thy former light restore,
> Should I repent me; – but, once put out thy light,
> Thou cunning'st pattern of excelling Nature,
> I know not where is that Promethean heat
> That can thy light relume.   (v, 2)

We can see here, in the narcissistic structure, the ever-present seeds of megalomania. How can we fail to suspect in Othello, who is not able to make himself totally, absolutely, unchallengeably master of Desdemona's desire, the desire to have right of life and death over her? Life and death; in other words he wants to have the power to give her life as well as death. His suicide must be understood in the same context. The Moor inflicts death on himself. He does not submit to it; he does not allow sentence and execution to be carried out on him. He makes himself master of his own destiny by an act equivalent to that of giving himself life. He sets out to rejoin his love, by means of the suicide through which he will accede at last to the undivided *jouissance* of union with Desdemona.

But, whereas suffocation respects unto death the integrity of Desdemona's body, whose perfection remains unimpaired by any wound, Othello kills himself by stabbing, as he relates his attack on a Turk, a 'circumcisèd dog'. He imposes upon himself this suicide by the sword, inflicting upon himself the castration that he abhorred in Desdemona. Thus Desdemona dies immaculate and entire, and Othello joins her after mutilating himself. Each has gone half of the way that separates him from the Other. Henceforth they are similar to the object and to its image in the mirror, though one cannot say which side the decoy is on, and which side the source of desire.

Othello and his double

Confronted by the effects of the tragic, especially when, as in *Othello*, this is a matter of purely internal mechanisms, without the gods showing themselves or speaking, one is bound to ask, 'Why?'

Why does death necessarily triumph over love? I have confined myself so far to situating Othello's desire between Eros and the death drive, without giving any explanation for this victory of the forces of death, although we saw what a dependable ally these forces could find in the narcissistic nature of Othello's object-investments. However, we still have to place a fundamental relation that governs others, the Othello–Iago relation.

Many commentators on *Othello* have realized that an analysis of the play must give a preponderant place to Iago. This mysterious character gives rise to very different interpretations. Granville Barker maintained that there was also a tragedy of Iago. It has even been suggested that the play should, by rights, bear the title *Iago* rather than *Othello*, so much does the ensign seem to dominate the course of the action: in turn creator, bringing Othello's jealousy to birth like an alchemist, and interpreter, offering to each individual the image that he demands (Granville Barker). He is compared to Shakespeare's other villains – Richard III and Edmund – but he surpasses them all. In the case of the other two villains, motives can be found for their evil. For Iago, all that can be found seems to be out of all proportion to the perversity he displays. The conclusion usually reached is that Iago is evil in essence rather than by reaction.

At all events, one cannot conceive of Iago in isolation. Some other term must be brought into relation with him in order to clarify the function or truth of the character. But it would be wrong to think that this other term might be contingent or interchangeable. In fact, behind Iago's proteomorphism, which enables him to succeed in his plans, there is something that one may define more specifically. Moreover, for all his cunning, his intrigue does not succeed; although his setting up of the infernal machine cannot be faulted, his plan fails. This failure should be ascribed not to some unforeseen accident, but to the very essence of the plan which, again, must contribute to the triumph of Cassio, which was also the outcome of Othello's secret desire.

For they cannot be imagined separately: Othello–Iago, Iago–Othello. They belong to that gallery of indissociable pairs – Dom Juan–Sganarelle, Don Quixote–Sancho Panza – to which Otto Rank drew attention in his study of the double. They are so inseparable that, even when their relations are considered as an opposition, the complementarity that unites them is always preserved. Thus, for Bradley, Iago is everything – devil, spirit of evil – but this means that Othello is nothing, little more than a puppet. For Leavis, on the contrary, Iago is merely a mechanism, a trigger added to an organization that is ready to function of itself, in which Othello is the only agent. How can we reconcile this difference of opinion, without ourselves falling into error? In fact, both theses are equally true and false. Iago is the revealer of Othello's conflict, but not a mere inducing agent. He is much more than the catalyst of Othello's jealousy. He gives body and credence to jealousy by extracting from the depths of his own envy the sympathy that it can assume in the desire of another. And, in another respect, does not Othello, so ready to submit himself to the signs already inscribed in him, drop the tunic of a warrior who makes and unmakes armies only to offer himself to movements and manipulations of which he is a passive toy, in search of a 'pleasure of his own of which he was himself unaware' (*S.E.*, x, 167)? Othello falls into Iago's toils only because he adheres strictly to his desire. But for Iago to be able to conceive the infernal machine, he must have been inspired by the heroic and monstrous elements in Othello's character. In the scene in which Iago plants the seeds of jealousy, it is not only Othello's peace of mind that is disturbed; it is above all that of the audience, in the position of the onlooker called upon as a witness.

Othello and Iago together seal a pact that binds them as closely as two lovers. Do they not end the scene on their knees, facing one another, invoking heaven to look favourably on their plans? Note the invocation of the forces of nature (stars, elements), which refers Othello back to his pagan gods and overshadows the God of his recent conversion:

> Witness, you ever-burning lights above,
> You elements that clip us round about, –
> Witness that here Iago doth give up
> The execution of his wit, hands, heart,
> To wrong'd Othello's service! Let him command,
> And to obey shall be in me remorse,
> What bloody work soe'er. (III, 3)

And Othello replies:

> I greet thy love,
> Not with vain thanks but with acceptance bounteous.

Having vowed to kill Desdemona and Cassio, Othello invests Iago with this new love:

> Now art thou my lieutenant.

And Iago concludes:

> I am your own for ever.

The modern spectator needs no knowledge of psycho-analytic interpretation to grasp that what he is witnessing here goes well beyond an alliance to carry out a task requiring the collaboration of two parties. What he is participating in is an intimate union, a joining together that becomes the cause of desire, the creation of an object that aims at the destruction of another desire. But it would be rash to see the situation in terms of homosexuality, without explaining what kind of homosexuality is involved. For although Othello several times speaks very highly of Iago, he never expresses himself in terms of desire, but simply praises his lucidity or his honesty. The place of the love-object is occupied by Cassio, a concern shared by Iago and Othello. If we recall that Freud sees in the process of paranoia a regressive path from homosexuality to narcissism, Iago stands before Othello like a mirror that makes his desire all the more unbearable the closer it gets to him. If Cassio has everything the Moor lacks, Iago is everything he is not. I believe that the endless arguments about the respective parts played by Othello and Iago in the jealousy and in its tragic outcome can be solved only if one accepts the identity of Othello and Iago. Othello and Iago are two sides of a single character. Shakespeare does his utmost to present them to us as utterly unlike each other, united by their very contrast.

The opposition is total, like day and night. Origin: Othello is a Moor, therefore a foreigner, Iago (despite his name) is a Florentine. Birth: Othello is a king's son, Iago base of birth. Faith: Othello is a convert and therefore a believer, Iago believes in nothing. Career: Othello is a great captain, Iago an undistinguished subordinate officer. Character: Othello is noble and generous, Iago mean and grasping. Temperament: Othello is passionate, Iago calculating. (Hazlitt was aware of this contrasted opposition.)

When Roderigo reproaches Iago for remaining under Othello's command after being passed over for the lieutenancy, Shakespeare shows the ambiguity of the relations between Iago and Othello in a play on words:

> Were I the Moor, I would not be Iago:
> In following him, I follow but myself.　　　　　　　　(I, 1)

What may be meant by this reversal, in the last resort, is that he *is* the Moor and, since therefore he is not Iago, he may be he whom the Moor serves, that is to say, Cassio. But this accession to the object of desire must pass through the channel of him who chooses it. It is not entirely surprising to the psycho-analyst that this answer to Roderigo should end with the line, 'I am not what I am' (I, 1), in which 'what I am not, I am' suggests the relation to the Other in the mirror, where that image is not outside where I am, since it is my gaze that constitutes it, but I am only in perceiving that image that I am not.

I have said little so far about Roderigo. He is Shakespeare's invention and might be seen as a mere cog in the machine, a part

necessary to the functioning of the plot, a character with no depth
and no interest. Nevertheless, he is part of the tragic structure and
cannot be dismissed so lightly. What does he amount to? To a simple
fool, one might say. His stupidity proves that if love can make heroes
lose their heads, so it can with fools. But this analysis is not enough.
We must see that Roderigo is the character that Iago chooses for all
his basest tricks; it is he who causes the brawl in the citadel, it is he
who is given the task of murdering Cassio. But he is one of the poles
of the desire of Iago, who tricks him out of his money. Thus he offers
himself as a mere instrument in Iago's service. But this same servant
will be the cause of Iago's perdition. The proof of Iago's guilt is
provided by the note found on Roderigo after his death. So, by this
unexpected reversal, the truth emerges through someone even more
gulled than Othello – Roderigo, the most child-like of them all.

There is an interplay in the Othello–Iago polarity of black and
white complexions. Honesty is on the side of the black, and blackness
on the side of the white. This black ram, who used trickery at the
beginning of the play, allows himself to be taken in by the appearance of the decoy in a world in which the whites counterfeit innocence and, under cover of their refined manners, use all the
falsifications of language, the secret conventions of glances, the
equivocation of the gestures of courtesy, to blur the transparency of
natural intercourse. Iago succeeds in making Othello believe that he
was wrong to leave his native soil and to breathe the air of Venice
where the whites are hypocritical, false, affected, treacherous, fickle.
Perhaps one should stress the notoriously dissolute character of
Venetian morals in this period, something often noted by travellers
of the time. This no doubt justifies Iago's words, which may be taken
as true:

> I know our country disposition well:
> In Venice they do let Heaven see the pranks
> They dare not show their husbands; their best conscience
> Is not to leave't undone, but keep't unknown.   (III, 3)

But this complementary narcissistic situation must, if it is to be
intelligible, be seen as part of another polarity. After introducing it
into psycho-analytic theory, Freud split narcissism into the opposition between Eros and the death drive. Iago is a figure whose link
with evil can be solved by no psychological explanation: neither as
jealousy of Cassio's promotion, jealousy of the Moor who, he says,
seduced his wife, or even, in the last resort, envy and spite at the
unreciprocated love he feels for Desdemona. Not even all this, which
provides the evil force with the reasons which motivate its action, is

enough to explain the Machiavellianism that emanates from Iago. (Iago has been seen as the new man of the Renaissance, the disciple of Machiavelli. His function far exceeds that contemporary interest.) His triumph is contained in two lines that illuminate Othello's conversion to his plan, when Othello says:

> Yield up, O love, thy crowned and hearted throne
> To tyrannous hate! (III, 3)

From then on, Othello's marriage will be a marriage with the death that was awaiting him from afar. He deceived death with this marriage, lured on by love. But Iago, that shadowy part of himself, wins in the end, so fulfilling his thanatophoric mission. Othello's and Iago's struggles are complementary and inverted.

What basically unites Othello and Iago is their common *méconnaissance* of their desire for Cassio. Othello does not see the love which underlies his favours to Cassio, or the aspiration – towards that which is outside his grasp – that this love attests. Iago does not realize that his thirst for revenge against a rival more fortunate in all respects is so strongly tainted with passionate desire that he will himself succumb beneath its weight. How else can we understand how Iago, the meticulous choreographer of this satanic ballet, when he holds Cassio at his sword's point, and is determined to kill him, misses this target that he stalks from behind and finds himself at that very moment overcome by some confusion that makes him lower his sword and wound his rival in the thigh, and not kill him (as Othello later wounds Iago without killing him, in the last scene). If it had not been an expression of his own desire Iago could not have invented the story of Cassio's 'dream', the phantasy of the night spent with Cassio that he insinuates into Othello's mind. The deception that motivates it does not diminish its power. For although he 'sets the scene' for Othello at this same moment, Iago is so caught up in his invention that he forgets to arouse the lack of the Other, imagining himself enjoying the scene in which he cherishes the hope of Cassio's demotion and Desdemona's disgrace. Similarly, when he deliberately creates misunderstanding by getting Cassio to talk about Bianca while Othello imagines that he is talking about Desdemona, in the scene that is acted out before him, it is he, Iago, who is won over just as much as Othello, by this masquerade that he has maliciously set up. For, in an earlier scene, he was the chagrined observer of the courteous exchanges between Desdemona and Cassio.

It has been pointed out that jealousy is not the monopoly of Othello in the tragedy. Iago, too, suspects his wife of having been unfaithful with Cassio and Othello, as if Iago was suggesting at the beginning of the play the jealousy that is still to emerge in the Moor, who has as yet no suspicion of his own jealous nature. In fact, Iago's feelings are closer to envy than to jealousy. Should we not, indeed, draw a distinction between jealousy and envy? In *Envy and Gratitude*, Melanie Klein differentiates between them. Whereas jealousy involves a preponderance of projection and admits the existence of a third party who enjoys the attributes of which the jealous individual is deprived, envy involves a desire for destructive introjection aimed at the direct degradation of the object of desire, without any intermediary, in the context of a dual relation. There is a further distinction between them, over and above the one drawn by Melanie Klein: jealousy is a desire addressed to the object, while envy is primarily an aspect of narcissism. While Othello is jealous (despite the narcissistic form of his object-investment), Iago is consumed by a thirst for mastery directed more at the desire than at its object, to which Othello is, for a time, still attached. Yet as soon as he attains his end of promotion to the lieutenancy and binds himself to Othello, his narcissistic mastery begins to crack. Swearing his fidelity to the Moor seems to make Iago's betrayal coincide with what betrays the Moor himself, his unavowed desire for Cassio.

It is as if there had been formed a 'set to partners' whose pattern of movement is not grasped by those who dance its figures. At the beginning of the tragedy, Iago speaks the language of envy, but advocates the domestication of desire in the cult of self – 'I never found a man that knew how to love himself' (I, 3). But Othello, preoccupied with his recent marriage, pushes into the background whatever belongs to the order of his more permanent satisfactions, those provided by the links binding him to his men. As soon as Cassio's fall is encompassed, it revives in Othello an unconscious homosexual love, but since this love is unacceptable it can be expressed only through the debasement and defilement of Desdemona. From now on, Cassio surreptitiously enters into Iago's desire, after the successful implantation of jealousy, undermining the security given by his feeling of having captured the Moor, though at the beginning of the play the ensign was more concerned to speak contemptuously of his more fortunate rival. So one comes to see that there is also a tragedy of Iago that is the exact replication of that of Othello. Shakespeare must be taken literally when he makes Othello say: 'By heaven, he echoes me!' (III, 3).

It is through this voice that the return of the foreclosed repressed is uttered. The words of old Brabantio surface and reappear with the self-evidence of a fulfilled prophecy. Othello had erased every trace of this utterance, and now it reappears in the mouth of Iago, bright and edged, like the two-handed sword of the day of judgement:

> She did deceive her father, marrying you;
> And, when she seem'd to shake and fear your looks,
> She loved them most. (III, 3)

From this moment on, Othello recognizes in Iago his double and other half. The death drive expressed through Iago seizes on this paternal speech as a speech of transgression; it only uses the spring of jealousy or of repressed and unacceptable desire in order to reach its true aim – to undo what has been done, to dissolve the ties of artificial bonds, to turn back the marriage partners – through the mutual annihilation of Othello and Desdemona, who had abolished the difference between them – each to the god of his or her race.

III SIGNIFIERS AND GODS

Marked signifiers

Suppose that we look in the tragic discourse for whatever stands out, is ineluctable or is suddenly revealed in a moment of transformation. Three motifs stand out in this way, one obvious (the handkerchief), the other two more subtle (the clown, and the hidden dagger with which Othello kills himself). I shall call these motifs marked signifiers.

Commentators have often expressed surprise at the presence of the clown; though it must be remembered that, in the Elizabethan theatre, a 'clown' is not necessarily a jester, but is sometimes a simple servant, of country origin. Shakespeare confines his intervention to two brief episodes, both in the third act. This is the act in which jealousy is implanted – it is as if its moment has not yet come in the hours of Othello's and Desdemona's happiness, and its time has already passed when jealous passion takes its tragic turn in the last two acts. In his two appearances, the clown serves as an intermediary between Cassio and Desdemona. On the first occasion, Cassio, arranging for music to be played for Othello, gives the clown a message to take to Emilia, herself acting as an intermediary for Desdemona. On the second, Desdemona questions the clown about Cassio's lodging. The clown stands between Cassio and Desdemona like a mocking image of their relations. These relations are secret and tender and remain innocent. Yet this innocence will not save them from Othello's delusional interpretation. The clown says some surprising things. With the musicians, his humour is cheerful and coarsely erotic, in his allusions coupling the sexual and anal thematics. With Desdemona, he carries his play on words to the point of incomprehensibility. Yet it may well be that there is more

meaning in what he says than first appears. The clown's jokes bring
out the very type of signifiers involved in delusional interpretation as
when, for example, Desdemona asks: 'Do you know, sirrah, where
Lieutenant Cassio lies?' (III, 4). The verb here has the triple meaning
of 'lodges', 'is untruthful' and 'is lying down'. And the apparent
hotchpotch of these answers is entirely typical of these jokes, double
meanings, or condensations that have their place in the primary
process and which re-emerge in humour and psychotic language.
Delusional interpretation loses no time in closing the gap between
the desire to know where Lieutenant Cassio is staying and the desire
to be with him, by means of lies, wherever he happens to be lying
down: to lie with him. And Shakespeare shows his usual insight
when he makes the clown say: 'I will catechize the world for him;
that is, make questions, and by them answer' (III, 4). The jealous,
delusional subject proceeds in precisely this way. From here on,
the character of the clown becomes a finger pointing at the eye and
ear of jealousy. What he will say is what the jealous man will see and
hear. This subversion of the signifiers can have tragic consequences,
as the end of the play will show. But it will nevertheless retain, for
all its derisive, absurd character, a comic dimension. (Buñuel's film,
El, one of the few instances of a truthful depiction of jealousy in the
cinema, was, I understand, a comic success in the country in which
it was filmed, a country with a Spanish culture, where questions of
honour are not taken lightly. Not that the classic authors of psy-
chiatry, least of all Clérambault, would have contested this. No doubt
one may attribute such defensive laughter, in which jealousy is the
affair of the Other, to *méconnaissance*.)
    This dimension of the comic in love, to which Lacan refers, is
worthy of further examination. The superego tolerates humour, but
laughter is the release towards the exterior of a tension, of an excess
of affect, in which is expressed the feeling of triumphing over the
object, in triumphing over all limitations. What one laughs at here is
not the jealous man, but, through the reversal of love into hate, the
overestimation of the sexual object of the Other. Jealousy is not
simply a matter of reversing the positive into the negative, but brings
out in its pure state the agglutination of an excess of signifiers. Such
a condensation remains silent in love or is untied only in the syn-
tagmatic chain of the innumerable qualities of the love-object that
are interposed between the desire of the subject and the phantasy of
union with him. The clown, an agent of mediation between the
protagonists, silences the harmonious sounds on Othello's behalf for
'to hear music the general does not greatly care' (III, 1), and replaces
them with the grunting cacophony of the signifiers exchanged
between Othello and Iago. In what the clown says there is an

exhibition of that 'extension of the sexual' that is related, not to what distinguishes the two sexes, but to what they have in common – the excremental. (See Freud's 'Jokes and their Relation to the Unconscious', *S.E.*, VIII.)

> CLOWN: Are these, I pray you, wind-instruments?
> FIRST MUSICIAN: Ay, marry, are they, sir.
> CLOWN: O, thereby hangs a tail.
> FIRST MUSICIAN: Whereby hangs a tale, sir?
> CLOWN: Marry, sir, by many a wind-instrument that I know.   (III, 1)

We shall see that this suggestive image of anality appears when the object that Desdemona lacks falls from grace.

The handkerchief, the second marked signifier, is the one by which Shakespeare signals to us. So much so that it has become a kind of veil drawn over the tragedy, for very little light has been thrown on it. I posed the question of its dual origin: is it a gift from the sorceress to the mother or from the father to the mother? I am tempted to see in this 'detail' standing out from the Shakespearean text the whole crux of the tragedy. The unformulated question, masked by the voices of the protagonists, is, what do the gods say of this union? The discourse that echoes it takes it up again in another form: who guarantees the awakening of desire and by what means? To this question no other answer is given in Shakespeare's text than the mystery of this dual origin, which shows us that what is at issue is not so much a question without an answer as an answer that cannot be regarded as simple. The handkerchief emerged from a matrilineal source seconded by the help of sorceresses, possessing a power of creation engendered solely by female forces, produced from the heart of these virgins whose only knowledge of desire is the traces left by the absence of its fulfilment. Alternatively, it is the gift presented by the father to the mother, to make up for what is lacking in her purely natural charm, where that natural charm cannot focus the desire of the Other, so that the piece of material itself becomes an object to be desired. In either case, the handkerchief is a signifier of desire whose signification is apprehended only when it is missing.

The close link between the handkerchief and castration is shown by the timing of its entry into the tragedy. It comes between Desdemona and Othello at the moment when, for the first time, Othello is complaining of having 'a pain upon my forehead here'. This is a reference to the horns that the Moor fears. But this metaphor and this fear are related to another pain in the forehead. Othello is an epileptic, and we are bound to link pain, pretended or true, with the attack he is about to undergo and of which it is perhaps the aura. But how rich in signification becomes Othello's refusal to let his forehead be bound by Desdemona, who offers that relief. 'Your napkin is too little', he replies. And it is at this moment that the little scrap of cloth falls as the remnant of an encounter marked with the prohibition that attaches to their desire, whether one calls it Othello's jealousy or desire for Cassio. (In Cinthio's story, Desdemona drops the handkerchief when Iago gives her his child to carry.) So Desdemona gives his gift back to Othello; in this gesture, she rediscovers the face of the solicitous mother and divests herself before Othello of the veil with which he covers his sex. We have seen that it is in Cassio, in his lieutenant, that he finds this indispensable complement that Desdemona lacks. Othello falls into his fit after evoking in unbearable detail the sexual scene between Desdemona and Cassio:

Lie with her! lie on her! – We say lie on her, when they belie her. – Lie with her! that's fulsome. – Handkerchief – confessions – handkerchief!

(IV, I)

The attack seizes him when he has grasped the relationship of speech ('It is not words that shake me thus'), the function of the handkerchief as a link ('Pish! noses, ears, and lips') and the dual role of the mouth as the organ of speech and the organ of the kiss. It is a revelation that becomes the condition of *jouissance* – by a return to language – giving back to the words their erotogenic value by veiling the connection that it has just suggested. 'Is't possible? – Confess – handkerchief! – O devil!' and he loses consciousness. The handkerchief, rejected by Othello as too small and returned to its possessor, brings together the impossibility of completely hiding the castration caused by the imaginary penis that the handkerchief represents in Desdemona and that other castration, of which Othello has a presentiment in the aura of his fit. This will expose him completely in the midst of his convulsions to the gaze of the Other, revealing in his illness what he had tried to keep hidden in Desdemona.

During this plunge into the night of consciousness, Shakespeare causes Cassio to pass over the stage, and he engages in a short exchange with Iago. The need for this dialogue totally eludes the spectator if it is not seen as yet another union of these two men, during Othello's fit, as in Iago's 'description' of the night when they were on guard and slept together. Cassio's appearance and exit, which leaves Iago to take care of the Moor, indicates the sequence of the permutations of the object of desire. When Othello returns to consciousness, Iago, instead of Cassio, is bending over him; the new tableau that he and the Moor form together is the sequel to the imagined abandon of Desdemona and Cassio, and to the phantasy in which Cassio embraced Iago in his sleep, taking him for Desdemona. The attack abolishes the abhorred vision of Desdemona in another's arms. But it makes it possible, in the very erasure of the intolerable, for the gap caused by this loss of consciousness to be occupied by that other scene in which, through the suppression of control in sleep, Iago and Cassio had let slip between them the first fruits of sexual pleasure. Othello comes to himself again in Iago's arms and sees in his gaze the image of his double; his identification with the desire of the rival becomes a desire for the rival. The chain of objects of desire stretching from genital love to narcissism has been run through, and ends with the phrase that enables Othello to identify Iago with the maternal Desdemona who was there before him: 'How is it, general? have you not hurt your head?' And Othello replies: 'Dost thou mock me?' For Othello, epilepsy is castration in the link it establishes between the pain in his head and the situation of the betrayed husband. The fact that Othello will not use the handkerchief to cover his wound shows that, although he cannot bear to leave the abode that allows him to veil female castration, his own wound will be exhibited openly. For Othello, the handkerchief represents a certainty: it is the index of a situation in which the presence or absence of the penis rests on visible signs, which must be inspected with the eye if a sense is to be made of them. For, like every jealous man, Othello is susceptible only to proofs that reinforce his desire, that is, which confirm his suspicions. 'Give me the ocular proof.' Give me visible proof that my love is a whore. 'Make me to see't.' Othello wants to see, as Oedipus wants to see. But neither of them has any ideas of what he is looking for. 'I'll have some proof,' Othello seems to be saying. We shall see yet another double meaning here. His desire is to have proof: his desire that his wife be proved a whore. This attachment to visible proof is again a sign of the return of the repressed. It is because he stole Desdemona in the night, eluding her father's eye, that he now needs to found this proof in what is visible. But the invisible that always eludes him sends him back to Brabantio's words: 'Look to her, Moor, if thou hast eyes to see. . .' Visible proof, then, is not only a form of surveillance, but an echo of the father's prediction.

Desdemona's supposed condition as a whore is essential to sustain Othello's desire. If all women are whores, then one can have lasting relations only with men, and one has the right to love women only as whores and to love the whore in them. But, in doing this, and moving as far as possible from the first love-object, the mother, one comes back to it without knowing. For, of all unfaithful women, the first was the mother, when the child discovered for the first time the existence of the secret relations she has with the father. So much so

that the man who flees women by debasing them to the level of
whores while preserving one of them platonically is closer than ever
to the mother when he is in the arms of a whore. (See Freud's
'On the Universal Tendency to Debasement in the Sphere of Love',
S.E., XI, 177.) And, in fact, Othello can give vent to the passion
within him only when he is able to treat Desdemona as a whore,
while in the heavens shine the chaste stars to which he cannot name
the cause of his desire. Love will have all sorts of debasements loaded
on to it, in which the love-object will suffer for its infidelity, growing
without knowing it into an unsuspected *jouissance*.

Lacking the handkerchief, Desdemona will arouse in Othello's
mind images that must be reinserted into the context of the phantasies that they connote. Their insistent accumulation shows how the
sexual and the repugnant go together for Othello just as anatomy
brings together the genital and the excretory. In these various
expressions, it is sometimes Othello who represents himself with the
characteristics he abhors:

> I had rather be a toad,
> And live upon the vapour of a dungeon
> Than keep a corner in the thing I love
> For other's uses.   (III, 3)

Sometimes he delineates and locates the representation of the cursed
object:

> The fountain from the which my current runs,
> Or else dries up; to be discarded thence!
> Or keep it as a cistern for foul toads
> To knot and gender in!   (IV, 2)

Sometimes this copulation eliminates all characteristics of sexual
difference, and the object is born by self-generation out of putrefying
matter:

> Oh, ay; as summer flies are in the shambles,
> That quicken even with blowing.   (IV, 2)

Othello does not base this ocular proof of Desdemona's infidelity, of
her condition as whore, solely on the fact of seeing the handkerchief
in other hands than hers; it is also because he has seen it in the
hands of Bianca the whore. 'If the whore has the handkerchief it is
because the woman to whom I gave it is nothing more than a whore,'
goes the argument. The handkerchief passes from hand to hand,
as the woman passes from the arms of one man to another. This is
what is to be demonstrated: the female chain that transmits the
penis is made up, as soon as they are dispossessed of it – as soon as
they are truly women – of whores.

So the circle of Othello's tragedy is closed, and fastened by the object of desire, the handkerchief. Once he is in the thrall of this search – the ocular proof he demands – Othello is unaware that what was being formed within him was in fact the completion of a circuit, which begins with the gift of the child – Othello himself – to the mother, and ends with the wages of the whore, the only gift that the mother deserves. And this circuit is formed by being closed upon Othello himself. It links two orbits. One is indirect, twists and turns, and follows the meanderings of the handkerchief from one hand to another, hidden from the sight of the Moor, and blindly passing between the objects of his desire. The other is immediate, and over-leaps all intermediaries to bind the eye that discovers it to the accoutrements of the whore. But the discovery of the handkerchief is indicative here of its absence on the person of its possessor, the fact that it is not where it ought to be: when she no longer has it, she is it. Where the circuit of desire is completed with the ocular proof provided by the object, the handkerchief, the subject begins to disintegrate.

This is the moment to introduce the dagger, which Desdemona is spared, since she must die intact, but which mutilates Othello, who must exhibit his wound at the moment of death. But this final mutilation, the full stop of this tragedy, is imbued with the lure that was the very motive-force of the tragedy. For Othello emerges from the tragic field by the same route that he entered it. The tragic was inaugurated by the disappearance of the object – the handkerchief – of which the possessor was dispossessed. Thus weapons will pass through his hands, as the handkerchief passed from hand to hand. Othello even goes so far as to act out before us the phantasy of the hidden other weapon. After lunging at Iago – he misses Iago as Iago missed Cassio – he is disarmed by Montano, but goes to get a second sword hidden in the bedchamber. With Othello disarmed a second time, the spectator can no longer expect further recourse to this procedure since it has already been used. At this moment, the phallic function gives way to the recognition of castration.

> Behold, I have a weapon;
> A better never did itself sustain
> Upon a soldier's thigh: I've seen the day
> That, with this little arm and this good sword,
> I've made my way through more impediments
> Than twenty times your stop: but, O vain boast!
> Who can control his fate? 'tis not so now.
> Be not afraid, though you do see me weapon'd;
> Here is my journey's end, here is my butt,
> And very sea-mark of my utmost sail.   (v, 2)

Even deprived of this last resource, Othello shows the glint for the last time of some dagger that comes from we know not where, the quickness of the eye deceived by that of the hand. Just when he has been disarmed and apparently rendered harmless, he brings out from some hidden source the dagger that will penetrate him. The recognition of castration was unable to prevent castration taking on for Othello the image of its negation, turning Othello, by these successive disarmings, into a kind of many-armed hydra. In the death that he inflicts on himself, cutting off the monster's head himself, he no doubt signifies the desire to join Desdemona in the beyond, adorned with those same attributes which he had to recognize, on their wedding night, that she did not possess.

The signs of the gods

I have seen in Othello's tragic end a fatal outcome obeying an implacable necessity. The image of this necessity is presented to us in the form of diabolical scheming. But we have seen that its mechanism, so blandly displayed to our view, has prevented us from hearing the echo of a prophetic speech. I now propose the hypothesis that the function of the mechanism is actually the unfolding of a fiction serving to disguise, faced with the marriage of Othello and Desdemona, this question of the consent of the gods. I acknowledged the signs of a transgression in Desdemona's elopement, which frustrates and castrates the father, old Brabantio. But those who represent Brabantio in the last act cut so pitiful a figure that it is difficult to see the dénouement as signifying paternal triumph. So the father and his representatives must be regarded as emissaries of a higher order, especially since the whole tragic progress turns on the power of representation of the signifiers, as the handkerchief shows. Desdemona's infidelity does not take place in reality; the prophecy is realized, rather, in phantasy.

From the initial situation in which Cassio represents what Desdemona renounces, the qualities possessed by her spurned Venetian suitors, and which the Moor lacks, the reversal of the signs will make the lieutenant into what Desdemona lacks and what the Moor refuses in his unavowable love. The phantasy of unconscious homosexuality that links Othello to Cassio, though never named or recognized, is deduced from the encounter of Othello's and Desdemona's desires. In moving to Venice, Othello disavows his peers and the gods of his birth and sees in Desdemona a love-object in so far as she herself disdains those to whom her birth entitles her as partners. But when Desdemona responds to him, Othello can read in her eyes only a refusal to allow herself to be desired by her countrymen that contravenes his secret desire to be like those very men who were meant for her. The haste to conclude the matter before other ties are forged suggests a feeling of 'before it is too late', as if to forestall each party's questions as to the destination of his or her desire. The abduction, carried out with the consent of the prey, following her inaccessibility to so many suitors, parallels Othello's adoption of new gods after so much determined resistance to escape enslavements. It is as if, in both seduction and conversion, there were deception in this search for the polar opposite.

The Christian God was betrayed by Othello's device of attracting Desdemona by the glamour of his distant origin, his fabulous exploits, his legendary bravery – all associated with his condition as a Moor. But Othello has denied the gods of his ancestors. He has been converted. This conversion is a betrayal for which he will be punished by the very means that assured him his triumph: deception and infidelity. The only unfaithful person in the tragedy is Othello, who forswore his gods. Thus a fateful alliance is formed between the Christian God, betrayed by the conquest of Desdemona, and the Moorish gods, abandoned by Othello. They both punish a man who has broken his ancestral ties in order to contract different ones.

This presence of the gods is felt particularly strongly in the last act, when both husband and wife die. We need to listen closely to hear how Othello transforms a crime into a sacrifice:

> thou does stone my heart
> And makest me call what I intend to do
> A murder, which I thought a sacrifice.   (v, 2)

And how insistent he is that Desdemona should die in a state of purity:

OTHELLO: Have you pray'd to-night, Desdemona?
DESDEMONA: Ay, my lord.
OTHELLO: If you bethink yourself of any crime
   Unreconciled as yet to Heaven and grace,
   Solicit for it straight.
DESDEMONA: Alack, my lord, what may you mean by that?
OTHELLO: Well, do it and be brief; I will walk by:
   I would not kill thy unprepar\`ed spirit;
   No, – Heaven forefend! – I would not kill thy soul.
DESDEMONA: Talk you of killing?
OTHELLO: Ay, I do.
DESDEMONA: Then Heaven have mercy on me!
OTHELLO: Amen, with all my heart!   (v, 2)

So it is not enough that he should kill her; she must also die religiously, in a Christian manner.

The improbability of the jealousy that breaks out when husband and wife have scarcely been reunited after their marriage has been remarked on more than once. This comes as no surprise to the psycho-analyst, for whom such things are not so unusual. But if we are to explain it from within the tragedy itself, do we not see it as the turning back upon him of the very thing with which he is accused: seduction by sorcery? Magic proves stronger than formal conversion. Othello is as suddenly overcome by jealousy as Desdemona was by love, the suddenness of whose love brought the Moor under suspicion of having instigated it by supernatural means. And if, as I have maintained, we see Iago as Othello's double, we will have a better understanding of the words he speaks as he stands over the Moor writhing in his fit: 'Work on, my medicine, work!' (IV, I).

Othello is black; he has emerged from a world of sorcery. Converted and married to the white Desdemona, he loses this blackness and accedes to the candour of the whites, which proves to be false. Desdemona's betrayal, in which Othello reads the reflection of his own betrayal, annuls this difference:

> her name, that was as fresh
> As Dian's visage, is now begrimed and black
> As mine own face.   (III, 3)

And it is as a black that he takes leave of life. Concerned as he is that Desdemona should die a Christian death, he is apparently unconcerned to make any preparation to commend his own soul to God. And yet when we examine the images of Shakespeare's language, in the monologue that precedes Othello's suicide, in the fable that enables him to leave the world by escaping the net that is tightening around him, we find scattered traces suggesting a return to his own gods:

> then you must speak
> Of one that loved not wisely, but too well;
> Of one not easily jealous, but, being wrought,
> Perplex'd in the extreme; of one whose hand,
> Like the base Indian, threw a pearl away
> Richer than all his tribe; of one whose subdued eyes,
> Albeit unusèd to the melting mood,
> Drop tears as fast as the Arabian trees
> Their médicinal gum. Set you down this;
> And say besides, that in Aleppo once,
> Where a malignant and a turban'd Turk
> Beat a Venetian and traduced the State,
> I took by th'throat the circumcisèd dog,
> And smote him – thus.   (V, 2)

The Indian, his tribe, the Arabian trees, Aleppo, a turban'd Turk,

Africa, the East: the whole of Barbary passes before our eyes in this final evocation in which Othello puts his original stamp on his end. The significance of his suicide, then, is not only that it enables him to join Desdemona, but that it accomplishes through death a reversal of his conversion, since in the eyes of the Venetians present he is – at the moment when he asks them to give a truthful image of him after his disappearance – the 'circumcisèd dog' he punishes.

So *Othello* would appear to be a tragedy of conversion. Through this conversion a double transgression takes place: transgression of the law of the father, by the abandonment of the faith of the ancestors, and transgression in the choice of the love-object. In taking Desdemona as his wife, Othello expresses a preference for the foreign woman over the girls of his own country. But it is because this rejection involves reversal that it is transgression. It is as if in binding himself in love to the image furthest removed from his mother – not other than his mother, but exactly the converse – it is still his mother that he finds. Unknown to himself, he commits incest, inside out, so to speak. In choosing her contrary, he falls back on the Same, the inevitable mother.

Othello wants Desdemona to be like his mother. He says as much when he shows her that the value he places on her person is linked to the value he attaches to his mother's handkerchief; she should be like the mother of earliest childhood, the mother as yet untouched by castration, provided with the veil, which hides her face from the world.

In the final analysis, then, Othello is a brother of Oedipus and Orestes.[7] He has gone to live in a foreign country, far from his father's sight. In saving himself from the desire to castrate his father, he has been unable to avoid satisfying this desire on the person of Brabantio. (Brabantio's social importance is attested by Iago, who warns Othello at the beginning of the play: not only is he nicknamed the Magnifico, but it is also said of him that his is 'a voice potential,/As double as the Duke's'.) This father arouses desire, which can only be conveyed through some talisman. He is the one to whom submission is due in that unconsciousness of homosexual desire[8] which bars *jouissance* in the love-object. Death, so often foiled, always avoided by a hair's breadth, all his miraculous escapes and victories, turn Othello himself into this talisman. But this safety, so often confirmed, stops at the marriage-bed. And it is not enough to have the innumerable enemy in his power by giving others to the death that he intended for the father alone, in order to be acquitted of the debt that this desire for death imposes. For the bed of love may also be the death-bed. Here the mirage is dispelled, and the demand that the talisman must come from the Other is revealed.

The gods who saw in this conversion a viaticum for a passage towards an impossible change of object were not deceived.

After representation: difference and mimesis

My analysis has revealed a difference. What this difference conceals is the gap that has always existed between the indisputable fascination that *Othello* exercises on those who see it, and a certain unease that the play arouses – a gap that has attracted the criticism of certain commentators. Indeed, one wonders whether these criticisms, which purport to discover certain 'weaknesses' in the play, have not sought the reasons for this unsatisfactoriness outside the operant effects of the spectacle, since none of them denies that the tragedy affects the spectator. *Othello* is not a work that can be rejected *in toto*; its unsatisfactoriness, the commentators believe, can be attributed to the improbability of its plot. In fact, this difference is the selfsame difference that exists between jealousy as a common human situation and insane jealousy, which is a form of madness. Now, there is nothing in the play to indicate that it is a question of insane jealousy, and it should be clear to everyone that what we are presented with is one of the more general forms of jealousy. Does not Othello say that he is not easily jealous? The difference between ordinary jealousy and insane jealousy is what is discovered behind the articulations of the tragic structure. If we are to perceive this tragic structure we must cease to look towards the jealous hero, who certainly attracts and holds our gaze, and follow the thread of the signifier in the unfolding of the play. The subject will be accessible to our investigation only as he travels along the circuit of desire. The difference will then be between the subject of the statement (*énoncé*) and the subject of the enunciation (*énonciation*)[9] – the difference between Othello as subject, as hero, and *Othello* as tragedy made up of the ensemble of the articulations between the various protagonists, marked signifiers, intersecting desires and personified forces in which the structure of the play may be read, which makes it possible to say that we are presented with the structure of insane jealousy and not of simple jealousy. The spectator, who is invited only to the display of simple jealousy, is caught up in the network of articulations, dominated, and delivered over to a feeling of unease. When his unease is not relieved by laughter, he will find bad reasons for locating the point where reason protests against what in all this appears to him to be unreasonable. In fact, he will try to elude the grasp of the secret reason for his *jouissance* and his unease. He will strive to prevent the forms of common jealousy from sliding towards the lethal figures to which Othello's story seems to be leading him. He will fix limits beyond which there can be no complete identification between Othello and himself. He will then give all the reasons that focus the difference between Othello and the spectator: blackness, the error of this 'mixed' marriage, the condition of women in the Republic of Venice, and all that. For the psycho-analyst, the difference is not reducible to these mere circumstances; it is rooted in foreclosed homosexuality, degraded into masochism. Between what Shakespeare presents to our senses and what he allows the unconscious to say there stands the difference that Freud aims to decipher. What must be restored is the thing that was offered on the stage, aimed to divert rather than to rivet the spectator's attention. What took place on the other scene must be the object of another reading, with the help of another type of link between its signifying elements, uttered according to another mode of scansion, marked by another punctuation, expressing a discourse that resists verbalization, being in itself a veiling of discourse, without which there would be neither tragedy, hero, spectacle nor spectator.

The tragedy mimes jealousy. It establishes, therefore, the difference between a common human jealousy and a tragic, theatrical jealousy. It is no longer, then, simple jealousy, but tragic jealousy and, as such, heroic jealousy. The differential gap becomes that between the spectator who is subject to common jealousy and that of the hero who is subject to an exceptional jealousy, that which strikes a man who has risen to the heights by birth and his own virtues. It is a jealousy like that of the gods, who are offended by Othello's success and happiness, given the innumerable obstacles to his accession to the generalship of the Republic of Venice and marriage with one of its patrician's daughters. It is a jealousy of the father who sees in the success of his son an abolition of the prerogatives that assure his paternal power and a sign of the desire to supplant him in his offspring. But what the tragedy reveals is that this jealousy is insane. This is the other difference – the one that is perceived only by the movement of the tragic structure that enables us to recognize in the relation between the elements of the work the face of madness. The exceptional situation, that of the hero, is reinforced by his blackness, which must be understood in its metaphorical signification. This heroic blackness makes Othello the character who bears within himself the mark of 'Long ago, a man came from afar off...A stranger...' But if all jealousy, even the commonest, does not bear within itself the germ of delusion, no spectacle of jealousy would be possible. Conversely, because this jealousy is delusional, the spectator, who will half-glimpse it in a flash, will reject it as unacceptable and attribute to the spectacle itself the cause of this rejection. Mimesis is deceptive mimesis in that it makes one believe in the identity of what it unites: common jealousy and heroic jealousy. In so far as it is a decoy, it attributes delusional jealousy to heroic jealousy and rejects delusional jealousy as too exceptional to be true. And when the spectator recognizes the delusional germ in jealousy, he escapes the taint of jealousy. 'Since jealousy is madness and since I am not mad, since I am the spectator of this play, then I am not really jealous.'

The representation of jealousy has realized its aim: to produce in the spectator the *méconnaissance* of his own desire.

3
Racine's *Iphigénie*
The economy of sacrifice

For the daughters of Thasos

Sacred!...The syllables of this word are already heavy with pain, the weight that loads them is that of sacrificial death... All our life is charged with death. But in me definitive death has the meaning of a strange victory. It bathes me in its glow, it opens up in me infinitely joyful laughter: that of its disappearance.

Georges Bataille, *Les Larmes d'Eros*

But if luck is with me, the thing we most desire is the one most likely to drive us to prodigality and to ruin.

Georges Bataille, *L'Erotisme*

I THE TWO *IPHIGENIAS*

Compassion and terror

Racine's *Iphigénie* is the tragedy of tears. It is for ever associated with Boileau's lines, which have become as well known as their subject:

> Jamais Iphigénie en Aulide immolée
> N'a coûté tant de pleurs à la Grèce assemblée.[1]

Yet it is surprising that these tears, which the court of Versailles shed more generously than 'la Grèce assemblée', should have been shed for a work that provokes such sharply divided opinions. So, one suspects that some change of course took place, away from the first intention of imitating Euripides – who, Racine tells us in his Preface to the play, 'was marvellously skilled in exciting compassion and terror, which are the real effects that tragedy should produce' (Racine, 51). The compassion that causes the tears is evident enough; but one wonders about the presence of terror, which seems to be well hidden, not to say totally excluded, in his play. No theme seems more likely to link terror and compassion in the pitiless decree of the gods than the sacrifice of a beloved daughter by her father. Can it be that the two thousand years between the Greek tragedy and

Racine's have seen a rarefaction, even the disappearance, of that *phobos* that was the most powerful link between the two halves of the tragic space, the spectacle and the spectator? We must seek, in the distribution of the effects of this sacrifice, the scar of something that in the earliest forms of tragedy derived from a ritual of sacrifice.

We feel the break between ancient tragedy and French classical tragedy. Yet Racine felt no such break: 'I was delighted to see, in the effect produced on our stage of everything which I have imitated from Homer or Euripides, that good sense and reason were the same in every century. The taste of Paris proved to be like that of Athens. Our audiences were touched by the very things which once moved to tears the most cultured people of Greece' (Racine, 51). So, for all the changes brought about by time, Racine argues that the two works had a comparable effect. It would be less than fair to accuse him of wanting to bathe in the reflected glory of Euripides. We must take his claim seriously and examine the related works in the light of their internal economies.

Here is a list of the thematic differences between Euripides and Racine.

In Euripides:

1. Iphigenia's marriage is a made-up story, a stratagem.

2. Achilles is above all a defender of honour and justice.

3. Menelaus is excitable, unstable, but capable of pity. Ulysses does not appear.

4. As soon as Iphigenia reaches the camp, Agamemnon's words imply unequivocally that the sacrifice is inevitable.

5. The meeting between Iphigenia and Agamemnon, witnessed by Clytemnestra, shows the tender relations between father and daughter.

6. Iphigenia is a young virgin, shy, timid, sweet-tempered, gentle, virtuous, brave.

7. Clytemnestra first tries to prevent the sacrifice, but finally submits to it.

8. Achilles, too, tries to resist, but gives up the idea of inciting a revolt without Iphigenia's consent.

9. Achilles and Agamemnon never meet.

10. Agamemnon gives way, and consents before a large army to the sacrifice of his daughter.

11. Iphigenia is either sacrificed, or is spirited away, and her place taken by a doe.

In Racine:

1. Iphigenia's marriage is a real possibility, decided on before the play begins.

2. Achilles is as much a warrior as a lover, eager to expend himself in the pursuit of love and glory.

3. Ulysses is cold, determined, calculating. Menelaus does not appear.

4. Agamemnon speaks with several voices; he changes his mind more than once.

5. The encounter between Iphigenia and Agamemnon takes place in a cold atmosphere, in the presence of Eriphile, a character of Racine's invention.

6. Iphigenia is a jealous, proud and vocal princess.

7. Clytemnestra resists the sacrifice to the end.

8. Achilles resists the sacrifice right up to the altar.

9. Achilles and Agamemnon come into conflict and dispute the possession of Iphigenia.

10. Agamemnon decides to keep his daughter, refusing her both to the Greeks and to Achilles.

11. Eriphile commits suicide, having been substituted for Iphigenia. Iphigenia marries Achilles.

These are the differences we have to account for. By comparing one tragedy with the other, and showing the coherent configuration which each tragedy possesses, we must try to explain how the tragic effect is achieved in each case. For Racine believed that there was a homology of structure between his work and Euripides', for all the modifications and innovations he introduced. Doubtless we need to take account of the transformation of the tragic feeling in two audiences separated by over two thousand years. But we contemporary spectators can listen both to Euripides and to Racine; there is some point in seeking the channels and forms in which tragedy continues to move us.

The marriage/sacrifice alternative

No overwhelming need forced Racine to choose the theme of Iphigenia's sacrifice. There was no circumstantial reason either. However, once he was prisoner of this choice, Racine looked around for bad reasons to eliminate the dénouement from his plot and spare us the sacrifice. He cites two arguments. First, it is unacceptable to 'sully' the stage with the murder of 'so virtuous and lovable a person as Iphigenia'. Second, he refuses to resort to 'a mere device', by which the virgin escaped and was replaced by an animal – acceptable to the Greeks but not to the taste of the French public. The first argument we are given is precisely that which eliminates the terror that tragedy should communicate. The second does not tell us why the seventeenth-century public, so concerned with verisimilitude, could not accept the substitution for the propitiatory victim of a doe, though it avoids questioning the basic issue: the legitimacy of a human sacrifice demanded by the gods. The precedent of Abraham's sacrifice cannot be invoked here. The god of the Greeks demands the sacrifice without explanation. He shows absolutely no concern for men. He exacts this tribute more or less as a part of his prerogative in the activities under his aegis. Artemis requires a victim, much as one offers bait in order to have good sport; the cruelty and pointlessness of her demand are not called in question. The God of the Jews gave Abraham the offspring he lacked, as testimony of his concern and desire to mark the patriarch with the sign of the covenant that he has contracted with him. If he takes back what he gave – however cruel the change of mind may be – God is within his rights, and moving to an end that it is not given to men to understand, but which is part of a line of conduct that never runs counter to his concern for Israel. We shall come back to this parallel, already noted by Kierkegaard.

It is this anomaly in the plot – the idea that sacrifice may plausibly be demanded but not carried out – that gives this tragedy its strange character. For this rejection has to be accepted throughout its course, and it imports into Racine's play everything that Euripides left out. The two tragedies have in common their protest against an iniquitous decree in which the cruelty of the gods and the prophets is compounded with the thirst for destruction inherent in the war. Not only does the sacrifice of Iphigenia not take place – the plot concludes with her marriage to Achilles, which is no longer opposed – but no sacrifice takes place at all.

Resorting to Pausanias, Racine introduces the providential character Eriphile, who provides the tribute demanded of the blood of Helen, whose secret child she is. But the device does not work. For, if one stops to consider the point of a sacrifice, it is clear that the death of Eriphile cannot be substituted. To begin with, she is not a fit object for such a ritual. The requirements of the rite always stipulate that the victim must be without defect or imperfection. What one is sacrificing is innocence. And what must perish must be free of any taint left on it by nature as a sign of some original disgrace or censure. By her birth (she is the offspring of a secret marriage), by her origins (she is the daughter of the sinner who must be punished), by her character (she shows every sign of a predisposition to misfortune), Eriphile is not a fit victim. Above all, she does not die in Iphigenia's place and in the way intended for Iphigenia. Seizing the priest's sacrificial knife, she plunges it into her breast, thus intending to bring a charge of murder against the future aggressors of her country. Her suicide becomes not an act of absolution, but evidence for the prosecution in the first of their crimes. In no sense can a suicide take the place of a sacrifice. The vigilance of those who look after prisoners condemned to death, preventing any attempt to shorten their own lives, and the macabre care that is taken of their health are well known. One can see how Eriphile's suicide serves to avoid the defilement of Iphigenia's murder; but it is this defilement itself that the character of Eriphile bears, and which is eliminated from the tragic space.

Both *Iphigenias* – that of Euripides and that of Racine – are based on an equivalence that is never stated except as an opposition: that of marriage and sacrifice. The ignorance in which the Greek camp is kept about what is being brought to birth makes them ready for either, and so the path to the altar becomes a one-way thorough-fare[2] for either eventuality. The weight is equal in both scales. The death would appease the gods and secure their protection. The union binding Iphigenia to the son of the goddess Thetis – thus strengthen-ing the line of the Atrides, which descends more distantly from the gods – confers on Agamemnon an additional authority in the con-duct of the expedition. Originally a mere stratagem, the deception about the marriage that drew Iphigenia to Aulis could quickly turn into a state event, as imposing as that of the sacrifice. This substitu-tion is so close a match that it becomes the subject of an equivocal passage in the encounter between Iphigenia and Agamemnon in Euripides:

> IPHIGENIA: Come quickly back from Troy, father – victorious!
> AGAMEMNON: But first I have a sacrifice to offer here.
> IPHIGENIA: Ah, I would wish to take part, in order to see at least what it is fitting to see.
>> (Euripides, *Iphigenia in Aulis*, 390–1)

This last sentence shows that this association is not fortuitous, but presupposes some element of the sexual. It is forbidden for a virgin to know the secrets either of sacrifice or of marriage. Agamemnon's reply, 'You will be instructed in them, and you will have your place by the lustral waters,' still plays on this equivalence: it is time for you to learn about the religious and sexual mysteries.

This impression is still stronger in Racine than in Euripides, for in his play the principle of marriage enters in even before the tragedy begins, and it is the subject of the first dialogue between Achilles and Agamemnon (who, in Euripides, never meet). In Euripides, what was at first merely a clever device to draw the victim on to the sacrificial floor becomes a reality at the end of the tragedy when Achilles, having taken offence at the use made of his name, braves the sarcastic remarks of the Greeks and claims the status of a man engaged to be married. So the element which in the antique tragedy steadily reinforces the equivalence between death and marriage cancels it out at the moment where the virgin's acquiescence leads her to a marriage with death. But in Racine, marriage becomes the objective of the whole plot, which therefore proceeds by reducing steadily the risk of sacrifice. This movement in turn opens up the possibility of suicide by another.

Agamemnon is trapped in this alternative between marriage and sacrifice. What is common to the two choices is that, either way, he loses his daughter. He must give her away to the bravest of the Greeks, in order to maintain the prestige of his high rank; but in doing so he adds to the power of the man to whom he gives her, however flattering the alliance with the son of a goddess may be. If, on the other hand, he obeys Calchas, he loses her just the same. The price he must pay for the realization of his personal glory is the loss of his dearest daughter. In the stratagem he devises in order to bring her to Aulis, Agamemnon can think of nothing better than this marriage, which shows that in any case, whatever the solution, he must undergo a dispossession.

It is this, perhaps, which explains Agamemnon's ambivalence, for he perceives that the death that is demanded by the gods is simply the beginning of his own death. This war, for which the Greeks are preparing with such enthusiasm, in which twenty kings will descend on an isolated Troy, this organized carnage in which he proposes to be the executioner – Agamemnon cannot enjoy the bloody profit derived from it, which is his by right, and go unpunished. The thing that gives Iphigenia's sacrifice its baffling character, which makes the demand of the gods seem so monstrous, is its anticipatory nature. For once, one must expiate the crime before committing it. It is clear from the outset how the action will unfold:

> We sailed; already, by a thousand cries,
> We threatened from afar the shores of Troy.
>
> (Racine, *Iphigenia*, I, 1:56)

It is Artemis who exacts this tribute and she, as goddess of hunting, knows what she is talking about. What she demands, she demands in view of what will follow, the events that the boundaries of the tragedy will not allow us to reach. In this sense Aphrodite is deceitfully invoked. Under cover of giving a wife to her betrothed, a bloody marriage is prepared, a Bacchanal of death dedicated to Ares. The death of Iphigenia and the sack of Troy will be the causes that will justify in the eyes of the gods Clytemnestra's murder of Agamemnon. The mechanism of misfortune that scourges the house of the Atrides is set once again in motion. Iphigenia's sacrifice, it will be said, was commanded by the gods. But the gods did not give their approval to the attack on Troy. 'If the Greeks wish to conquer Troy,' they say, 'then Iphigenia must be sacrificed.' They do not say that the Greeks must conquer Troy, or that it is a good thing that they should do so. This is the trap of the oracle; it is the things it does not say that delimit the area for the reversal of the proposition, on which the consequences of this elision will be mapped.

Euripides' two *Iphigenias*, *Iphigenia in Aulis* and *Iphigenia in Tauris*, are bathed in a remarkable atmosphere of religious impiety. Nowhere is the word of the gods honoured. At every opportunity, the principal characters stress its iniquitous character and seek in it no source of occult wisdom. Jealousy, the 'secret envy' of the gods, is not even conceived as a punishment of hubris. Those who utter prophecies are condemned as harshly as those who listen to them and go off in pursuit of mirages:

But the divine geniuses who are called *wise* deceive us no less than our winged dreams. In the intentions of gods no less than in those of men there are many troubling things. And this above all suffices to undermine their wisdom: it is to see a mortal man of good judgment perish because he believed the words of oracles. And this will be attested by those who know his story.   (Euripides, *Iphigenia in Tauris*, 90–1)

It is Agamemnon's son who says this. Is this not an attack on his father for believing Calchas and sacrificing Iphigenia?

But sometimes Iphigenia attacks the gods themselves and challenges their logic: 'As for Artemis, I find her guilty of hypocrisy! Her purity! Any man who has touched blood or a woman in labour or a corpse, Artemis calls unclean and bars him from her altars; yet she herself delights in these murderous sacrifices!' (Euripides, *Iphigenia in Tauris*, 84–5). In the end, she reaches the explanation that Freud would not have rejected: 'I believe that the men of this country, being murderers, impute their own savagery to divine authority!' But this truth is softened with an acquittal of the gods: 'I do not believe that any god is evil!' This impiety on the part of Euripides, so clearly manifested in *Iphigenia in Tauris* – written shortly before *Iphigenia in Aulis* – explains perhaps why Agamemnon finds no voice to defend him in the second play. His acceptance of Calchas' decree is interpreted as an act of madness. All those who speak of it say that his mind has turned. But for all that the sacrifice does indeed take place. This proves beyond doubt that the true desire behind his consent to the sacrifice is the one desire that stokes his thirst for Trojan blood, and which by an unexpected reversal justifies this sacrifice as a talion-payment unusual only in being exacted before the offence. Whoever wishes to shed blood must pay in advance for the blood that he will shed.

In Racine, it is true that Achilles and Clytemnestra both set about criticizing the soothsayers and also blame Calchas' decrees, but the attacks on the gods are perhaps less frank. On the other hand, the revolt against the father is given free rein. In Euripides, Clytemnestra is finally resigned to the sacrifice and sadly accepts her daughter's decision, just as Achilles accepts the decision of his betrothed, who wishes to subject herself to the paternal will. In Racine, the mother and the son-in-law struggle to the end, forcing Calchas to change his views. This different arrangement does not simply reflect an evolution in *mores*. It reminds us that although Charles Mauron is right to speak of a return of the father in Racine from *Mithridate* onwards – that tragedy immediately preceded *Iphigénie* – nonetheless Racine subjects the father to assaults from which he does not emerge enhanced. It can be no accident that this displacement which makes the father the privileged target occurs in a context where love has assumed an important role, and that the father's final decision should take him outside the sacrifice/marriage dilemma and make him save Iphigenia in order to reappropriate his child.

So the object of the father's attack – the thing that opposes his decrees and prohibitions – is the object of desire that he possesses and which forms the focus of the struggle.

One sees how hubris, excessive pride, took shape. In it was condemned the excess that strove out of pride to reduce the gap between man and the gods without naming the end pursued: *jouissance* and the object through which it passes. In Racine, the veil is torn away, but the action has its counterpart: the uncovered Eros unveils the image of his shadow, the black Eros of Eriphile towards whom the tragic is displaced.

Kingship between the force of expenditure and the force of calculation

This Agamemnon has inspired many contradictory opinions. Some recognize a certain nobility in him, a kingliness that is no less worthy than that of the *Roi-Soleil*; others accuse him of mediocrity and ambitious greed. The second reproach is not entirely unfounded. But what monarch aspiring to a high destiny could escape such a charge? More marked in the construction of the character is the overwhelming weight of the virtues and powers that are piled on his head: 'father, husband, king, great Atreus' son': the enumeration of titles suggests the reasons for his satisfaction. The speeches addressed to him never fail to recall episodes in which his glory was enhanced.

Achilles

This is what differentiates Agamemnon from Achilles. Achilles has his entire destiny before him: he runs after a fate that he knows to be a glorious one. His movement is a perpetual effort to hasten its progress. Achilles with the winged feet[3] is the wind that no longer blows at Aulis. What prevents him from giving full vent to the forces he contains is not so much the work of the gods as the royal will of Agamemnon, on whom every decision depends. Achilles devours time; he would prefer to longevity 'a short life followed by long renown'. He moves by leaps and bounds. He does not try to please the gods, nor to bend himself to their will. On the contrary, he does not fear to enter into competition with them. He is moved neither by a sense of resignation, nor by pious submission, but by a burning love of action, even though he knows that he must espouse the fate that the gods have allotted him. In relation to the gods, therefore, Racine's Achilles is a force that expends itself lavishly and which finds satisfaction only in exhausting itself in some cause that makes an appeal to his native nobility. By virtue of his rank and title, Agamemnon acts as a mediator between him and the gods, who are called to witness: 'My only honour is to follow you.' And for Achilles, to follow can only mean to overtake.

If I am inclined to read in Racine this new relation of rivalry between Agamemnon and Achilles,[4] which is more marked than in Euripides, it is not only because Iphigenia is more obviously in contest, but because the sets of forces that they personify are opposed to one another. With Agamemnon, the possessor of unequalled acquisitions, goes a cast of mind concerned to preserve as much as possible of the wealth he has accumulated, and to increase his fortune and glory. The king–father is subjected to this contradiction which he cannot reconcile, having to destroy what he wishes to keep (Iphigenia) or to preserve what he wishes to destroy (Ilion). The only alternative that he has to offer in this opposition is that in which he gives what he wishes to keep (through marriage) or loses what he wants to get (the spoils of Ilion). With Achilles goes an energy that reduces to dust whatever it touches and which gets satisfaction from approaching the promised annihilation, in defiance of the course of time. Sacrifice is also part and parcel of the cause of Achilles, who cannot see the danger, because his life is entirely devoted to this consummation, with no other reflection than what will survive him in his own legend. We shall see that this ruthlessness in violence will summon up its exact inverse in another figure of the tragedy.

Menelaus

If Racine made love a part of the character of Achilles, it was not simply to depict a hero who conformed to the taste of the time; it is also because he had to displace the impact of desire as it is present in Euripides. We know that he sacrificed the character of Menelaus and replaced it by that of Ulysses, who never appears in the ancient tragedy, although he and Calchas together control the situation. The priest, the mouthpiece of the gods, inspires fear, and demands the submission of the Greeks in the execution of the sacrifice. But Ulysses strives to fan the flames of war in the Greek camp, brushing aside whatever opposes his thirst for conquest – a conquest that is not at all a matter of revenge, but is activated solely by a desire to appropriate to himself the wealth of the enemy. It has been said that the character of Menelaus, the fair-haired Menelaus, would have been intolerable to the French public. This character, as deceived husband, would have tilted the play still further towards bourgeois comedy. But nothing justifies this judgement in the ancient context. The scene in Euripides between Menelaus and Agamemnon may at times take on the acrimonious, sordid tone of a family quarrel, but at a deeper level it suggests a conflict between two brothers whose blood ties fail to temper contrary desires that drive them to inevitable characteristic extremities as soon as their alliance ceases to unite them in common interests. Menelaus' final reversal, when he no longer demands the sacrifice of his brother's daughter, is no less moving. But this act is not enough to extinguish the passions already aroused. The beast is unleashed; it moves into the Greek camp where no one can restrain it, where one can only permit it to take its course, or else exploit it.

Ulysses

Racine remodels this ineluctability by eliminating the intermediaries and directly substituting Ulysses for Menelaus. It is usually said that for Racine Ulysses represents the politician. Above all, he represents a value complementary to Achilles – and this not only in mythology, but also in the terms of the tragedy. To Achilles' principle of individual consummation he opposes, in order to serve the warrior's appetite, the principle of larger dividends. Individuality, as an entity of no consequence, is even condemned when it endeavours to follow its own ends. So the salvation of Iphigenia, when her father seeks to preserve her, condemns Agamemnon without extenuation because he 'dare not buy glory with a little blood' (1, 3:66). His reticence and his reserve are such that his influence weighs heavy. He frames the play – he is present only in the first and last acts – and Racine leaves it to him to sum up. It is for him to draw up the account of the unexpected dénouement, since there is seen emerging a still more advantageous solution: the gods appeased, Agamemnon delivered from possible rancour, Achilles gratified in his matrimonial desires. A good omen: with Eriphile's death, we have the first head to fall in the ranks of the enemy. Ulysses supports Racine's dramatic intention and assists him in his search for a compromise that will satisfy the taste of the time. He is to be one of the two poles between which the Racinian tragedy oscillates. He represents the pole of that solution that closes the tragic action by displaying all its knots untied, all its forces neutralized. The other pole, Eriphile, who is also an invention of Racine's, is opposed to any solution of that kind.

With the character of Ulysses, however, the meaning of the sacrifice is revealed. In Euripides, Ulysses must lead a troop of soldiers to seize Iphigenia. The gods are appeased in the end by the violence that the sacrifice seemed to hide in itself. In Racine, Ulysses is the guarantor of the rites that must be carried out so that the expedition that the Greeks have decided on may go forward. Here, too, he is opposed to Achilles who, while believing in the prophecies that determine his destiny, does not admit of intermediaries between the gods and himself, and feels no hesitation in challenging the judgements of the soothsayers and ignoring their decrees:

> What is a seer?
> A man who, if he's lucky, tells a little truth
> And a lot of lies.   (Euripides, *Iphigenia in Aulis*, 402)

In Racine, no explicit accusation is made against Calchas. But never for a moment does Achilles stop to consider whether he is under an obligation to carry out Calchas' command. Furthermore, he even attacks the altar:

> He's at the altar. Calchas is distraught.
>   (Racine, *Iphigenia*, v, 5:122)

But although the character is in this point identical in Racine and Euripides, the modification introduced by Racine, who transforms the valorous Achilles into the amorous Achilles, gives meaning to the opposition between the two tragic writers. In ancient tragedy, each passion, bearing within itself its own excess, also brings its own censure, and the reversal of which it is the object survives, as after the crossing of a critical point at which any desire, however legitimate, suddenly gives way to the resistance which it has just broken. The conflict is born not so much from some reason of state directed against a private feeling as from the clash of two non-coincident feelings. A desire is always opposed by another desire, one form of madness by another. The character of Ulysses disturbs this equilibrium obtained by the confrontation of two disequilibriums. The distribution of forces operates between the characters more than within each character. To the ravages of love, the irresolution of an ambition too dearly bought, Ulysses opposes the force of calculation, which chance places at the service of desire. He is not even the cunning Ulysses, whose malice will always leave some scope for humour. Here Racine, who was reminded of Homer for the character of Achilles, speaks for himself alone when he gives the tragedy its regulatory pole – the resolution of tensions into a movement towards the aim dictated by interest alone, obtained at the lowest price: a little blood buys a lot of glory.

In Racine, then, Agamemnon is caught up in the sweep of the combined passions of Achilles and Ulysses: the force of expenditure, less concerned with the result of its action than with the display of its energy; and the force of calculation,[5] where the commitment to the enterprise is less important than the expected benefit of its operations. The reversals will be imputable in part to the relative strength of these energies at different moments in the tragedy. Outside the vice in which he is caught, the king would turn his daughter away from the path to the altar. When Achilles is abused and neutralized, he gives in to Ulysses. But when Achilles takes the offensive, he responds in language that Ulysses would approve. In the end, detaching himself from both, he disengages the issue constituted by the life of his daughter, which he preserves for himself alone. In short, he can free himself of Ulysses only to come within range of Achilles, who also wants to take his daughter away from him. So Agamemnon has not so much to choose between saving his daughter or losing her as between the various ways of giving her to some other: to the gods, who exact that tribute only from the powerful, who owe them that tribute as the due of their power; to Ulysses and the army, of whom he expects great sacrifices, which demand some return on his part; to Achilles, whose rivalry and rebellion are worthy of the party he represents, who alone has the weight to replace, *qua* husband, the prestige of the father.

In Racine, these three influences – those of Calchas, Ulysses and Achilles – share the area of the conflict, whereas in Euripides, Achilles, however touchy he is about his honour and however much he may wish to help Clytemnestra and Iphigenia, nevertheless keeps a respectful distance from Agamemnon. In the end, even he takes part in the sacrifice, despite his initial intention of preventing it by force, being dissuaded by the victim herself, who makes clear the meaning of the law. His revolt is nothing compared with that of Racine's Achilles, resolute to the end, who even takes his struggle to the altar despite – perhaps because of – Iphigenia's submission to her father's command.

Agamemnon's hesitations, the shocks he receives from various quarters and Achilles' total challenge of his authority are set in contexts where they respond to different needs. In Euripides, the actual execution of Iphigenia is for the father a virtual castration that fulfils the desire of the gods, who might be thought to be jealous of the power accumulated by the King of kings. The balance between temporal power and spiritual power has been maintained, and the price of the sack of Troy has in a sense been paid in advance. In Racine, where the sacrifice does not take place, the challenge to the royal power is made more explicit through the voices of the men. In Euripides, Agamemnon suffers not so much *qua* father as *qua* rival son of the gods. In Racine, Agamemnon pays for his condition of father under the attacks of his brother (Ulysses) and his son (Achilles). Calchas may become more discreet, since what is lost by one hand is retrieved by the other. In any case, in that century of absolute monarchy it is shown that power cannot be concentrated indefinitely, but that it is fragmented after having been condensed ('father, husband, king, great Atreus' son'); it is not preserved for ever, but is dispersed and transmitted; it does not increase in an unlimited way, but decreases and runs the risk of dissolution.

Agamemnon's conflicts of conscience reflect the competitive struggle between his ego and certain of his objects, some of which must elude him, and whose antagonistic interests dispute each other's right to survive. And if, like Charles Mauron, one can speak of the return of the father in Racine after *Mithridate*, *Iphigénie* shows this father exposed to blows that deprive him of much of his prestige. The sacrifice of the sacrifice was certainly worth that.

The pact and sexual prohibition

At the origin of the tragic situation, both in Euripides and in Racine, we find an indissoluble bond established by a pact. This is the oath made to Tyndarus, Helen's father. His daughter's suitors, too numerous and too infatuated, bitterly dispute the privilege of winning her. For fear that the dissatisfaction of a rejected suitor might engender discord, before any choice is made the girl's father binds the suitors by an oath, by which they commit themselves to unite against any future ravisher. Of course, this excessive precaution does not remove the danger, since a stranger later emerges, unbound by any oath, and free from the threat of punishment that this coalition might exact, and carries off this same Helen, the object of desire and cause of discord.

It is this pact that Agamemnon has invoked in order to unite the kings of Greece in a punitive expedition. But a pact between men is nothing if it does not have the assent of the gods. The pact is one boundary of the tragic space: the long chain of kings assembled at Aulis forms a circle at whose centre the edict of Artemis requires Iphigenia's sacrifice. It is Ulysses who closes the circle of this chain, when he demands that the gods' interdict be removed, that is, satisfied. Not that he submits out of respect for them, nor yet that he sees the avenging of a humiliating offence as above any other cause; rather in the name of that conduct that does not turn aside at the sufferings that it must undergo, and pursues unflinchingly the aim it has set itself. Now, one of Racine's innovations, found nowhere in Euripides, is to proclaim on several occasions that Achilles has not subscribed to this pact:

> *He* was not Helen's suitor; never swore
> To Helen's father to defend her troth.

> (Racine, *Iphigenia*, II, 3:78)

Since he has not been one of Helen's suitors, he is involved in the undertaking only as a heroic quest. He hastens wherever the scent of battle draws him. It is not simply that Achilles has to be innocent of this earlier passion, so that his love for Iphigenia should have the required nobility and purity. It is also because by virtue of this fact he places himself in an exceptional position among the sworn kings.

In fact, what this great gathering of kings shows is that in the name of love and fidelity a bloody orgy is being prepared, dedicated not to Eros but to aggressiveness. In the name of the rancour once aroused by the demand that they give up all claim to the beautiful Helen one finds, in these former suitors of hers, more than a simple satisfaction of the interests of the ego, an ego that loves itself only in its own aggrandisement, an ego jealous of affirming its mastery.

> Behold the honour flowing from her blood,
> The Hellespont whitening beneath your oars,
> Perfidious Troy abandoned to the flames,
> In chains its people, Priam at your knees,
> Helen by you restored to Menelaus,
> The prows of your fair vessels garlanded
> To this same Aulis sailing back with you

In glorious triumph, destined to resound,
Undying, down the centuries to come.

(Racine, *Iphigenia*, I, 5:68)

In the name of this chain of desires Artemis demands that before there can be any armed engagement a victim must be sacrificed to her, with which the Greek camp must be marked, as by a wound imposing the seal of castration. The pact had meant the renunciation of the object. Under the pretext of having right on their side in the present, the desire to avenge the outrage is silent about this renunciation, accepted in bad faith in the past.

Achilles, who seems to be in the front rank of the revengers, escapes this conjuncture, therefore, and fights only to enhance his own glory. From a basis of narcissistic affirmation, of the appetite for conquest, from which Agamemnon's future son-in-law is not exempt, Achilles proclaims the rights of Eros. For, in the last resort, it is Eros who is the cause of contention between Agamemnon and the son of Thetis. In all respects, then, Achilles is indeed the Oedipal hero, recognized by Charles Mauron. It is as herald of Eros – a positive, affirmed Eros – that he speaks and acts. His strength, placed at the service of the pact of alliance, will be detached from that and placed under the banner of his desire for the most enviable creature in the Greek camp: the daughter of the leader of the coalition. This is one of Racine's most fundamental innovations, but it was not entirely of his own making.

It would be more correct to say that Racine opened up a hidden element of the Euripidean situation. For one cannot say, if one reads the text attentively, that there is no love in Euripides. It is met at every turn, but it is supremely expressed in two ways: either through the tender relations that grow up between Iphigenia and her father, which are much freer in their expression than in Racine; or in the very strongly marked form of prohibition. And we find this fear – whose singular absence in Racine I have already noted, though Racine recognizes its eminently tragic value – arising before any image of an encounter between the sexes. One has only to think of the moment when the surprised Achilles comes face to face with Clytemnestra:

Goddess of blushes! Who is this?
I see a lady richly endowed with comeliness.

(Euripides, *Iphigenia in Aulis*, 396)

Informed about his situation, he bursts out: 'It would be overbold of me to pursue an encounter with a woman.' And when Clytemnestra holds out her hand to him, believing that she is addressing him as her son-in-law, he exclaims in embarrassment: 'What are you saying! I, take your hand? Could I look Agamemnon in the face if I touched what is forbidden?' Later, Achilles avoids Iphigenia, advising Clytemnestra not to bring her before him:

> Don't bring your daughter out to see me; let us
> Avoid, Madam, all risk of earning the reproach of fools.
> (Euripides, *Iphigenia in Aulis*, 404)

One might almost say that the ancient tragedy is imbued with an atmosphere of sexual suspicion. Iphigenia hides herself from the sight of men, and when, with her father, she ventures a remark about her future condition as a wife, her father's reply reminds her of the ignorance in which her condition as a girl must keep her.

It is less important that we should see this as a reflection of the *mores* of the time than that we should understand these *mores* themselves as testimony of the fear in which the sexual is held. Racinian *galanterie* seems unaware that its own foundations are nourished by this fear. The tragedy would not have its full effect if some mediator did not take over responsibility for this fear. And not even Achilles' vitality – not even his furious, blind fascination,[6] which emerges above all in his conflict with Agamemnon, who regains his resolution only at the moment in the tragedy when he struggles for his daughter with this man chosen to be his son-in-law – can create an impression of the sacred, a constricting feeling of horror, of impending doom. Achilles is the image of a transgression in the course of realization, unaware of itself in its fulfilment. He lacks the stigma of some transgression already committed, which has savoured the taste of perdition and always draws it back to the target in which it sinks and exhausts itself. Could Iphigenia help us to feel it?

The virgin and her rivals

Set against the male conflicts, Racine's female world does not show the same tensions. Iphigenia is flanked by her mother, Clytemnestra, and that new figure, Eriphile, whose sombre colours throw a sinister light on the tragic space.

Clytemnestra

There is not much to be said about Clytemnestra. The differences in the treatment of the character in Euripides and Racine are insignificant. It is usually said that Racine's Clytemnestra is more regal, Euripides' more familiar. However, this becomes far from clear if we see her through the eyes of the Argive royal power. This mistress–wife who dominates the scene from her arrival and dares to confront Agamemnon is no different from Racine's enraged mother; the French woman is more capable of argument, despite her bursts of sarcasm and anger, while the Greek woman is more moving, more painfully wounded. But, in each case, it is the feelings of a mother that are conveyed, with no room for hesitation. It has been said that Achilles and she defend the rights of the individual. But this is hardly correct. Achilles wishes to enter upon the path of glory that leads to his death. Clytemnestra demands above all the life and safety of her daughter, beside which nothing else matters, no interest counts, no divinity is to be heard. It is in this sense that Freud remarked that the demands of the superego were weaker in women, which is certainly not pejorative in its implication, since it testifies to an unlimited love of life and, no doubt, is accounted for by the part played by women in creation. Given the demands of the situation, Clytemnestra is the least tragic character – though this does not reflect adversely on Racine – because she is the most affected by the situation, though the least torn by her contradictory desires.

Iphigenia(s)

The power of Racine's genius is shown by the fact that his Iphigenia cannot be conceived without Eriphile. Modern commentators (Goldmann, Mauron, Barthes) stress this – so much so that one wonders whether without Eriphile the original actress, La Champmeslé, could have moved the assembled court of Versailles to tears as she did. Euripides' Iphigenia, with her simple youthfulness, which plunges her in spite of herself into the tragic, is a moving figure. In Euripides, when Iphigenia sees her mother, she runs towards her father:

> Oh, mother, don't be angry if I go before you;
> I want to put my arms around him and hug him close.
> (Euripides, *Iphigenia in Aulis*, 388)

Racine inverts the sense of this encounter:

> I for the Queen respectfully made way;
> Can I not detain you for a while,
> And in your presence manifest my joy?
> (Racine, *Iphigenia*, II, 2:74–5)

The precaution of that 'don't be angry' will later make possible the moving exchange between father and daughter. It will enable her at the moment of the dénouement to obtain a place in the desire of the father by an identification with the paternal ego-ideal which the mother cannot reach, whereas in Racine, submission to the mother shows the way to the displacement of jealousy towards Eriphile. It is no longer the mother who is the obstacle, in the father's way, but the rival woman whom she suspects of competing with her for her lover's heart. Hence the coldness that emerges during the encounters between daughter and father in Racine, in which all charm has disappeared, sometimes draining the emotion from the scene and leaving a lack, sometimes substituting for the complaint of an Orphic song a 'message' that is no more than a piece of rhetoric. Tenderness for the father will have to be sought where the desire of the Other wishes to eliminate it: in the reply to the lover determined to dispute her with the man who enjoys a love that is due to him. Charles Mauron thinks that the relative success of Racine in depicting Iphigenia's situation derives solely from his concern to concentrate on the passions and on his inability to appreciate the values represented by the sacrifice. The emotion aroused in Euripides by Iphigenia's acceptance of sacrifice gives her farewell an astonishing verisimilitude, by virtue of its unmotivated, irrational character, moved solely by identification with the object of paternal desire through the ways of the ego-ideal. This must, in Racine, be transferred elsewhere and also, a crucial fact, it must change sign. In Euripides, Achilles' revolt is reduced to silence by Iphigenia's will. The acceptance of the sacrifice is transformed by paternal identification into a positive value. In the end, the marriage/sacrifice equivalence makes the two terms coincide, but by transforming the ascent to the altar into a marriage with the father, in which the daughter receives his power, at the same time as she marks it with the wound that she inflicts on this power by her death. Passing into the kingdom of the dead, she recalls the initial meaning of the metaphor: in the course of time, the doe has been substituted metonymically for the virgin of the original sacrifice. On this day, for Artemis, as she awaits the great hunt that is about to take place, there is a return to the primary meaning of the sacrifice, and, as in time immemorial, the virgin takes the place of the doe. But this substitution for the doe of the sacrifice, and the return of the doe at the last moment – this operates a second metaphorical leap. Iphigenia saved, carried off by Artemis, is in her second life or, to put it another way, in a miraculous extension of the first, herself a priestess dedicated to the cult of Artemis: responsible, against her will, for human sacrifices that she does not carry out, but which she consecrates.

Too little has been said about the curious destiny of the gentle Iphigenia. *Iphigenia in Tauris* – written before *Iphigenia in Aulis* – may depict her as a shy girl, unhappy at being chosen for such a task. But this Iphigenia, in Tauris, proves to be of an infinitely less gentle character than the virgin of Aulis. In the famous recognition scene, Orestes, wanting to prove that he is a son of the house of Agamemnon, and fully acquainted with the history of the place, offers some interesting evidence. It is in the virginal chamber of Iphigenia that the spear of their ancestor, Pelops, is hidden, 'that old spear which Pelops hurled when he killed Oenomaus [his father] at Pisa and won his daughter Hippodamia!' (Euripides, *Iphigenia in Tauris*, 98). This reminiscence is particularly apt in the circumstances, since Iphigenia has been given responsibility for blood sacrifices. And although it is true that she dislikes her office, disappointment and anger give rise within her to a passion that is the contrary of compassion. Having dreamt of the death of Orestes, which frustrates his hopes of flight, she wishes that the wind might drive Menelaus and Helen to the shores of Tauris, 'that I might take due vengeance and make a second Aulis for atonement here! Aulis! where Greeks took hold of me as though I were a calf to slaughter me, while my own father officiated as priest! How can I ever forget that day?' (Euripides, *Iphigenia in Tauris*, 84).

This, then, is an Iphigenia consumed by understandable and justified feelings of resentment and vengeance, which are absent in the sacrificial victim at Aulis. One cannot accuse Euripides of neglecting the coherence of his characters from one tragedy to the other or of subordinating them to different tragic circumstances.

The similarity of the Greek and French works cannot be accidental. Not only because *Iphigenia in Aulis* refers back necessarily to *Iphigenia in Tauris*, but because Racine considered writing an *Iphigenia in Tauris* and even left a plan for the first act. This plan contains the idea of a love intrigue between the son of King Thoas and Iphigenia – a theme not in Euripides – just as the plot of *Iphigenia in Aulis* was altered by the transformation of Achilles into a lover. But the document is interesting for another reason: it provides a comparison between Iphigenia's dream as given by Euripides and as Racine proposed to describe it.

A comparison of the two dreams is certainly rewarding. Here is the dream as it appears in Euripides' *Iphigenia in Tauris*:

> I dreamt I had escaped out of this land
> And lived in Argos. There I and my maidens
> Were sleeping, when the earth's shoulders heaved and shook.
> I flew outdoors, and stood and watched the house –
> Plinth, pillar, coping, roof – reel at one blow
> And crash to earth. Out of the ruin which
> Had been my father's house one column stood;

And from its head flowed golden hair; it spoke
With human voice. And I performed for it
My murderous rite for strangers, sprinkling water
As though on one destined to die, – and weeping.

(Euripides, Iphigenia in Tauris, 75)

Explicitly, this dream alludes to the collapse of the 'house of Agamemnon', that is to say, of the Argive royal house. It elides the stages of the murder of Agamemnon and the murder of Clytemnestra. It refers to Orestes' survival, but announces prophetically that Orestes will soon be sacrificed. However, this manifest content is more complex than it seems. Iphigenia is in Argos, carried back to the past, yet at the same time in Tauris in the present, since she is carrying out her sad priestly duties. One may see the dream as condensing a scene from the past and a scene of the future; that is to say, as rendering a fear or a wish-fulfilment.

Let us not forget that this dream is an undreamt dream, a fictional dream; so we should not ask of it more than it can tell. But, at the risk of betraying the Freudian method, that is to say, treating the dream not as a riddle, but as a succession of images coherently linked in sequence, I shall attempt to interpret it. This interpretation will try to rediscover the meaning that Euripides, consciously or not, meant to convey to the Greek public.

Confronted by such a dream, any analyst would think that he was faced with a dream of the primal scene. The child, a girl, is awoken in the middle of the night by the noise of her parents' sexual relations. This noise disturbs her; she wants to get up in order to see and understand what is happening, or escape the disturbing strangeness that surrounds her. She is the witness of the actions of the parents united in sexual relations and thinks that they are destroying one another, the mother getting the worst of it. She sees or imagines her father's sexual organ, which she wishes to appropriate for herself either in itself or in the form of the child that the penis engenders and which may be its substitute. She is afraid that if she seizes it, she will destroy it.

This is the phantasy reduced from the dream in Euripides.

How does Racine transcribe it into the scheme of his own tragic language? What his Iphigenia says amounts to this: 'I thought I was at Mycenae in my father's house: it seemed to me that my father and mother were swimming in blood and that I myself was clutching a dagger with which to cut the throat of my brother, Orestes.'

My interpretation is confirmed. Racine stresses what Euripides' dream does not bring out, the thing which the whole tragedy invites us to imagine: the identification of Iphigenia with the father's penis,

which underlies his virile position. This is apparent in the tragedy at
Tauris and completely concealed at Aulis, where she represents the
innocent sacrificed doe.

Her character in *Iphigenia in Aulis* is deflected by Racine, who
gives her feelings of rivalry, hostility, even sadism, towards Eriphile.
In short, by introducing love into his tragedy, Racine does more
than present a feeling capable of moving an audience; he includes
in his range of emotions the necessary value of hate and also its
consequence – the masochistic reversal that is expressed in her final
consent.

So Charles Mauron is right to see Eriphile as Iphigenia's repressed
double. Iphigenia and Eriphile are opposed not as night and day,
but as dawn and dusk. There remain in Iphigenia remnants of the
night that the dawning day has not yet chased away, just as Eriphile
shines with the muted glow of nightfall.

Iphigenia's violence, directed at Eriphile, has the function of
expressing within the register of lover–beloved relations the element
that is aimed at the rival (the mother); and this is not expressed
within the register of father–daughter relations in which the mother
would naturally be included. In any case, it is Eriphile and not
Clytemnestra (as in Euripides) who bears the father's coldness and
the lover's lack of concern and who will soon be accused of
treachery.

> You triumph, cruel one, and brave my grief.
> I had not felt the weight of all my ills,
> And you compare your exile to my fame
> But to enhance your unjust victory.
>
> (Racine, *Iphigenia*, ii, 5:82)

We must not be misled here: when in the following act Iphigenia
demands that Eriphile be freed, it might be thought that, although
she seems concerned to be forgiven for her earlier accusations, she is
removing to a safe distance a dangerous rival whom nothing would
make her keep near her. When she asks for Eriphile – 'Do not
condemn her to behold us' – she removes her from her own
proximity. Perhaps passion had already prompted the presentiment
that there was more than a rival to be feared in Eriphile: the threat
of a misfortune still less exorcizable, in her irresistible inclination to
misfortune:

> the dead,
> Lesbos, the torch, the ashes – by these things
> Your love for him is graven on your soul,
> And, far from hating this grim memory,
> You still delight to talk to me of it.   (*Iphigenia*, ii, 5:81)

The Iphigenia who speaks like this, who reads into the heart of another woman, is herself a woman, not a virgin. Her consent to the sacrifice is not, can no longer be, that of an innocent girl, but the expression of a choice between two loves: love for the father and love for the lover. (In Euripides, the Oedipal guilt, the guilt of the daughter at the forbidden love she feels for her father, encourages the conversion of this object-love into narcissistic identification with her ego-ideal. In Racine, it might be said that this guilt bears primarily upon the love felt for the lover, who is abandoned to the rival, Eriphile, the mother-substitute. This in effect culminates in the return to the parental fixation on the paternal object, and its incestuous character demands sacrificial expiation.)

Certainly Achilles understands the choice. The abandonment of the lover and the return to the father mark the fixation on the parental object. The desire for a *jouissance* obtained through the father's desire can be fulfilled only through masochistic exaltation, and its reward will be the attainment of a glory that will rival that of Achilles.

> If I've not lived at great Achilles' side,
> I hope at least a smiling future joins
> My memory to your immortal deeds.   (Racine, *Iphigenia*, v, 2:116)

The further the tragedy proceeds, the more Iphigenia's object-love, Iphigenia's love for Achilles, gives way to the narcissistic love of paternal identification. The scene in which she confronts her father, knowing her fate, no longer has the supplicatory aspect it possessed so strongly in Euripides, in which the daughter is deprived of all power before her father: 'but my tears are my one magic'. In Racine's play, it is to Achilles that she addresses her patriotic speech, when refusing his help.

Just as Racine's Achilles is a mixture of Euripides and Homer, it might be said that his Iphigenia is a mixture of *Aulis* and *Tauris*.

What lies behind this transformation? An individualization, a humanization of the character? The interest that is no longer confined to the tragic situation, as systematically embodying its tension in its form, but which becomes internalized in the conflicts that reside in the characters? No doubt, but also an economy that shifts the terror at the carrying out of the sacrifice into personal conflict. On the one hand there is the noble spirit of Achilles, eager to be consumed, and the renunciation of the object after the struggle against the rival and the return to a narcissistic identification with Iphigenia's paternal idea. To this there must correspond another negative value, in which tragedy is rediscovered in the spectacle of a misfortune whose sole cause is the cause of the misfortune, in which is seen the mark of the fatal power of the gods, and which assumes the mask of an irresistible aspiration to the *jouissance* of destruction. This is Eriphile.

Eriphile or the tragic rediscovered

Roland Barthes makes the following just and lapidary judgement on *Iphigénie*: 'Without Eriphile *Iphigénie* would be a very good comedy.'

This seems to mean that, without this character who is Racine's special addition to Euripides' scheme – everything else being at most in the nature of substitution (replacement of Menelaus by Ulysses), modification of feeling (Achilles the lover) or shift in the final solution (marriage instead of sacrifice) – *Iphigénie* would allow the survival of only the first of the Aristotelian tragic 'effects', compassion, which is compatible with the spirit of comedy; the second, terror, which properly belongs to tragedy, would disappear completely.

The place left vacant by terror is related to the disappearance of Iphigenia's sacrifice; this is taken by Eriphile's suicide, which cannot actually take its place.

What this amounts to is that we owe all the specifically tragic power to Eriphile, both in her life and in her death. (In *Le Dieu caché*, Goldmann opposes the tragic universe of Eriphile to the providential universe of the rest of the characters in the tragedy.) Why, apart from the motives that he gives, which are scarcely convincing, does Racine balance things in this way? Eriphile is a counterweight that holds the balance equal with Euripides' tragedy, and compensates for the introduction of the love theme between Achilles and Iphigenia, the opposition between Ulysses' calculation and Achilles' impetuosity (interest opposed to love) and the elimination of the dénouement involving sacrificial murder, on which the entire tragic sense of the ancient play is focused, and all its cruel, senseless, absurd and remorseless character.

Barthes, Goldmann and Mauron all feel that the tragedy revolves around Eriphile. 'Her Eros is the most tragic that Racine has defined,' says Barthes. Mauron sees her as Iphigenia's dark double and devotes most of his study to her. Eriphile is usually seen as a figure of jealousy, treachery, hate. We are taken in by this appearance if we confuse what is externalized by a dark power and projected on to others with the labour that is expended by this power on its object, the heroine's ego, which must succumb at the end of the tragedy:

Ah! Beneficial perils: Useless hopes!   (Racine, *Iphigenia*, IV, 1:98)

Is this not like a motto on a coat of arms? If we allow ourselves to be taken in by Eriphile's jealousy and her overtly expressed desire to harm and ruin her unfortunate rival, we run the risk of losing the thread meant to guide our reading of the tragedy. Eriphile is doomed to misfortune: the misfortune she causes others is no more than a slight deflection of the misfortune that must devolve on her:

> Give scope to my dejection and their joy.   (*Iphigenia*, ii, 1:70)

To give scope to her dejection is to set free this repressed contrary destiny, where all the other characters strive to avoid evil, accept compromises dictated by circumstances and exploit every possible chance of success. Eriphile must always dwell on her 'woes', as Doris remarks to her, stressing their cumulative character:

> Your grief with every step grows more profound. (*Iphigenia*, ii, 1:70)

Our suspicion that this grief is a self-wounding necessary to her existence is confirmed for us by the exposition of her masochistic phantasy:

> In the fell hands of this fierce ravisher,
> I long remained unconscious and inert.
> At last my sad eyes opened to the light,
> And seeing myself embraced by bloodstained arms,
> I shuddered, Doris, and I feared to meet
> The savage face of a wild conqueror.
> Carried aboard, I cursed his violence,
> Averting still my horror-stricken gaze.
> I saw him. There was nothing fierce in him.
> I felt reproach expire upon my lips;
> I felt my heart declare against me; I
> Forgot my anger and could only weep.
> I let myself be led by that kind guide.   (*Iphigenia*, ii, 1:73)

Love can be aroused in Eriphile only from her collusion with misfortune; the object of desire can only be something which attacks and wounds. Love, nourished on the ravisher's *jouissance*, is indistinguishable from annihilation.

We see how this love value complements, in Iphigenia, the acceptance of her destiny as a victim, out of love for a sacrificial father. If we ask ourselves by what penetrating perspicacity Iphigenia could guess what underlies her desire –

> Those arms you saw streaming with blood, the dead,
> Lesbos, the torch, the ashes – by these things
> Your love for him is graven on your soul,
> And, far from hating this grim memory,
> You still delight to talk to me of it   (*Iphigenia*, ii, 5:81)

– one might reply that in some geometrical locus, the phantasies of the two heroines coincide. Conversely, Eriphile, who cannot bear Iphigenia's happiness, envies her still more when she sees her as a victim, since this, for her, is the most enviable state of all. When Doris expresses surprise –

> What strange obsession's power
> Can make you envious of her destiny?
> She dies within the hour. Yet, so you say,
> Never were you more jealous of her luck   (*Iphigenia*, IV, 1:98)

– she declares her vocation for death, in order to take the place of her who in her misfortune excites the desire of Achilles the saviour, formerly Achilles the ravisher.

All these cumulative touches show with startling clarity Eriphile's tragic despair. Here, terror, which we have so far sought in vain and which must reach its acme in the suicide, resumes its place – a vengeful suicide, thrown in our faces like an accusation, which nevertheless appeases the gods' thirst for blood: a suicide that does not fulfil the same function as a sacrifice, but which takes up where the sacrifice left off.

Sacrifice is intended to seal the alliance with the gods and to obtain a guarantee of their benevolence and protection. (The silent jealousy of the gods, their 'secret envy', which is presented in Euripides without explanation – thus enhancing the tragic sense – is replaced by the human, explicit jealousy of Racine's Eriphile.) Sacrifice forces man periodically to recall, through the mutilation that he has to inflict upon himself, his original castration. Here, the transgression is manifestly sexual – Paris's abduction – and the sacrifice is demanded as the price to be paid for the punishment of this transgression; for the punishment may, in its excessive reaction, constitute a new transgression. The excess of the punishment would exceed the excess of the crime.

We have seen that, in Euripides, love was by no means absent, being present above all in the forms of its taboos. In Racine, love is authorized between Achilles and Iphigenia, and, apart from Calchas, there is nothing to oppose its free expression. But we then pass from forbidden love to the cursed love of Eriphile and from guilt to masochism. This accounts for the overwhelming need which Racine felt to invent Eriphile. Henceforth, the sacrifice becomes inevitable, since its cruel, senseless and vicious character is largely compensated for by the interiorization of guilt and the establishment of a negative passion, as cruel, senseless and vicious, if not more so, than the decree of the gods. Through the pure cultivation of the death drive, of

which the suicide is the culmination, the subject becomes the plaything of the gods.

But the sacrifice cannot only be a tribute paid to the gods; it may
be the sign of a kind of balance-sheet, where Achilles represents one
way of setting out the account. For him, at any rate, glory is an
expected gain, for which one offers one's life in exchange. But even
before she is asked to do so, Eriphile is ready to offer hers, with no
compensation:

> Perish I must, and, by immediate death,
> Bury my shame for ever in the tomb.   (Racine, *Iphigenia*, ii, 1:74)

This desire springs from the intolerable sight of others' happiness,
intolerable for someone who believes that she has never been the
object of any desire:

> Placed among strangers from my earliest days,
> Neither at birth nor later have I seen
> Mother or father ever smile on me.   (*Iphigenia*, ii, 1:71)

Thus this longing for death is effectively counterbalanced by no love
attachment; love can spring only from the destruction of which the
subject is the victim. This free force, set against no emotional investment, is therefore always in excess. It is this force that suicide must
discharge and finally liquidate utterly. In the process, other people
are affected, or she hopes they will be:

> A voice from within me ordered me to go,
> Told me that my unwelcome presence here
> Might bring perchance my ill luck here with me,
> That, if I mingled with this happy pair,
> Some one of my mishaps might spread to them. (*Iphigenia*, ii, 1:74)

Only the absolute sacrifice of suicide, as provocation of meaningless-
ness, can release the tension in the subject.

Right up to the moment of her death, Eriphile refuses to acquire
sacrificial value, since she denies Calchas any religious function in
escaping his 'profane hands'. Her suicide is a purely tragic act in
which the girl is totally identified with the misfortune to which she
aspires, for no reason.

The act is all the more tragic in that Eriphile's destiny – as
Barthes notes – is related to that of Oedipus. Not knowing who her
parents are, she must be born and die in one day. The opportunity
of discovering that she comes of illustrious birth is transformed into
lethal fate. The broken promise and the deception of the signifier
have once again outwitted the individual who staked everything in
the game.

What we have here is a rediscovery of the tragic sense.

In the final analysis, beneath the refined language of affected gallantry and courtly preciosity, three of Racine's characters aspire to death: Iphigenia, out of duty and obedience; Achilles, out of thirst for glory; and Eriphile, out of a predilection for misfortune. In the last act of the tragedy, we witness a race to the altar. The question is, who will get there first. Euripides' economy concentrates the power of divine cruelty on Iphigenia alone and silences the revolt of the Greeks, intent on death. Furthermore, the male supremacy that motivates the concern to preserve the life of every fighting man tells against any weakening of one's forces before the encounter with the enemy. There is a sentence spoken by Iphigenia that is difficult for us to hear fully with our contemporary ears, and which was already beginning to seem shocking in Racine's time: 'One man is of more value / Than a host of women' (Euripides, *Iphigenia in Aulis*, 419). The concentration on this one character gives the sacrificial death its emotional effectiveness. Pity and terror are produced not only by the innocence of the victim, but by the fact that this death must also be a sign of rejoicing. In secrecy and solitude, Iphigenia may shed tears over the cruelty of the fate that is hers; before the Greeks, this sacrifice must be a joyful celebration and, as she offers her head to the ritual consecrations, she calls on the officiating priests to rejoice:

> Praise Artemis with dances,
> Queen Artemis the blessed; circle round
> Her altar and her temple.   (*Iphigenia in Aulis*, 422)

By this means, the Euripidean situation condenses the effects of the tragic to the maximum. It directs them upon a single character, who, applauding her own death, proud of her high destiny, experiences mingled pain and joy in the sacrifice. Thus the chorus accompanies her last steps to the altar:

> You who rejoice in human sacrifice,
> Dread goddess.   (*Iphigenia in Aulis*, 423)

It can be said without fear of error that it was not only the sight of Iphigenia dying that the French public could not accept; even more, they were unable to accept the example of identification offered them, where the sacrifice was linked with a Dionysiac ritual still imbued with its original joy.

In Racine, death is displayed; it may be reached in the desire for a glorious destiny (Achilles), for a duty carried out in joyless submission (Iphigenia), or through personal and emotional inclination (Eriphile). But this merely shows us how far we have come from the primitive signification of sacrifice. The celebration is now a sad act.

Christianity has done its work. It leaves the tragic with no other means of expression than the vocation for suicide.

This comparison gives us some notion of the gulf that separates the two conceptions of sacrifice.

Sacrifice is bound up with the oracle. It is resorted to for the sake of benefit, gain, appropriation; and its counterpart, the assurance that one will keep what has been acquired or increase its value, is the consent of the god, who is appeased by the sacrifice. In Euripides, Agamemnon finally surrenders to the glamour of numbers:

> I must do this.
> Look at this fleet of war-ships marshalled here, this huge
> Army of bronze-mailed warriors from the Hellene states,
> Who cannot sail against the walls of Troy, or raze
> That famous city to its foundations, unless I
> First sacrifice you, as the prophet Calchas commands.
>
> (Euripides, *Iphigenia in Aulis*, 412)

The sacrifice represents the portion that is reserved to the god, which one subtracts from one's own wealth in the hope of future increase. But as such the sacrifice represents some excess to be wiped out; it is the surplus that must be drawn off. The sacrifice makes sacred in its wastage an immunization by loss, by loss consented to, rather than a calculation of future advantage. A sacrifice as advantageous submission may be replaced by a sacrifice as *jouissance* in wastage.

For Euripides' Iphigenia, this *jouissance* is her identification with the *jouissance* of celebration, a heroic identification that brings the gods closer. For Racine's Eriphile, this sombre double of *jouissance* is linked to the pure pain she is seeking. What Eriphile has to defend herself against when confronted with Iphigenia is not loving Achilles, but loving in Achilles the cause of all her misfortunes:

> ERIPHILE: *I*? Stoop to love a frenzied conqueror,
> Who still all bloody comes before my eyes,
> Who, torch in hand, intent on murder, burnt
> Lesbos to ashes?
> IPHIGENIA: Yes, false-hearted one!
>
> (Racine, *Iphigenia*, II, 5:81)

Desire is punished not because of the forbidden character of its object, but because of its aim, which here is masochistic pain. In this alteration of the signification of sacrifice we see the extent of the gap that separates the Dionysiac ritual celebrations and the performance at the court of Versailles.

In this sense, the idea of sacrifice is entirely subverted. Eriphile's sacrifice costs nobody anything. It is her destiny and her *jouissance*. It appeases no god, since no one has been dispossessed of her: she has no family to feel her loss. She is not a counterweight to the warrior's power. Royal magnificence will be exhausted in the ruinous war, without any prior obligation to pay tribute. It is love that will pay, love alone.

In its horror, the sacrifice of Iphigenia was in a sense a sequel to the feast of Atreus. The gods' vengefulness drives Agamemnon, faced by the carnage that he is about to commit, to devour his own child. The sacrifice of Eriphile is a self-devouring in which tragedy rediscovers that primitive vocation which is illustrated by *The Bacchae* of Euripides, the devouring by the mother of the fruit of her own womb. Eriphile is a daughter of the blood of Helen.

The gap that separates ancient tragedy from French classical tragedy is the gap between infanticide and suicide. Both tell of a striking gesture of expenditure, a pure extravagance, quite unconcerned with preserving one's dearest goods, to the point of destroying one's very life for the *jouissance* of the cult that is the cult of *jouissance*.

Violence and nomination

No analysis can confine itself to the exploration of thematic forms without concerning itself with the very form of tragedy.

Let us take Euripides: a quasi-linear action, which moves closer at each step to its dénouement, with no unexpected reversal, interrupted by the chanting of a chorus that duplicates the scene and comments on what it sees there, expressing what it feels. It is a drama displayed before us, which simultaneously uncovers and exhausts its possibilities, in which each character enters and speaks of his deeds, his case, his misfortune, and from which at last there rises the voice of the victim, high and exemplary, while for some the moment of supreme pain, for others the moment of combat, has come, a moment in which a thunderclap announces the miracle.

In Racine, each act, right up to the last, produces its intention and its frustration. In the first, it is the attempt to deflect Iphigenia from her chosen way, and its failure; in the second, we await the celebration of the engagement, and this engagement is broken off; in the third, the engaged couple are reunited, only to be separated once again by the announcement of the sacrifice; in the fourth, we have the preparation of the sacrifice and the refusal to consent to it; only in the last act is the victim rescued and the marriage confirmed. Again we note the interiorization of the conflict, which no longer emerges from a raw, fixed situation, given once and for all, and where the purpose of the entire tragic development is to show its ineluctable character; but from a shifting conjuncture, each flow being followed by its ebb, each phase balancing the preceding one by a process of subdivision.

The breadth of the Euripidean discourse is now followed by a syntax, a prosody, under which the fragments of discourse turn symmetrically upon themselves in a counterpoint of exquisite perfection. But the essential difference is that of the opposition between the alternate chanting and discourse on the one hand, and the intrinsic development of discourse on the other. In the first of the two systems, the chanting finds its contrary in the discourse; this last contains the elements of the pulsion which it releases in lyrical expression, where freed emotional energy bursts forth, rises and exhausts itself until a new discourse returns it to a waiting state. Terror is born from this periodic movement as much as from the covering of one form of expression by that which it masks. The characters may say what they have done and nothing more, since the chorus will tell the rest. And it is from their union and separation that the sacred effect emerges, sometimes from a discursive speech, sometimes rising in a chant that imposes its rhythm on the traces left by the silence of the discourse.

Racinian discourse expounds, distributes, organizes, diversifies, develops and even, on occasion, pleads. The Racinian line is incandescent, it burns; but it burns like ice. The homogeneity of the speech deploys within it a space that is proper to it and which belongs to it alone. Contradiction becomes internal to it, between its own unified elements. As Roland Barthes says: 'To speak is to do and the Logos assumes the function of Praxis, and takes its place: every disappointment in the world is taken up and redeemed in speech, action empties itself, language fills itself' (Barthes, 1963, 66).

So violence and terror become pure nomination; in a sense, this nomination is deprived of all its emotional elements. In purifying itself, it seems to weaken its sacred power. But we must not condemn it too hastily. It extracts from the primitive tragic milieu its essential element, speech, which had difficulty communicating through the heterogeneous forms of discourse – that of the chorus and that of the characters – and of which the whole tragedy, by this play of oppositions, becomes a dialectical celebration.

Racinian discourse takes as its task the celebration of language alone, of pure language that is a substitute not only for action, but also for feeling: for the effective and the affective. Racinian tragedy might be understood as a cathecting of language. Perhaps this accounts, by way of counterpart, for the appearance of those characters who can experience only a negative passion, in which language falls apart, cedes, ceases to exercise the rule of an impeccable syntax over the world of affects, and expends itself, loses itself, breaks its bonds and affirms its vocation for annihilation, with no other reason than an inner call towards the abyss. Here speech is no longer its sovereign order. The gods no longer preside over this excess, the gods pass, the excess remains, calling for its own destruction. And the Dionysiac force emerges again as a challenge to language, to the order of labour. It returns through the festival, claiming its right to an expenditure without profit, with no other aim than itself. It is here that tragedy is born again. Henceforth, in the silence of a lethal *jouissance*, the festival of language becomes the tomb of language.

II THE TWO INFANTICIDES

Euripides wrote *Iphigenia in Aulis* in the year in which he died. Its posthumous performance caused the Athenians to award him the laurel crown, which he won rarely and never without difficulty. It was also in Macedonia, where he ended his days, far from Athens, that he wrote, shortly after *Iphigenia in Aulis*, *The Bacchae*. Now, the two tragedies have something in common: they both deal with an act of infanticide in the course of a ritual sacrifice. Iphigenia, having been demanded by Artemis, ends her earthly life at the altar for the glory of her father, after a doe has miraculously died in her place. Pentheus dies during a Dionysiac ritual, torn to pieces and devoured by his own mother, at the height of the sacred ecstasy. The situations are both similar and contrasted.

The Dionysiac ritual and the punishment for absence from it

That Euripides the blasphemer should have devoted his last tragedy to celebrating the cult of a god has caused some surprise. As if this god were like the others in the Greek Pantheon, as if one had forgotten that tragedy derived from that very god! From him and from the tragic author. In glorifying Dionysus, in showing him proving his divine origin, the tragic poet weaves a crown for himself. It is a marvellous opportunity to remind the public of the power possessed by the bard, of the magic he has at his command, and which both require certain duties in return. The Dionysus of *The Bacchae* is quite simply the poet himself, or the ancestor from whom the poet sprang, from whom he derives the tragic gift. (Just as the sacrifice of Iphigenia for the success of the Greek expedition is a fine opportunity for the tragedian to quit the stage on the image of devotion to the popular cause.)

That this return to the sources should have revitalized the tragic poet, then living in the very spot where tragedy originated, and that Euripides should then turn to the East – this permits us to envisage the point at which the death of tragedy coincides with its birth.

Never was the vindication of chant over discourse, dance over rhetoric, passion over eloquence, madness over reason, more strongly affirmed. For language it is a struggle against the thing which exceeds and overflows it on all sides, and through which it has conquered an empire that periodically succumbs to the pressure of the thing that resists it. The epiphany of the sacred regains, in a cyclical return, its dominance over linguistic construction. But, as we know, it is not so much a struggle between passion and language – between Dionysus and Apollo – as a struggle between one logos and another, with no certainty that either has finally triumphed. It is a victory of language over chant, but a penetration of chant by language and a return of chant within language. Tragedy is the representation of this alternate process of inscription and effacement, in which each term strives to absorb the other.

Let us now consider this tragedy, the only one concerned with the Dionysiac rite to be preserved, the only one that in the language of mature tragedy speaks of its origins.

The originality of *The Bacchae* is not that it shows us desire and its various disguises, but the return of 'barred desire', which is manifested with untameable violence and frenzy. The frenzy, the delirium, the pursuit and the murderous determination are the consequence of the refusal to pay homage to *jouissance*. With our Judeo-Christian ears, we must listen to a language that has long been foreclosed, in order to understand that it may be blasphemous and sacrilegious to refuse to honour pleasure, the festival, drunkenness. This is by no means the same thing as infringing the prohibitions that surround them.

In this respect, those in our cultural world who have looked for the return of Dionysus have no doubt been those most marked by the Judeo-Christian seal. For what is required is not the celebration of Eros, but that which in the myth of Dionysus is bound up with the punishment which the god inflicts on those who do not recognize his divinity and who are set to wander in the depths of frenzy. It is this that accounts for the approval given to a sacrifice that is pure consummation, delight in destruction, the expression of a cruel eroticism that is alone capable of evoking that which unites, in the sacred, horror and ecstasy.

The paradox of *The Bacchae* lies in its constant interplay between madness and reason. *The Bacchae* is usually thought of as an orgy of unreason, an uncontrolled delirium of the senses. Yet the chorus suggests that this madness is not unrestrained. The sacred delirium is contained within certain limits:

> The celebrant runs entranced. . .
> And with shouts he rouses the scattered bands,
> Sets their feet dancing.   (Euripides, *Bacchae*, 186)

Such madness is not to be feared by those who give themselves up to it: 'for a chaste-minded woman will come to no harm in the rites of Bacchus' (*Bacchae*, 191). Whereas the virtuous Pentheus, that wild-eyed monster, who despises the effeminate god and forbids the practice of his rites, is a virulent blasphemer who on a number of occasions is treated as insane by Teiresias – 'He speaks like the madman he is' (*Bacchae*, 191) – yet madness is not part of the homage paid to Dionysus; it lies in that other delirium, infinitely more subversive, that wishes to subject the world to his law, that is to say, to his desire. Pentheus' authoritarian character is revealed in his interrogation of Dionysus, in which he tries to subject the god to a cross-examination in theology:

> PENTHEUS: Is there a Lydian Zeus, then, who begets new gods?
> DIONYSUS: No; I speak of your Zeus, who made Semele his wife here in Thebes. . .
> PENTHEUS: Is this the first place where you have introduced Dionysus?
> DIONYSUS: No; every Eastern land dances these mysteries.
> PENTHEUS: I believe it. Oriental standards are altogether inferior to ours.
> DIONYSUS: In this point they are superior. But their customs are different.
> (*Bacchae*, 195–6)

In the course of the tragedy, Pentheus' puritanism melts away, to be quickly replaced by the desire to see without being seen, to surprise the Bacchae, among whom is to be found the tyrant's mother, whom he has severely condemned. In the same way, he had condemned his aunt, Semele, Dionysus' mother, accusing her of having given in to lustful desires with a mere mortal, and so rejecting the thesis of the divine identity of her seducer.

Here, reason and restraint involve acceptance of the Dionysiac cult; rejection of it is a sign of madness and excess. Pentheus' sin is that of narcissistic self-satisfaction – the pride that makes him deny not only Dionysus, but also his mother and grandfather. The chorus says of Dionysus:

> His enemy is the man who has no care
> To pass his years in happiness and health,
> His days in quiet and his nights in joy,

Watchful to keep aloof both mind and heart
From men whose pride claims more than mortals may.

(*Bacchae*, 194)

This is a condemnation of sophistry and a denunciation of a tyranny whose pretensions are excessive, since it attempts to shut out desire from man, not being able to master it.

The acceptance of desire, the cult of drunkenness and ecstasy are not the only domains of the Dionysus of *The Bacchae*. The doctrine that Euripides puts into the mouth of the god is imbued with Orphism and includes the theme of accession to a truth. When Pentheus alleges his right, based on force, to chain up Dionysus, the god replies: 'What are you saying? What are you doing? Who are you? You do not know' (*Bacchae*, 197).

Here, the two vocations merge: the cult of Dionysus, the guardian of terrestrial life, and the cult of Orpheus, the mediator with the beyond.

In another register it is interesting to compare these questionings with those that Oedipus had to face, and to link these questions through the mediation of Dionysus, to desire and *jouissance*.

Ritual is, we know, one of the manifestations that elucidate the subordination of desire to the universe of rules. It is a return of the repressed that enables us to witness, through certain ritual practices, the disguised expressions of desires whose prohibition would be absolute if they were expressed outside the limits of the ritual.

The devouring of the child in the course of delirious orgies seems to have been attested in several rites, at Orchomene, Argos and Thebes (where the action of *The Bacchae* takes place). The cause is always the same: some failure to acknowledge the divinity of Dionysus. This punishment takes the form of an excess of desire, for the Maenads eat the raw flesh of animals, but not that of human beings. If in the course of Maenadic delirium women may devour animals alive, it may be taken as an equivalent of or a euphemism for cannibalism. The sacred frenzy seems to bring them back to practices that certain specialists in prehistory have described: hunts, chases, unrestrained sexual activity and the devouring of animals. (When the victim pursued is a human being, the death is fictional.) The devouring of human beings and even of one's own children abolishes the frontier between the animal kingdom and the human, since it is a common form of behaviour among animals. This might signify that the refusal of desire, of drunkenness, of ecstasy brings with it a reaction in the form of its exasperation to a proto- or pre-human level. So desire must be a qualifying function of the human being, and he who refuses it can no longer belong to the community of men.

But what does it mean to refuse oneself to desire? In fact, one cannot escape it. Madness, which Freud links to narcissism, is the punishment for trying. It attacks the Minyades, the Proitides, the Cadmean women, for refusing to give in to the god's injunctions. The refusal of desire is more precisely the refusal to celebrate desire, that is to say, the mutation of natural desire into human desire, the passage of desire through the universe of rules – since it is inscribed in a rite of which desire itself is the base – thus passing from *jouissance* to pleasure. (As Bataille and Lacan show in their writings.) The Dionysiac ritual, then, is not a natural ritual; on the contrary, it is the culturation of the natural. If the cultural excludes it, the punishment of the god will fall: the Dionysiac rite becomes frenzy sent by the god, in which the symbolic collapses again under the pressure of the repressed, and the mother, instead of devouring the living flesh of fawns, tears at her children's entrails.

This return to the state of nature coincides with the agrarian origin of the rites concerned with the expulsion or putting to death of winter on which the myth of Pentheus in its various stages is exactly modelled: disguise, exposition to the ridicule of all, concealment in a tree, persecution and stoning, dismemberment of the victim and cutting down of branches, decapitation and the fixing of the head on the temple. The affirmation of the naturalness of man goes further, then, than his identification with the animal kingdom; it is pressed to the point of his participation in the agrarian world.

Maternity and paternity in Dionysus

The argument of *The Bacchae* shows, from its very first line, that the problem embodied in the tragedy is that of the filiation of the god. Is Dionysus born from the coupling of a mortal and an adulterous, sinful woman, or is he the son of Zeus? This is the question that will be resolved at the cost of the life of whoever doubts the divine origin of Dionysus. It is a question of knowing in what way such a question is bound up with the outcome of the tragedy. Why does the punishment sent by the god consist in having a child–king devoured by his mother? This original devouring mother, whom psycho-analysts encounter in the exploration of their most disturbed patients, is a phallic mother.

The myth of the birth of Dionysus tells how Zeus shelters the embryo in his thigh in order to bring the interrupted pregnancy to term. What does this signify, beyond the usual explanations that it is an equivalent of adoption or initiation? I am tempted to see it as the expression of a phantasy, that of being born not from the mother's womb, but from the father's sexual organ. Euripides says:

> Twice-born Dithyrambus! Come,
> Enter here your father's womb.   (Euripides, *Bacchae*, 197)

It might be remarked that, although the Dionysiac cult was celebrated exclusively by women, women were no more than Dionysus' followers. In this way, the god received as his share the attributes of the exuberant virility of his father, Zeus. Moreover, one should note the extreme phallicism of the Maenads, 'hurling the thyrsus like a spear', covered with snakes and displaying a quite masculine physical strength.

> You could see Agauë take up a bellowing young heifer with full udders, and hold it by the legs with her two arms stretched wide. Others were tearing our cows limb from limb, and you could see perhaps some ribs or a cleft hoof being tossed high and low; and pieces of bloody flesh hung dripping on the pine-branches. And bulls, which were one moment savagely looking along their horns, the next were thrown bodily to the ground, dragged down by the soft hands of girls – thousands of them; and they stripped the flesh off their bodies faster than you could wink your royal eyes.   (*Bacchae*, 204)

This state contrasts oddly with their state when asleep, when they preserve all their femininity, lying 'chastely', as the Messenger testifies, recounting what he has seen to Pentheus. But, as soon as they awake, the sacred delirium seizes them. This nocturnal rite, in which the activity of waking in the middle of the night is accompanied by an unleashing of energy that contrasts with the peace of sleep, suggests a comparison with sexual activity.

Pentheus' desire to attend this ritual is, then, to be compared with the child's desire to see his mother during the nocturnal sexual activities she shares with the father. No doubt this phallicism of the Bacchae expresses a sadistic phantasy-conception of coitus as devouring, but it also testifies to the boy's rejection of the passive feminine position during coitus and to his fear of undergoing castration by the father. Hence the attitude, both curious and frightened, before the spectacle, in which all the danger seems to come from the mother who devours the child and the father's penis in the course of the embrace. We should remember Pentheus' repeated reproaches about Dionysus' effeminate appearance and the need he feels to reassert his own virility: 'I must not be laughed at by the Bacchae – anything rather than that' (*Bacchae*, 207).

The deeply-rooted phallicism that imbues the play, despite the frequent invocation of the mother goddess, Cybele the Great Mother, gives some inkling of the fifth-century Greek sense of an irreversible progress from the maternal divinities to the paternal divinities. For, although it is true that the Dionysiac rite is inseparable from the agrarian rite and that Teiresias declares that the first essential principle of human beings is 'the goddess Demeter; she is the Earth – call her by what name you will', whereas the second is 'the juice that streams from the vine-clusters' (the liquid that is both nourishing and seminal), Dionysus cannot rest until he has obtained recognition of the Name-of-the-Father, that is to say, of the fact that he is 'son of Zeus'. Thus he will manifest himself to the Bacchae in the thunderbolt, armed with the paternal attribute with which he strikes Pentheus' palace, just as Zeus presented himself before Semele. The chorus comments thus:

> Do you see, do you see the flame of Semele's tomb,
> The flame that remained of the lightning-stroke?

And, later, hailing Dionysus: 'Oh, what a joy to hear your Bacchic shout! You have saved us. We were deserted and alone: how happy we are to see you!' (*Bacchae*, 199–200).

This is perhaps why Pentheus, who mocked the effeminate Dionysus and promised to sever his head and cut off his blond curls, is earlier morally castrated and derided in female disguise, as he wanders in his emerging delirium, before being seized and torn apart by the Bacchae. The phallic power must remain the attribute of Dionysus alone, who inherited it from Zeus. Those who resist the appeal of desire, of the festival and of drunkenness will be the victims of the Bacchae, who will seize the whole body of the blasphemer. 'They will kill you if you are seen there dressed as a man,' Dionysus warns Pentheus. One might note here what Teiresias says of Dionysus: he is god not only of ecstasy and drunkenness, but also of frenzy. 'He also in some degree shares the function of Ares, god of war.' It might be thought that the implacable aggressiveness shown by the Bacchae in their erotic activity is expressed all the more freely because their refusal of Dionysus encourages a diffusion of the drives that leaves the field open to the exteriorized expressions of the death drive.

Other powers devolve on Dionysus: prophecy, which, owing to its greater proximity to the unconscious, makes the ecstatic situation a source of knowledge. Lastly, and it is surely not the least of his weapons, the lure which enables him to win in the end. Pentheus sets out in pursuit of Dionysus, but is in fact chasing a phantom: 'Thereupon Dionysus – or so it seemed to me; I tell what I thought – made a phantom figure appear in the palace courtyard; and Pentheus flew at it and kept stabbing at the sunny air, imagining that he was killing *me*,' says Dionysus (*Bacchae*, 200–1). In the end, the king gives in, exhausted. The madder of the two at that moment is certainly not the god, who is guided by a remorseless plan. This is only the beginning of the misfortunes he promises, since the Messenger, having told him what he saw on Cithaeron, arouses in Pentheus a fatal desire to attend the Maenadic rituals. Dionysus sarcastically asks the insidious question 'And what has betrayed you into this great eagerness?'

The representation of the primal scene

The tragedy of *The Bacchae* is of absorbing interest, both because of the scarcity of extant documents on the Dionysiac rituals and because of what it tells us of the strange behaviour of those women of Thrace or Phrygia. And yet neither reason explains the emotion we feel. If we centre our attention only on these general aspects, we run the risk of falling into the same trap as Pentheus himself. Pentheus wishes to purge his country of the Bacchic ritual, which he sees as a new scourge. He sets out to annihilate it with all the energy at his command. Yet it is he who will be put to death at the end of the tragedy. What Pentheus cannot be admitted to see in the spectacle, which he imagines before taking part in it, is the reason why he is interested in it. His reason is that his mother is the principal attraction. The Euripidean development shows us with great precision the change of direction taken by Pentheus after the herds-man recounts to him the delirium of the Bacchae rising at a signal given by his mother Agaue, chasing goats, tearing heifers apart, throwing bulls to the ground, abducting children from their homes, giving suck to young fawns and wolf-cubs, bathing in blood, in-vulnerable to the effects of fire or steel. As he listens to this account, Pentheus feels that 'this outrageous Bacchism advances on us like a spreading fire' (*Bacchae*, 205). He wants to join battle; and at this moment he, who despises Bacchus, falls under the yoke of desire. His thirst for blood is in no way less than that of the Bacchae. His pulse beats with the same impatience as that of his mother. From that moment, he enters Dionysus' net, agreeing to dress himself as a woman, which, by a magic transformation, brings about the change in him by which he identifies with his mother. 'Well, how do I look? Do you think I stand like Ino or like my mother Agaue?' (*Bacchae*, 210). From this moment he falls completely into the possession of Dionysus, to whom he passively gives himself. In his growing delirium, he sees Dionysus as a bull and becomes the plaything of the god's manipulations. Dionysus ridicules him before the assembled Thebans. 'You are a man to make men fear,' he says to Pentheus, disguised as a woman. He sets up in Pentheus the femininity to

which he was so strongly opposed. Pentheus now shows concern
about his hair and his clothes, like the most coquettish of women.
And the god triumphs over him in a refrain that the chorus takes up:

> What gift of heaven should man
> Count a more noble prize,
> A prayer more prudent, than
> To stretch a conquering arm
> Over the fallen crest
> Of those who wished us harm?   (*Bacchae*, 209)

Victory is the castration of the adversary. What Dionysus is revenging, though it is never mentioned, is perhaps the martyrdom that he
was subjected to in the persecution of the Titans. Pentheus and
Dionysus are cousins, since Agauë and Semele are sisters. It might
be supposed that there is a corresponding relation here to that between Semele and Hera. In each case, Semele represents the good
mother, while Hera and Agauë represent the bad maternal imago
that will have to be dominated. The punishment of Pentheus, who
dies under the blows of Agauë, would therefore revenge the death
of Dionysus at the hands of Hera.

The derision to which Pentheus is subjected is merely the prelude
to the tragic, as if the tragic had to be born and to generate its
effects from its antinomian polarity. In fact, in this situation – the
death of the hero falling in battle against Amazons – the satiric pole
and the epic pole are joined. (We are reminded of Kleist's *Penthesilea*,
which must have owed a great deal to Euripides.) But the tragic
essence, the very centre of the tragic, is revealed in the ritual murder
by a mother in the grip of delirium, tearing apart a son whom she
does not recognize from behind the veil that covers her eyes.

Pentheus' desire is not only to see 'sights he should not see', which
is already enough to mark him out as an expiatory victim, to the
delight of the Bacchae. He even goes as far as incest. (Cadmus,
father of Semele – Dionysus' mother – is also the father of Agauë,
Dionysus' aunt. He is also an ancestor of Oedipus.)

PENTHEUS: Yes, I can picture them – like birds in the thickets, wrapped
in the sweet snare of love.
DIONYSUS: That is the very thing you are going to look for; and perhaps
you will catch them – if you are not first caught yourself.
                                                  (*Bacchae*, 211)

There is a strong sense of sexual possession here. Awake and lucid,
Pentheus wants to see the Bacchae; his delirium reveals that he
wants to possess them. For behind each of the Bacchae is Agauë,
whom he seeks as object of his desire. Anticipating the success of his
enterprise and having conquered the perverse god, he imagines him-

self being fondled in his mother's arms, returning to Thebes in triumph. This ordeal will put the hero to the test of having to seduce his mother in order to possess her and she will see him die, possessed and destroyed by her, herself inspired by the breath of Dionysus.

As soon as Pentheus' incestuous desire is affirmed, the chorus at once turns on him and denounces his plan, although it is quite clear that the young king is no longer in a state to carry it out. This is more in the nature of a justification of his forthcoming execution than a warning of danger. His delirious mother will deny him as he denied her: 'Who gave birth to him? For he is not born of woman-kind, but of some lioness or the breast of Libyan Gorgons.' Death will be his punishment for having wished to 'dominate the Invincible'. We do not know whether this accusation concerns the conflict be-tween Dionysus and Pentheus or whether one may already think that it is some transgression that is being punished, that of the incest-prohibition, which can be recognized in the desire to see 'things one should not see'. The meaning of the blasphemy is modified; Pentheus' delirium allows his desires to find expression, repressed beneath his thirst for blood, thus showing the substitutive character – displaced, in every sense of the term – of this violence. Pentheus, therefore, has committed a double crime: the refusal to recognize Dionysus when he is lucid, and incestuous desire when he is under the control of the god. Acceptance of the Dionysiac cult is, in the end, the best way of rendering to desire what is its due, of forcing the excess that it expresses into a system of exchange.

The account of the scene of the last meeting between mother and son allows us to feel once again the identity between the incestuous relationship and death. This last exchange between Pentheus and Agaüe is reminiscent, in its contrasting as well as its complementary details, of the last meeting between Orestes and Clytemnestra. Orestes becomes mad after the murder; Agaüe is mad before it. The Erinnyes – like the Bacchae, nocturnal powers – will appear wearing snakes in their hair, as do the Bacchae. Clytemnestra bares her breast in order to remind her son of his original bonds and his earliest feelings; Pentheus, trying to get his mother to recognize him, strokes Agaüe's cheek like a child. ' "Mother!" he cried, touching her cheek, "it is I, your son, Pentheus, whom you bore to Echion. O mother, have mercy on me; I have sinned; but I am your son: do not kill me!" ' (*Bacchae*, 216). It is no use: just as Agamemnon's son refuses to hear his mother and ruthlessly plunges the sword in her breast, so

Agaüe was foaming at the mouth, her eyes were rolling wildly. She was not in her right mind; she was under the power of Dionysus; and she would not listen to him. She gripped his right arm between wrist and elbow; she set her foot against his ribs; and she tore his arm off by the shoulder. It was no strength of hers that did it; the god was in her fingers and made it easy.   (*Bacchae*, 216–17)

Only Aeschylus could have equalled the horror that Euripides conveys at this moment; the last of the tragic poets rediscovers the primal excess that inspired the first. But the scene does not end in terror. Pentheus is decapitated and his head stuck on the end of the thyrsus as a trophy, since Agauë believes that she is carrying a lion's head on the end of this spear and is proud of the phallic ornament she means to devour: 'Come now, join in the feast!' she says to the chorus. She then appears before her own father, Cadmus, and it is his sad task to bring her back to reality. Cadmus gathers together the scattered fragments of Pentheus' body, giving vent to his sorrow at the double affliction of the death of a grandson and the murderous delirium of a daughter. (This provides some justification for the interpretation of this myth as the expression of an initiation ritual in which the passage from childhood to adulthood involves two aspects: the death of childhood and the resurrection of the grandfather in the form of the adult.) To this mourning is added the mourning of his daughter when she realizes what she has done. The death of Pentheus is certainly a castration for Cadmus, for by it he is deprived of male heirs – this only grandson was cherished as the hope of his line.

At this point a new ritual succeeds the Bacchic ritual, moving in its nakedness, terrible in its content. Imagine this father and daughter kneeling before what is no longer a body, but a heap of severed remains, to which they try to give back a human appearance as if they were trying to create a new birth. 'Come, father, help me,' says Agauë. 'Lay his poor head here; as far as we can, make all exact and seemly. O dearest face, O young fresh cheek; O kingly eyes, your light now darkened! O my son! See, with this veil I now cover your head, your torn and bloodstained limbs' (*Bacchae*, 224).

One cannot help thinking that after this, after this illuminating return to its origins, tragedy could only die in turn. Certainly, Euripides is the equal here of Aeschylus at his greatest.

Agamemnon and Agauë

Iphigenia at Aulis and *The Bacchae* represent, then, two cases of infanticide. As Marie Delcourt reminds us, infanticide was the least serious of familial crimes. Parricide alone was inexpiable. It was not the putting to death of a child as such, but the reason invoked for it that gave the act its gravity. The examples of Iphigenia and Pentheus are not unique in the stock of Greek myths. Above all, there is the case of Medea: and Marie Delcourt gives many other examples (Delcourt, 1959, 56). These may be grouped under two headings, which correspond to the situations in *The Bacchae* and *Iphigenia at Aulis*; that is to say, infanticide committed in a moment of aberration (Leucippe killing her son Hippasus, Athamas his son Learchus, Lycurgus his son Dryas; it should be noted that in the last two cases a son is killed by a father, who is able to mask feelings of hostility towards a potential rival) or during a religious sacrifice. Let us leave on one side the cases in which the father's cruelty is directed at a pregnant daughter whose offspring constitutes a threat to him. Marie Delcourt remarks that the mother does not figure in the mythological context but is replaced by a mother-in-law or female relation.

So, just as the mythological projection establishes a constant link between matricide and madness, and just as madness is a cause or consequence of the murder, so infanticide obeys definite psychological contexts. If committed by the mother, it can take place only in a state of mental disorder. (Medea is a special case, for she kills her children in a state of lucidity. And it should be noted that despair following disappointment in love and jealousy are at the root of an act whose aim is to deal a mortal wound at Jason, who has betrayed her. Her reasons, then, are profoundly linked to sexual passion.) Committed by the father, the act may be either the result of a moment of aberration, of some fatal error, or a precaution to eliminate some future danger for moral or religious reasons. (One is reminded of Laius leaving Oedipus to die on the hillside.)

Thus infanticide is always in the case of the mother, sometimes in the case of the father, an expression of madness and, in the case of the father alone, an exercise of power. So the two cases of *The Bacchae* and *Iphigenia at Aulis* represent the extreme situations of this conjunction, since they describe for us the whole course of Agauë's delirium and Agamemnon's command.

It may well be that these extreme cases convey a truth that profoundly concerns the relations between child and progenitor. The *Oresteia* shows the physical link between the child and the mother, in which some disruption gives access either to paternal speech and its law, or to psychosis when the speech of the father has not been heard and recalled by the mother. Contrariwise, *The Bacchae* presents us with the punishment of a couple: mother and son who refuse to honour pleasure and desire.

The murder of the son by the mother, like that of the mother by the son, are established, therefore, in a context of psychosis (cause or consequence); hety unite the significations of the incestuous love union and the relation to death. Their outcome is not so much castration as tearing to pieces (Pentheus) or vampirism (Orestes).

In the case of the sacrifice of the daughter for and by the father, things are presented quite differently. In the tragedy of *Iphigenia in Aulis*, the father does not himself put the victim to death, nor does he demand it. He obeys the command of the soothsayer, who is the mouthpiece of the gods. It is the law that demands this death; the father finds it hard to submit to it. The gods demand what is dearest to one; usually a son, an heir. Infanticide, then, is also a sign of the mutilation of the father. And it comes as no surprise that circumcision should have originated as a substitute for human sacrifice.

Henceforth the sacrifice of the daughter – who cannot blame her father for it, since he is merely the instrument of the gods' desire – takes on particular signification. It is a mark of the father, a trace, a scar of the wound that is inflicted on him, but it is also an accession to a preferential status above the brothers and sisters and above the mother, since the bond with the god is the sign of a union between them of a unique kind.

One may find here an expression of what has been called the female masochistic movement of turning aggressive and erotic drives back upon the subject. The desire for the father's penis is realized through a renunciation demanded by the ego-ideal. Although the sacrificial murder may have the incestuous connotation that I suggested in infanticide by the mother, it operates here through the ceremonial of the marriage with death, which presupposes its mediation by a complex institutionalization. Ritual may refer us back through human sacrifice to the remote past, but there remains a difference between the frenzy of divine possession occurring in dreamlike trance and the pomp of a religious service officiated by a high priest before the army and the kings gathered around their leader.

In this second case, the direction of the movement is reversed. Before this army and these kings, brought together in an alliance, sworn to defend the freedom of the Greeks, will be practised an archaic form of sacrifice, since animals have long been substituted for human beings in this type of ritual observance. The gods' demand for a human sacrifice is a reminder of the original ritual, just as the sacred delirium of the Bacchae is a reminder of the original human condition. The ancient tragedy preserved this contact with the myth of a past whose forms still remained alive. The French classical tragedy, rooted in a different subsoil from that of myth and ritual, is no more than distantly indebted to them. It could therefore evade the sacrifice, preserving its metaphorical value, and substitute the suicide for it, thus paying the death drive a due that history tends to

forget. Nevertheless, Racine's Iphigenia, in her final consent,
operates a reversal that places her in a situation comparable with
Euripides' heroine, establishing, like her ancient model, an identical
relation to the father. What Racine subverts, at this moment of the
tragedy, is the dénouement of sacrifice. Euripides' Iphigenia is both
sacrificed and saved: sacrificed because she leaves her people,
abducted by the goddess; saved because her life is spared, a doe
dying in her place. Racine's Iphigenia is entirely saved, and
promised the happiness of marriage; but, in compensation, Artemis'
thirst for blood finds its counterpart in Eriphile's suicide. Between
the two stands the sacrifice of Isaac, who is also saved and also
replaced by an animal, but given back to his father with no other
benefit than that of survival. Lucien Goldmann is right to note in
Racine the presence of the *Deus absconditus*, the God of Jansenist
Port-Royal, who is entirely alien to the gods of Greece.

In *Fear and Trembling*, a work shot through with the passionate
desire 'to enter into an absolute relation with the absolute', Kierkegaard compares the sacrifice of Iphigenia by Agamemnon with the
sacrifice of Isaac by Abraham. He compares the tragic hero, a being
of compassion and admiration, with God's elect, a being of silence
and fear. One may weep for Agamemnon, but 'no one can shed
tears over Abraham. You approach him with a *horror religiosus*, as
Israel approached Mount Sinai' (Kierkegaard, 86). Let us leave on
one side for the moment, however important it may be, this difference between the Greek gods and the God of the Jews, and ask
ourselves whether Iphigenia is for Agamemnon what Isaac is for
Abraham. If we suppose that Abraham's desire is God's desire, any
comparison becomes superfluous, for it is obvious that Agamemnon's
desire is not Artemis' desire. Agamemnon's desire is a desire for the
sack of Troy, for which the goddess's approval of the actions of the
expeditionary force is indispensable. And although there may be
some grandeur in the silence of Abraham, who refuses to question
the divine command, one cannot but be surprised at the silence of
Agamemnon, who never asks himself the question, 'Why is Artemis
so cruel?' It is in order to punish an unjust action, in the balance of
conflicting powers, that Artemis demands through Calchas this
victim so dear to the Greeks. When Kierkegaard writes: 'And who,
watching Agamemnon with envious eyes, would be so barren as not
to weep with him?' (Kierkegaard, 86), he is not faithful to the
tragedy. For although some people may weep for him, many dis-
approve of him. Agamemnon, says Kierkegaard, 'has the consolation
of being able to weep and complain with Clytemnestra and
Iphigenia'. Although this may be true of Iphigenia, who indeed, at

the moment when she consoles herself, has converted her sacrifice into glory, it is not so of Clytemnestra, who remains outraged by this act that mutilates her in her flesh. This is because her desire cannot coincide with Agamemnon's. That is why many regard him as mad. Why would these Greeks, no less pious than Agamemnon, risk so severe a judgement if they did not suspect that there were impure motives in the affair that had led the king astray in his desire?

In fact, there is something to be said for seeking the cause of his desire here, rather than abandon oneself, in fear and trembling, to the mystery of Abraham's compliance. To say of Abraham that he has an ultimate *telos* before which he suspends the moral process, that the end of his sacrifice is beyond morality, is to set up within him a relation to the Father that infringes his being as a patriarch, as the progenitor of a chosen people, beloved of God, while the sacrifice of Agamemnon infringes his *having*, his prerogatives. The accumulation of his possessions infringes his being as a competitor of the gods, whose anger recognizes in his election as King of kings the seed of an excess which must be prevented from swelling. That is why many rituals show all-powerful sovereigns misled and humiliated by priests. The God of the Jews circumscribes this problematic area by addressing himself not to kings, but to fathers – to that father in particular who has received paternal sexual potency as a gift, when normally he would have despaired of making fruitful the object of his desire, who was not Hagar but Rebecca.

The reference to duty is the product of the secondary elaboration. That is why it is not possible to confine oneself, especially so far as Agamemnon is concerned, to the thesis of submission to a higher duty. Even in the case of Iphigenia, that analysis would be inadequate, for we see very clearly that her conversion is something quite different from acceptance of a duty and even from mere submission to a paternal command. Her conversion can only be that of her desire: the desire of a virgin, the promise of being a woman, a desire for life, for fecundity, the desire for the desire of her father, the city, Greece; the narcissistic desire of sexuality, of death and of memory.

The opposition between the aesthetic and the ethical that Kierkegaard develops is not, to my mind, convincing. In fact, Abraham and Agamemnon are both caught up in the same ethical or aesthetic circle, but they do not speak of the same father or of the same child. The idea of an aesthetic religion borrowed from Hegel should perhaps be related to a religion of the representable, as opposed to Jewish aniconism, in which Freud sees a decisive advance of spirituality.

This no doubt is the ultimate reason that makes Racine, in his *Iphigénie*, recoil before the representation of this sacrifice, for to show us this sacrifice is to show us the God who demands it. Being unable to reconcile himself to presenting us with a *deus ex machina*, he presents us instead with what is a logical substitute: the suicide of Eriphile, the only character motivated by true love in this hybrid, half-Greek, half-Christian tragedy, which tosses all the Greeks, together with the servant of their gods, Calchas, back among the mere pagans:

> 'Stop!' she cries. 'Come no nearer, villain. Stop!
> The blood drawn from my noble ancestors
> Can shed itself without your impious hands.'
>
> (Racine, *Iphigenia*, v, 6:124)

With the sacrifice of Eriphile, the *horror religiosus* reigns once again over the stage; and the sacred, in which ancient tragedy was steeped, returns after having apparently been eliminated. The Racine of Port-Royal is not completely liberated from the model of Euripides. His sacrifice would, after all, have been that of the tragic *phobos*, for which he substituted the Racinian line, that doe, or ram, of the religion of beauty.

The economy of sacrifice

The myth of the death of Pentheus represents a reproduction of the myth (and ritual) of Dionysus. The Bacchae are transformed from the god's officiating priestesses into a vengeful pack of women. In putting Pentheus to death, they merely repeat the action of the Titans, who once dismembered Dionysus as they now dismember Pentheus. While Dionysus is attacked by the Titans, set on by a jealous Hera, behaving like a fairy-tale stepmother (the bad double of the mother), Pentheus falls into the hands of his own mother, possessed by the divine delirium. The infanticide is committed here in the crude form of a mother devouring the fruit of her own womb. The ritual is swamped by the ecstasy, and no doubt one should speak not so much of a sacrifice, in the strict sense of the word, as of a bloody outburst that occurs in a secondary state. How different from sacrifice, in the strict sense, performed according to a ritual, with a precise aim, in the name of a particular god, according to prescribed norms!

The tragedy combines in itself the ecstasy of the festival, the ordering of ritual and the power of speech. Each of these aspects reveals a different origin, whose mode transcends the particular and constitutes a new form.

The same effect is produced in the passage from the ancient tragedy to the French classical tragedy. Here the field is entirely conquered by language, which has merged beneath its dominance the heterogeneity of the various types of signifier: dance, chant and speech. Similarly, at the level of the signified, the passions have been reshaped. The action of the gods is scarcely perceptible in the seventeenth century; they no longer appear, but remain in their celestial realm. Man is no longer possessed by the trance that the gods send upon him. Already, in the ancient tragedy, man was merely the artificer of his own destruction, the gods acting as his allies along this fatal way. French classical tragedy attenuates divine intervention to an extreme degree. Racine's 'psychology' aims at greater verisimilitude than that of the Ancients. This psychology, so flattering for the consciousness, which grasps all its various subtleties, is in fact more closed to the unconscious than the ancient tragedy.

Civilization and disguise have worked together, and the false lure of 'verisimilitude' has played its mystifying role. Nevertheless, the Racinian line remains. The 'screen of beauty', to use Lacan's phrase, reveals, through the medium of style, the jewel that 'psychology' appears to have destroyed. Racine could, like Euripides, write an *Iphigenia in Aulis* and even an *Iphigenia in Tauris*; but he could not have written a *Bacchae*. The century of Louis XIV and Port-Royal would not have accepted it. The crushing censorship shows us all that has been lost, all that the monarchy of divine right and the eldest daughter of the Church proscribed. But however heavy the repressive apparatus of the unconscious may be, the return of the repressed is inevitable. Shakespeare and the Elizabethans brought the tragic back to life, as today Genet and others are re-discovering things long since forgotten.

Periodically, the tyranny of language becomes over-severe, and sparks off a rebellion of the impulse conveyed by music and dance, challenging the hegemony of speech. The lyricism that underlies language may compensate for the damage done to it by the formal construction of discourse, without the actual presence of the dance and chant being necessary. (The living substance of the primary process has become particularly sensitive to the secondary, trans-formational elaborations of 'pure' formalism.) Racine's *Iphigénie* belongs to this linguistic domain; Euripides' *Iphigenia* is in a middle zone; while *The Bacchae* is in a more nocturnal realm, more steeped in sexual associations. *The Bacchae* shines with an eerie brilliance, and, being farthest removed from contemporary themes, it conveys a profoundly disturbing mystery. The morality of tragedy sustains the affirmation, beyond religion, of the rights of the tragic and its indissoluble link with the unconscious.

Confronted with the frenzy of the Bacchae and their sacred delirium, any psycho-analyst is bound to be reminded of the phenomenon of mass hysteria. Today this phenomenon has almost disappeared in its more serious forms, but it still survives in certain cultures. One has only to re-read the classic texts to be convinced of this link. What are we to infer from this? Not that there is a direct connection, which would tell us nothing, for the pathologizing of the sacred simply produces the sacralizing of the pathological. But that there is some link is obvious enough. Although the Greeks perceived and established through ritual and myth the link between the sacred delirium and the Dionysiac, we will recall that it was through the mode of hysteria that Eros showed Freud the way to a scientific conception of desire. Here is the crossroads between Dionysus–Eros and desire on the one hand, and the Bacchanalia, sacred delirium and hysteria on the other. Just as Dionysus was the least accepted and the least loved of the gods, the god who had to struggle to get his divinity recognized, so of all the discoveries of psycho-analysis desire was the most bitterly resisted when Freud submitted the results of his enquiries to the medical and scientific world. Even today, it is in this same world that the most stubborn resistance is encountered. The refusal of desire, the refusal of the Dionysiac, on which a whole civilization has been built up, has led to a hysterical efflorescence. By a curious reversal, the apparent sexual liberation of today is accompanied by a demand for toxicomaniac pleasure that is reminiscent of Dionysus. However, we must not be misled: the appetite for drugs is the exact opposite of a Dionysiac search; it is its Mithridatization.

But to return to our three plays. A relation to sacrifice may be constructed in the following way:

The Bacchae represents, at the close of the great period of ancient tragedy, the origins of that same tragedy, and of human sacrifice practised during a sacred frenzy as punishment for the refusal to sacrifice animals to a god who is the god of *jouissance*, of ecstasy. It is a sacrifice for the desire of the god.

Iphigenia at Aulis represents, at the very end of the life of the last of the great tragic writers, a human sacrifice, which, although heroic, marks a return to ritual forms that were already archaic at the time when it was supposed to be carried out. Its purpose was to assure the success of an undertaking based on revenge and profit. It is a sacrifice for the desire of the father.

Racine's *Iphigénie* represents, by means of another language, a sacrifice that does not take place; however, it will be replaced not by the death of an animal victim, but by that of another human victim, who transforms the acceptance of sacrifice by her suicidal refusal ever to be the object of any desire. It is a sacrifice for the desire of desire.

This thematic relation suggests, in a parallel way, a reflection on the genre. *The Bacchae*, giving us a representation of representation, sets before us one of the origins of tragedy: the origin of the Dionysiac ritual, linked here with that other possible origin, that of the epic ritual; for Pentheus is a hero, despite the contempt in which he is held. *Iphigenia at Aulis* allows us to follow the whole process from its earliest forms to the point to which Euripides brought it. Between the sacrifice carried out in the context of a mystery and the sacrifice set in a human conflict (within the same character or between different characters) is traced this itinerary of communion. We weep for Pentheus and Agauë and even for old Cadmus. We will not weep for Agamemnon or for an Iphigenia taken up to the heavens (there is no question of Tauris in *Iphigenia at Aulis*). The idea of a passage to a better world in the beyond becomes clearer. We can see why the subject tempted Racine – tempted and repelled him. Every sacrificial situation must remind the Christian of the passion of Christ. Iphigenia survives and prepares herself for a kind of happiness appropriate to her gods, her blood, her race; Eriphile raises her protest against a religion that she challenges, opens up once again the way to the sacred, which reaffirms its links with an untamed desire by which she becomes exhausted and loses herself in the death she gives herself. Which of the two women has achieved grace? The question is left open, and is taken up again by the Aricie–Phèdre dyad, which brings Hippolyte to his death – the hero who opens himself to desire. The sublime leap of *Phèdre*, the return into the religious orbit of *Esther* and *Athalie*, bring this blasphemous activity to an end.

After this, French classical tragedy will also come to an end, just as Greek tragedy died with Euripides. *Iphigénie* is not yet the end of classical tragedy, but with it disappeared any possibility of believing in the Dionysiac sacrifice of Greek tragedy. Racine's *Iphigénie* does without sacrifice.

Epilogue

Oedipus, myth or truth?

If *Oedipus Rex* moves a modern audience no less than it did
the contemporary Greek one, the explanation can only be that
its effects do not lie in the contrast between destiny and human
will, but are to be looked for in the particular nature of the
material on which that contrast is exemplified. There must be
something that makes a voice within us ready to recognize the
compelling force of destiny in the *Oedipus*. . .His destiny moves
us only because it might have been ours – because the oracle
laid the same curse upon us before our birth as upon him.

                                                    Freud, *S.E.*, IV, 262

Psycho-analysis has little prospect of becoming liked or popular. It is not merely that much of what it has to say offends
people's feelings. Almost as much difficulty is created by the
fact that our science involves a number of hypotheses – it is
hard to say whether they should be regarded as postulates or
as products of our researches – which are bound to seem very
strange to ordinary modes of thought and which fundamentally
contradict current views. But there is no help for it!

                                                    Freud, *S.E.*, XXIII, 282

The *Oresteia, Othello* and *Iphigénie* reveal the most shadowy, the
most hidden side of the Oedipus complex. They show the underside
of this complex, since on each occasion the conclusion leads to the
death of the object of desire at the hands of the desirer: mother by
son, wife by husband, daughter by father. The reverse of the complex is profoundly opposed to its obverse. What has been revealed to
us are its reversals, its inversions or its disintegration before the work
of the death drive. Thus we have seen the positive Oedipus structure
break down and form the nodal points of primary masochism linked
to the symbolic relation with the mother, of psychotic homosexuality
degraded into masochism and of moral masochism and the suicidal
feminine. The negative Oedipus complex necessarily refers back to
the positive Oedipus complex and even to the ensemble they form in
the developed formula of this structure.

For that is the essential nature of this complex. It never exists in
the simple state, but is always double. It never exists in an integral
state, but survives only in a vestigial state. It never exists in a conscious state, but remains in an unconscious state.

It is this conjunction – and, of course, the disjunction with which it is indissolubly bound up – that Freud was describing when he wrote:

For one gets an impression that the simple Oedipus complex is by no means its commonest form, but rather represents a simplification or schematization which, to be sure, is often enough justified for practical purposes. Closer study usually discloses the more complete Oedipus complex, which is twofold, positive and negative, and is due to the bisexuality originally present in children: that is to say, a boy has not merely an ambivalent attitude towards his father and an affectionate object-choice towards his mother, but at the same time he also behaves like a girl and displays an affectionate feminine attitude to his father and a corresponding jealousy and hostility towards his mother...Analytic experience then shows that in a number of cases one or the other constituent disappears, except for barely distinguishable traces; so that the result is a series with the normal positive Oedipus complex at one end and the inverted negative one at the other, while its intermediate members exhibit the complete form with one or other of its two components preponderating.

(Freud, *S.E.*, XIX, 33–4)

This chain of which only traces remain shows that the structure, even when it is appreciated in terms of the arrangement of relations that constitute it, may be assessed on the basis not only of what it holds outside itself, but also of that within it which witnesses to exclusion.

'Exclusion' must be understood in the full sense of the term, that of banishment from a certain area. As early as 1900, in *The Interpretation of Dreams*, Freud affirmed as much:

When I insist to one of my patients on the frequency of Oedipus dreams, in which the dreamer has sexual intercourse with his own mother, he often replies: 'I have no recollection of having had any such dream.' Immediately afterwards, however, a memory will emerge of some other inconspicuous and indifferent dream, which the patient has dreamt repeatedly. Analysis then shows that this is in fact a dream with the same content – once more an Oedipus dream. I can say with certainty that *disguised* dreams of sexual intercourse with the dreamer's mother are many times more frequent than straightforward ones.

(Freud, *S.E.*, V, 397–8)

It is logical, therefore, to conclude this study with an examination of the Oedipus complex. We have to choose between two approaches. The first would be to consider the Oedipus complex as a complex constitutive of subjectivity. This would take us well outside the limits of this book. The second would be an examination of the facts that lead us from the myth to Sophocles' tragedy. It is the second approach that I have chosen, taking as my starting-point the most recent work of mythologists (Marie Delcourt), Hellenists (J.-P.

Vernant) and anthropologists (Lévi-Strauss). This will give me an opportunity to take stock of the way in which the epistemological break introduced by Freud has been capable of influencing specialists who often declare themselves to be receptive to his work, even when their own work is not directly influenced by it.

I

Unspeakable acts – I speak no more of them.
Hide me at once, for God's love, hide me away.
(Sophocles, *King Oedipus*, 64)

The function of the myth

That the psycho-analyst is right to concern himself with tragedy rather than with myth is proved overwhelmingly by the example of Oedipus.

The question is the following: why did Sophocles' tragedy become for a whole civilization the very essence of tragedy, providing the ground for a commentary taken up again and again, from Aristotle to Heidegger, while Freud, whose interpretation of the play was the keystone of his system, had so much difficulty in being understood? (It is worth noting that Sophocles himself had the same trouble, at least at first. He did not win the prize in the year he presented *King Oedipus* – the public preferred the tragedy offered by Aeschylus' nephew.)

Marie Delcourt's *Œdipe ou la légende du conquérant* is one of those books that every psycho-analyst should read. It does not matter that the opinions expressed by the author about psycho-analysis show signs of a particular period, when Freud was banished from 'thinking' circles. The work's Adlerianism is obvious enough, as is the author's reluctance to take account of the notion of libido, which is both misunderstood and rejected. It should not be thought that the psycho-analytic interest is subordinate; the book ends with a challenge to Freudian theory. But the work is so rich, so illuminating in its detail, that it is worth forgetting for the moment the dismissive judgement passed on psycho-analysis and examining its content.

Like most modern mythologists, Marie Delcourt no longer sees myth as an expression of a spontaneous impulse, with no cause beyond itself, but derives myth from ritual. This derivation takes place, she thinks, in several stages. First, there is ritual to attain a particular result: 'If you want a certain thing to take place, submit to this ritual.' Then the ritual practices become enriched and more complex as the rite is preserved, modified and dissociated from its original causes: 'One submits to a particular practice in particular circumstances' – forgetting why one does so. In a secondary way, one can explain the practice by reference to the divine command: 'Because an oracle predicted that...one performs such and such a ritual.' Gradually, the ritual becomes attached, not to man's desire, but to the history of the god, which is recalled in its various episodes by the ritual practice.

There is much to be said for this interpretation, for it excludes the merely gratuitous in the development of rituals and myths. Both obey a particular requirement – whose nature is not explained – and are governed by a particular economy. They undergo distortions that present us with complex, composite, stratified objects. So far, Freud would agree on all points with the modern mythologists. He would no doubt have more reservations about the relations between myth and history, and he would hardly accept that myth had no function in relation to historical truth. Historical truth and material truth are for him in a non-univocal relation, the first being related above all to desire.

The history of desire is never at the disposal of anyone wishing to find its sources or roots. He must be content, by means of an approach disconcerting to those who are unfamiliar with it, not only with provisional truths, as in all scientific exploration, but with truths established *a posteriori*. Factual history is certainly the history of events in the past, but a history that includes, over and above what we learn from acts or great achievements, what we learn of their hidden elements in relation to a possibility that is never exhausted by what the real actually gives us. We are especially impressed by the human effort that went on demonstrating a determination to protect from the effects of time the things that only man's memory could preserve from destruction. We are less inclined to realize that history is always a secondary piecing together of a network originally experienced as separate elements. This reconstruction, which is the basis of a memorial text, is not carefully set down merely in the interests of scholarly record.

Historical writing, which had begun to keep a continuous record of the present, now also cast a glance back to the past, gathered traditions and legends, interpreted the traces of antiquity that survived in customs and usages, and in this way created a history of the past. It was inevitable that this early history should have been an expression of present beliefs rather than a true picture of the past; for many things had been dropped from the nation's memory, while others were distorted, and some remains of the past were given a wrong interpretation in order to fit in with contemporary ideas. Moreover people's motive for writing history was not objective curiosity but a desire to influence their contemporaries, to encourage and inspire them, or to hold a mirror up before them.   (Freud, *S.E.*, xi, 83–4)

Marie Delcourt's work does not, of course, correspond with Freud's conception. In any case, Freud's examples do not illustrate the case of Oedipus, but that of Moses – which inevitably provoked disagreement in some quarters. Whether or not he was mistaken in his interpretation of the case is actually less important than what he taught us to seek behind the myth: the repression of the unconscious. This approach may also be applied – at least in principle – to Greek mythology, so rich in stories of astonishing truthfulness, without claiming to be a substitute for the traditional approach, whose requirements are not exactly the same as those of psycho-analysis.

It is well known that the discussion of myths has raised the problem of their genetic explicative value. This is because scholars have wanted to limit the extent of the explanation of factual history in the strict sense. But pose the hypothesis of a factual history of desire – that is to say, a history that tries to bring back into the account everything that a social imaginary[1] sets up as structures in parallel with the unfolding of the facts and lying behind the versions of historical knowledge that necessarily exclude it – then myth has a significative function equal in interest to that of official history. It is not absolutely necessary, even if theoretically it were always desirable, that all the bridges linking one with the other be built. Perhaps it is a question of two parallel ways that are destined to meet only by becoming tangled together.

'True' historical truth, however shocking this proposition may be to historians, cannot be material truth. Even with the most banal material fact, who can safely ignore the dramatization of phantasy, the force not only of what has been actually lived through, but also of what was hoped for, the effect of hoping for certain answers left in the air at the whim of the other, of the furtive recording of its complications, its deceptions and its retreats? Here a field of possibility is opened up, which the factualness of desire outlines or fills in as best it can. The factual history of desire is given as a hypothetical factualness superimposed upon a lost trace. The access to the truth, Freud boldly said, can only pass through an examination of its distortions. This is a formidable task, given that distortion is usually measured against the truth, whereas for Freud the truth is to be deduced from the distortion. In this respect, myth is revealing, for the fiction in myth is not gratuitous and it is constructed not in order to entertain, but in order to further the function that brings it to birth: to give simultaneously form and outlet to desire. The finished, elaborated product of the myth is a scar which has closed above a wound which needs to be hidden. The text is not only a palimpsest of the myth, the product of additions written one on top of another, but above all an enigmatic image, or one with a superficially smooth surface, masking with pseudo-logic what needs to be concealed and sealed. In this respect, myth can only be a tattered and patched narrative, in which essential pieces of the puzzle are missing.

Can we agree with Marie Delcourt about the pedagogical function of myths, whose role seems to be, by virtue of the exemplary cases they recount, to persuade? And how can one explain satisfactorily the constant revision to which they are subjected? 'They are modified because new intentions are inserted into them in place of those that have ceased to be understood' (Delcourt, 1944, 222). It is clear that, however malleable mythical material may be, it is important that some nucleus of meaning should be preserved if the whole myth is not to become obsolete. For the problem is not so much a matter of the coherence of the myths as of the mode of intelligibility that they presuppose. This is especially interesting in the case of Greece, where the myths are inserted into a system of fairly loose beliefs held in place by no rigid dogmatism. The meaning of their transformations therefore poses the problem of a limit of communicability. The pedagogical value, the intention to persuade, must take account of the fact that most of the time – and this is so of the myths that became tragic themes – they seem to suggest not so much an example to be followed as a psychical reality to be exorcised.

Can we not, therefore, regard the pedagogical or persuasive value as a secondary determination, a justification of an activity that might be said to have been sacred and impure, since myths are compared to 'the transposition of a ceremony, the opening of a closed tabernacle and the solemn revelation of mysterious objects, sight of which is normally forbidden' (Delcourt, 1944, 50)? Yet nothing could be more dangerous than to approach this mystery outside the mythical context, just as psycho-analytic interpretation is resistant to any immediately vouchsafed generalization that has not passed through the mediation of a material whose theoretical development extends its limits, but which is inconceivable without them.

The notion of the transposition of a mysterious reality, of a memory – 'But what the legends teach is never simply a memory, it is always a transposition in which the old reality is decipherable only at a second reading' (Delcourt, 1944, 226) – poses implicitly, once more, the question of the meaning of the transformations. We must discover by virtue of what principle a particular feature disappears, another takes its place, or is replaced by a third with a similar, but subtly different meaning. To say of the 'subconscious' (*sic*) or psychical tendencies that they can come into play only 'to fix certain mythical themes, to give them exceptional popularity and vitality' (68) without actually creating them, or to disseminate a myth, 'to snatch it from oblivion' (229), or again to encourage its inscription in the context of the family (69), would be acceptable if one were able to maintain a more convincing hypothesis about the conditions of the genesis of these mythical projections. In fact, Marie Delcourt constantly oscillates between a sociological explanation, which she tries to avoid, and a broader explanation that she is looking for but cannot find: 'So the sociologists will be tempted to reduce our legends to mere initiation rites. I believe that they have a deeper, more general, also a more religious signification' (57). Elsewhere, she rejects – and one can see why – an approach free of any concrete substratum in the analysis of the religious. Hence, the transformation of myths will obey mechanisms suggesting a comparison with 'the creations of fictional genius' (14). But do such creations escape the unconscious?

For, to maintain that 'subconscious tendencies collaborate with the memory, but not with the story-telling genius' (words with which the book ends) – is not this to neglect the Freudian interpretation of remembering? Is it not to misunderstand the link between the products of the fictional genius and the story-telling genius?

The unfaithfulness of this mythical memory no doubt makes it very difficult to interpret things. The tangle of Greek legendary projections is perhaps more difficult to understand; because they are not content to classify the natural world as do the myths of primitive peoples, which enables a Lévi-Strauss to propose a formalization of them; because they are not subjected to a referential principle that places them under the aegis of a monotheism; because they do not obey a regulated ordering into a strict hierarchy, as in the cases of the heroes and divinities of other religions. There is also the question of their link, which is more difficult to detect here than elsewhere, with the Indo-European religions, for example. Does not the major difficulty lie in the fact that the object exposed by myths always preserves a direct contact with that from which they emerge, namely desire? The transformations of poetic invention can only be explained by an attempt to reconcile with the facts a psychology of 'natural' desires to which the structure of desire remains resistant. Thus a political pole will be opposed by an emotional or fictional pole, so divesting desire of its erotic charge, forgetting that Oedipus and Dionysus sprang from the same ancestor. For invention and story-telling are acceptable when it is a question of transforming an overtly embarrassing, even odious, feature – and this is intuitively accepted as 'natural' – but the idea that invention or story-telling have a function not only of attenuation or accommodation, but also of censorship and mask, seems difficult for mythologists to accept. This being so, would it not be useful to privilege the reading of whatever elements in the myth are resolutely contradictory, irreducible to the arrangements of a psychological understanding and, above all, unique? For the myth of Oedipus is the exemplary myth, since it is the one that links the question 'Who am I?' with the questions 'Whose son am I?', 'Whose father?' The question 'Why is there something rather than nothing?' can itself be posed only by linking its terms by generation. It is legitimate, then, that the question 'Who am I?' – itself a concatenation – can be answered only by a question concerning concatenation.

It may be useful to recall here the opinions expressed unambiguously, and with his usual boldness, by Freud:

In the first place, it seems quite possible to apply the psycho-analytic means derived from dreams to products of ethnic imagination such as myths and fairy tales. The need to interpret such productions has long been felt; some 'secret meaning' has been suspected to lie behind them and it is to be presumed that that meaning is concealed by changes and transformations. The study made by psycho-analysis of dreams and neuroses has given it the necessary experience to enable it to guess the technical procedures that have governed these distortions. But in a number of instances it can also reveal the hidden motives which have led to this modification in the original meaning of myths. It cannot accept as the first impulse to the construction of myths a theoretical craving for finding an explanation of natural phenomena or for accounting for cult observances and usages which have become unintelligible. It looks for that impulse in the same psychical 'complexes', in the same emotional trends, which it has discovered at the base of dreams and symptoms. (Freud, *S.E.*, xiii, 185)

For Freud, one principle dominates psychical activity, individual or collective: the pleasure principle, which has as its corollary the avoidance of unpleasure. But reality regularly frustrates man and does not allow him to realize his desires, despite the many displacements that are held out to him by way of diversion or substitution. 'Myths, religion and morality find their place in this scheme as attempts to seek a compensation for the lack of satisfaction of human wishes' (Freud, *S.E.*, xiii, 186). All three are collective social means of releasing group tensions. It is Freud's view, then, that one must interpret them in this way: let us apply to them the principle of the Oedipus legend, in the double process that led to its construction and to the deconstruction that it had to undergo through the distortions of the censor.

II

Marie Delcourt breaks the Oedipus legend down into a series of remarkably synonymous acts that were later brought together to form the legend as we know it. Each of its stages – the exposure of the child, the murder of the father, the victory over the Sphinx, the riddle, the marriage with the princess and the union with the mother – is part of a single context, the conflict between the generations. The most important element is perhaps this constitution of the hero 'after the event', since Oedipus, according to her, is 'the very type of those heroes of an essentially, if not uniquely, ritual origin, whose acts are anterior to the person' (Delcourt, 1944, 13). As if their beings were the product of the welding together of their havings, a welding that makes them come together as a being who existed before them without ever having been.

Thus, just as the time of experience is anterior to the time of signification and just as repression works on remembering, so here perhaps one may infer that the censor will work at the level of ritual, which is already memory. The 'person' in this case is certainly a later product, reshaped and distorted many times by repeated censorships.

In an illuminating work published in 1912, Ferenczi wondered how this myth was able to focus this complex so finely. This is his reply:

Significant but unconscious physical contents (aggressive phantasies against the father, sexual hunger for the mother with erection-tendencies, dread lest the father would avenge the sinful intent with the punishment of castration) procured, each for itself, indirect symbolic representatives in the consciousness of all men. Men with special creative capacities, poets, give expression to these universal symbols. In this way the mythical motives of exposure by the parents, victory over the father, unconscious intercourse with the mother, and self-blinding, might have arisen in individuals independent of one another. In the course of the passage of the myths through countless poetic individual minds, one that Rank has made probable, condensation of the separate motives led secondarily to a greater unity, which then proved to be durable and which was fashioned anew in much the same form by all peoples and at all times.   (Ferenczi, 265–6)

This interesting interpretation rather ignores the role of the censor. However, one factor seems decisive: the passage through the imaginary creation of the poet, that is to say, the reshaping of the unconscious by the phantasy of desire. For that is what the Oedipus complex is before it becomes a historical reality: a phantasy of desire which, since it has passed through the unconscious of a poet of genius, Sophocles, has become a reality of a cultural order: a tragedy.

The exposure of the child

Although Marie Delcourt is adept at discovering beneath each of the 'mythemes' the common denominator of the conflict between the generations, both in the exposure of the child and in the murder of the father, and although beneath the myth one can discover the old base of the 'ordeal', the initiation ritual, as other scholars have maintained, I must nevertheless admit that these interpretations leave my desire for meaning unsatisfied.

We learn that the practice of exposing a child on a mountain or immersing it in water is equivalent to a trial. Exposure on the sea in a chest represents a transition between the two. As Marie Delcourt points out (1944, 23), earlier versions of the Oedipus story made use of one or other of these practices. The alleged deformity used to justify the exposure of the child is more or less a pretext, and the oracle is certainly one: it is as if it had taken the place of a former legal power that has since come to be regarded as excessive. For, of the three mythical children exposed – Oedipus, Paris and Atalanta – the last is exposed solely on the pretext that she is a girl, whereas her parents wanted a boy. All this shows that the infirmity, the cause invoked to justify the exposure, was based on highly variable criteria. The restriction that required that the exposure should take place within a strictly limited time after birth reveals a desire to guard against motives that the deformity might hide or only partially justify. In any case, a link established between the legends and archaic customs shows that bastards were subjected to the same treatment: 'strange as it may seem, both categories of child were treated in the same way' (Delcourt, 1944, 24). It might be thought that the sign of non-conformity attaching to the child at birth – and expressed most strongly in illegitimacy – indicates an exceptional case in procreation, and makes it possible simultaneously to focus the signs of some defilement that may have no known origin and those of some as yet unforeseen deed by virtue of which the exposed child reveals capacities denied to ordinary people. The important factor is that survival should in every case be interpreted as the sign of an exceptional destiny. (The comparable elements found in the stories of Oedipus, Paris and Atalanta – removal to a different country after birth, upbringing by substitute parents or benevolent animals – cannot obscure the fact that the misfortunes caused by Paris were the consequences of a sexual abduction; and that Atalanta, exposed for belonging to the wrong sex, spent a large part of her life competing with men in the activities of hunting.)

One cannot entirely separate the exposure of Oedipus from those situations in other legendary contexts in which mother and child undergo this fate when there is some doubt as to the legitimacy of the child – where the mother invokes sexual union with a god. The divine origin of the child, born outside wedlock, is then attested *a posteriori* and explains the brilliant destiny that awaits him – especially since the fulfilment of this destiny often involves a more or less involuntary parricide, foretold by an oracle.

This destiny, then, is the result of a transgression. It is a transgression when the mother has adulterous sexual relations with a mortal. This mortal then turns out to be a hero, who transmits to his offspring a heredity that will lead him to challenge the law and carry out other striking exploits. It is also a transgression when it is a god (Dionysus) who seduces the mother, in the sense that this involves a crossing of the barrier that separates gods from men. In any case, the son, whose survival is the sign of divine favour, will in his turn be a hero or a demi-god. In the case of Oedipus, one may reverse the stages of the legend. It is not because Oedipus was predestined that he killed his father and slept with his mother: it is because he committed these acts that he had to be predestined.

The theme of moving to another country, which is encountered with remarkable frequency, emphasizes a necessary break in the narrative, a break by which the child will be brought up, educated, by others: beneficent animals or persons of humble station. The fact that the second part of the hero's life leads him to feats of valour, during which a more or less accidental parricide takes place, should not make us conclude too hastily that it is resentment, caused by the rejection expressed in the act of exposure, that dictates some obscure act of revenge. It might be thought that in order for the deed to be directed at the parent, it must pass through a period of dissociation and distancing – or latency, as the psycho-analysts call it – so that the deed may be done in ignorance of the kinship relation. It is like the family romance, in which the child, in his day-dreams – themselves dissociated from the rest of his psychical world – imagines himself not to be the son of his parents, so that his desires may be more acceptable. This is an apt reversal: it was on behalf of the apotheosis, of the evil to be avoided by the community, that the child was exposed; the sequence of the hero's exploits, often regarded as beneficial to the community, then includes the accidental death of the father.

The earlier versions that have survived speak only of parricide, not of incest. But sexuality is involved more than one might think: the original sin is sexual, since the mother often has to undergo a chastity test and is exposed with the child. Because she has given birth to a child outside marriage, she must provide proof – here the myths of Oedipus and Dionysus concur – of some other paternity or of the divinity of the father. This is what happens whenever the child is saved. The accusers, often the child's maternal grandfather, die at the same time. In a certain group of legends, mention is made only of the evil associated with the child, which represents a danger to the whole community and must therefore be sacrificed. But here again his heroic, and therefore beneficial, quality is acquired when he survives. The sexual sin, present even in the first case, may suggest that it was the object of a censorship in the second. Similarly, it becomes an element of the final incest committed in ignorance.

The legend of Telephus (Delcourt, 1944, 5) is related to that of Oedipus. But is it not significant that whereas the sexual conflict concerns the father and the daughter, and the ordeals are undergone above all by the daughter, the theme of incest by the son, who also performs exploits and slays monsters, is nonetheless introduced? This incest is avoided because the mother belongs to Hercules, does not wish to have any other lover and displays her hostility to the man whom she does not know is her son and whom she is prepared to kill. It is as if the absence and the desire of the father were assigned the separating role that the father plays when he decides on the exposure. The distributive value of the affects in this legendary group shows that the struggle for power between the generations is not enough to relegate incest to a secondary position.

In short, the legend of the exposure followed by survival – the only case that concerns us here, since those in which the child perishes do not call for comment – is a retrospective explanation: 'The practices deriving from the myth of the exposed child had to be applied to people who in one way or another were *intruders* or, to put it another way, men forced to conquer the place they wished to occupy and to which they had originally no right' (Delcourt, 1944, 40). This is obviously the case of Oedipus Tyrannus. If we then interpret the meanings of these convergent contexts, we see that the distancing caused by a change of country is evidence of separation from the mother through the action of the father. The stigmata of evil are the indices of a message; it signifies not only that the man who will kill his father and impose himself by force on the mother's kingdom is a monster, but that it is monstrous that such desires should be even thinkable. For, as Marie Delcourt observes, 'The poets have never brought themselves to depict a conscious parricide.' And we know that Solon's code did not mention any penalty for parricide, for to punish it was to envisage it. The ambiguity of the charge to be laid against the father in the act of exposure – which would result in too precise an indication of the son's intentions concerning him – has left its mark in the tragedy. Jocasta says to Oedipus:

> As for the child,
> It was not yet three days old, when he cast it out
> (By other hands, not his) with rivetted ankles
> To perish on the empty mountain-side.

(Sophocles, *King Oedipus*, 45)

The servant declares that it was Jocasta who gave him the child to get rid of. The thesis by which his role becomes that of a mere carrier, like that of the lie, does not account for this silence about the father, who fails to concern himself with the practical details of so serious matter.

Marie Delcourt's remark about parricide forces us to abandon any hope of rediscovering an original content that has undergone no distortion or substitution. It is enriched in *King Oedipus* by a development that is no more than hinted at in the myth, but which Sophocles brings out into the open. It is true that 'almost all newborn children exposed are the sons of a god, that is to say, of an unknown father' (Delcourt, 1944, 159) – at least in the cases in which the overcoming of the woman is associated with the conquest of power. But it is at the moment when the hero, seeking to learn who his father was, hears the first clues about his origins in the account of the messenger from Corinth, when he learns he is not the son of Polybus and Merope, that he calls himself the child of Fortune, of Happy Meeting. This is not simply an apotropaic declaration. The chorus takes up the idea and begins to dream about this mythical generation; the place of the exposure is transformed into the scene of a coupling between a nymph and a god.

In many legends, the deformity is reduced to its minimal expression, consisting only in the following remarkable feature: it is the youngest and weakest of the sons (Freud notes that it is often the favourite child) who will triumph over the persecuting father (or one of his substitutes).[2] The claim to divine origin is an ostentatious way of expressing the hero's relationship with the god; this relationship confers such power that the act of parricide is no longer necessary for him to prove that he is his father's match: his survival is the first sign of this.

A psycho-analyst would have something to say about the detail of the pierced feet. With Freud, he would suppose – though no doubt the view would be challenged – that this mark is the scar of a displaced primal castration, inflicted by a father wishing to avoid any danger of future incest, or at the least a practice comparable with circumcision. Psycho-analytic material points conclusively enough to an equivalence between the foot and the penis for such a hypothesis not to be gratuitous. The clear etymology of Oedipus' name (the swollen-footed), which is distinctive because a rare feature in these legends, allows us to link him to his lineage. To be more precise, only when he turns out to be the son of Laius (the man of the people) does the detail that identifies him with his grand-father become clear, not so much as a feature inherited from him and a sign of actual relationship, but as explaining the significance of the act of his father that unites the son to his own father, Labdacus (the lame). It should be noted that Laius does not pierce Oedipus' feet; he binds them together, whereas Labdacus walks with his feet splayed out. It is through his concern for his people, then, that Oedipus finds, through the same act of exorcism as that by which his father claimed to have saved the city, confirmation of his divinatory power. This power accords with the exceptional gesture of the father who excluded the son simply for being his child.

Recognition by means of the mutilation of the pierced feet, which easily bears a 'psychological' justification, survives here in the form of a trace. The scar is not so much an index of deformity as the brand placed on the subject in that place through which he was able to recognize himself in the Sphinx's questions (which all concern walking). This was because he had been previously marked as having 'monstrous' feelings for which the father, after the event, provided the cause, so endorsing them by means of this 'signature' left on the exposed child. Just as Oedipus begins his second life as a child – a life in a new country – by the act of the messenger who unties the bonds binding his pierced, new-born limbs, so he will begin his second life as a man after untying the bond that is strangling his mother and by piercing his own eyes.

The act of exposure, like casting adrift in a chest, or ritual immersion, seems to be an attempt to inaugurate an 'absolute beginning' (Delcourt, 1944, 56); the time-lag which prevents this beginning from coinciding with birth will show later, in each of the myth's episodes, that it is above all a desire for an indefinitely renewed origin. So Teiresias recommences the father's action by exposing Oedipus to the city, just as Oedipus will expose himself by self-blinding and will place himself once again in the hands of the gods, restricting himself from any longer seeing those who see him exist.

The exposure is compared by the mythologists to the practice of the *pharmakos*: out of fear of mysterious forces (which Marie Delcourt hesitates to term divine, so archaic is the period to which she refers), out of fear of some unknown sin committed, which causes the anger of the unleashed elements or the misfortune that under-mines the group, there is born the desire to transfix evil, to enclose it in a single being on whom the whole weight of the sin will fall. He is responsible for it by his mere existence, if not by his actions, and must be excluded, punished and exterminated in order to rid himself of defilement and to appease the maleficent powers. Yet it should be remembered that the stoning of the *pharmakos* and the expulsion from the group with a tiny amount of food was accompanied by chastisement of the genital organs. Behind this configuration, one finds the signification that, in an attenuated or distorted form, might be assumed by the experiences associated with the initiation ritual at puberty. But, to establish this connection is to link the ordeal to sexuality and not solely to admission among adults to a share of the responsibilities of power. In any case, the privilege of power frequently goes with sexual privilege. How else is one to understand that success in the ordeal brings the victor the hand of the princess by way of reward?

What these rituals suggest is that they are an attempt, at the very moment when puberty reveals a new sexual thrust which reawakens everything that had preceded it in the domain of desire, to achieve a mutation that finally breaks the knot that binds the child to the mother. At the extreme, the secret of initiation might appear a mere trick, since it reveals nothing, and since the exclusion of women is scarcely justified. Men's desire to share a secret among themselves in which women shall not participate, far from answering the question, refers us back to it precisely because only women possess the property of producing children. They alone know how to bind children to their bodies well after birth. The role of the father, in the very question in which it is considered, transforms into a secret the question that he leaves open. The hollow in which it is inserted – not every sexual act culminates in generation, but there is no generation not preceded by a sexual act – is carried back to the relation between man and nature and between man and his fellow men. The secret, then, is to be kept among men, just as the woman keeps what the man deposits in her, and in which he no longer has a share, and just as the child is born of the desire that the mother has for him, when she asks herself what becomes of the erect penis that has ceased to be in her. This void, which it leaves after its withdrawal, continues to accompany each stage as more room must be made in her belly for the child that she will see only when the process finally separates him from her. Although initiation opens up a certain mastery, it does so not by replacing one progenitor by another, but by a capacity for decision whose aim-inhibition (the conquest of the mother) is the essential stage that privileges the trace over the event.

To introduce the event into the recommencement will be the

temptation of the tragic hero. Thus Oedipus preparing to leave
Thebes asks to return to Mount Cithaeron, but adds:

> And yet I know,
> Not age, nor sickness, nor any common accident
> Can end my life.   (Sophocles, *King Oedipus*, 66)

This takes up, with a new twist, Teiresias' prediction: 'This day
brings you your birth; and brings you death' (*King Oedipus*, 38).

The Oracles

The oracle may not be considered as a mere artifice, and it is all too
easy to regard it as the expression of transcendent speech. Through
it is expressed the reminder of a forgotten speech. But here memory
and oblivion are not to be thought of in terms that allow them to
overlap.

Thus one is struck when one observes that there are two oracles in
King Oedipus. The first is invoked by Jocasta:

> An oracle was given to Laius –
> From Phoebus, no; but from his ministers –
> That he should die by the hands of his own child,
> His child and mine.   (*King Oedipus*, 45)

This prediction, then, is made by the god's intermediaries. The
second oracle is that which Oedipus receives from Apollo, here
designated by one of his most common epithets, Loxias (the oblique),
which predicts for him with almost imperious detail both incest and
parricide. Why, then, should Marie Delcourt write that Laius'
oracle (for it is undoubtedly this oracle that she is referring to – she
quotes lines 713 and 1176) 'announces after the birth of the child
and too late for the misfortune to be avoided that the new-born will
kill his father'? No doubt this is in order to underline the feeling of
fatality that must hang over the whole play, but this makes
Sophocles say more or less than he actually does say. A distinction
must necessarily be drawn between Sophocles and Aeschylus concerning the prohibition prescribed by the oracle.

In Aeschylus, whose tragedy of Oedipus has not come down to us,
the sin, the product of the prohibition and its transgression, is
described in *Seven Against Thebes*, performed in 467 B.C., less than
twenty years, or a generation, before *King Oedipus*. The chorus says:

> For I speak of a sin sown long ago –
> Which brought swift punishment then,
> Yet now abides to the third generation –

When Laius disobeyed Apollo,
Who from his Pythian shrine at the world's navel
Three times in oracles warned him,
If he would save his city,
To die without issue.
Mastered by the rashness of love
He begot for himself, to his own doom,
The father-killer Oedipus,
Who sowing seed in the forbidden field,
His mother's womb in which he grew,
Endured the bloody harvest of his act;
For the spirit of madness brought them together,
And their understanding was taken from them.

(Aeschylus, *Seven Against Thebes*, 110–11)

In the lost Oedipus play, the sin of the son must pay for, but cannot annul, the sin of the father. In Sophocles, there is no solution either to the prohibition or to the transgression. One cannot say that the aesthetic criterion or formal requirements alone explain this disappearance. The omission is then interpreted by relating it to the notion of responsibility to be found in the historical, mental and social contexts. Thus Vernant writes of *King Oedipus*: 'In the context of the *city*, man begins to test himself as a more or less autonomous agent in relation to the religious powers that dominate the universe, more or less master of his acts, having more or less control over his political and personal destiny' (1972, 5). I cannot help noting that these characteristics are much more applicable, as commentators have always realized, to Aeschylus than to Sophocles and very little indeed to Euripides.[3] If the progress of the tragic consciousness does move in step with the social consciousness, a movement of that kind in the evolution of social consciousness, which allows itself to pose the question of responsibility without reference to prohibition, presupposes a quite considerable time-lag at the level of social change.

Yet there is a line spoken by Oedipus that touches in an allusive way on guilt about a father's sin:

Now found all evil and of evil born.   (Sophocles, *King Oedipus*, 64)

It will be said that the public was sufficiently aware of this guilt for Sophocles not to have to name it. But the whole point is the absence of this naming, the fact that it does not need to be said because it is understood between the author and his public. For the impact of this line, far from referring back to the explicit prohibition, reopens the question 'What, then, were they guilty of?'; for the absence of progeniture is one of the worst evils, since there would be no one to perform the father's funeral ceremony on the day of his death.

For it will be observed that this absence of explicit prohibitions corresponds to the absence of a theme dear to Sophocles: precisely that of excusable guilt.[4] This means not only that simply by moving round the nucleus, which is the axis of certain related problems, discussion remains possible; but also that this discussion compels recognition by not having to name the nucleus, by maintaining it in absence. Another alternative would be to split this nucleus. So one would try to separate incest and parricide.

Parricide and incest: the first approach

Though parricide is the most horrible of crimes, it cannot be denied that the severity with which it is punished is bound up with an implicit regicide. But the question is, why are forms of succession by violence so constantly repeated throughout history and legend, which also never fail to condemn them? Even when the elimination of the chief moves from the level of the tribe or clan to that of the family, it is still regarded with horror. Although social practices must account for certain persistences in legendary themes, what does the constant recurrence of the same figures in the stock of legends indicate, if not that this mass of words always covers some silence, about something that must not be said?

Although she relates the group of legends about exposure on the mountain and those about casting the child adrift in a chest, alone or with his mother (the second case being associated with sexual sin), Marie Delcourt finds in the conflict between son and grandfather – the latter often paying for the survival of the child with his own life – no indication which allows us to relate them to Oedipal incest. Although immersion acquires the value of a probationary trial, we know that it also has two other meanings: purification and rebirth. That this new life, of which the miracle of survival was the augury, should hold out the promise of kingship, has been linked both to the character of the intruder who carves out a place for himself to which he has no right, but which he seizes, and also, in an apparently contrary way, to the heroes who take possession once more of what belongs to them, returning to a land that has been plundered. It should be remembered here that Freud, on the basis of a study of dream-symbolism, showed over half a century ago the identity in signification between entering the sea and penetrating the mother on the one hand, and emerging from water and being born on the other. The connection discovered by Marie Delcourt (1944, 22) appears to be much more significant, since the new heroic life,

already prefigured in the feat of survival, is connected with possession of the mother, as is shown by the frequent though not invariable
presence of the mother with the child in the chest. (Not to mention
the ship-symbolism, which still holds in the analysis of the dreams of
analysands the same value as representation of the genital organs,
usually female.) Incest seems to remain in a relation – if only one of
disjunction – with the mythical context, by that stage in its development that preserves only the most distant connection between purification and the sin, which is dissociated from it. For, if survival is
the very sign of the proof of divine kinship, why is the ordeal duplicated by a signification of purification?

In Sophocles, the discovery of the parricide proceeds step by step
with the discovery of the incest; the two crimes are linked, and the
horror at the second is as great as the horror at the first. The servant
who relates Jocasta's death and describes Oedipus' blinding does not
dare to refer to incest explicitly in front of the chorus. But the blind
Oedipus, speaking after his self-mutilation, proclaims it openly.

The stock of myths has not always called Oedipus' mother and
wife Jocasta. She has also been Epicaste, Eurygonia, Eurygane,
Eurygania, Erigone and Euryclea. Examination of the legends in
which these characters figure shows that censorship or displacement
has effected a disconnection between mother and wife. Thus
Euryganea is the name of Oedipus' wife in the legends in which
incest does not occur. However, it is after Jocasta's death that
Oedipus marries her and gives her four children. Eurygania,
daughter of Hypophas, is the mother of Oedipus' children in other
legends, but Oedipus marries Epicaste, who gives him no children.
In other versions, Euryclea is Oedipus' mother and Laius' first wife;
Oedipus marries his father's second wife Epicaste, after killing Laius.
So reworking of the myth leads to these apparently incomprehensible
results, but they all have the same result: they do not allow it to
emerge that Oedipus has married his own mother, who is the wife
of the man he killed, his father; and the woman gives him four
children (as evidence of the sexual relations he has had with her).
Hence the various operations that split off the incest: the dissociation between Laius' two wives, and dissociation between wife and
mother.

Obviously, it would be wrong to think that incest would be
regarded as a less serious crime. Sophocles' genius gathers together
these scattered elements and links them to the parricide. But this
gathering together must be counterbalanced by a degree of *méconnaissance*.

A new disjunction appears by means of the time-lag between the
two oracles in the tragedy – the one given long before to the father,

which does not mention parricide and omits both the cause of the prohibition to procreate and the prediction of the union of the child with the mother; and the oracle that occurs within the time-scale of the tragedy itself, which is given to the son and which announces the imminence of the incest and parricide.

Incest, we know, is a major prohibition, mother–son incest being most particularly subject to prohibition. (Father–daughter incest, which, in certain conditions, is possible in a matrilinear system, is forbidden in a patrilinear one. Mother–son incest is always forbidden.) By centring matters on the rite of the struggle between the young king and the old king, and discovering in it the seed of the legendary figures of the struggle between son and father, an attempt has been made to deny that the mother can be the cause of contention, and to see the throne itself as the object of the son's envy. This is to deny infantile sexuality in favour of only those interests of the adult that have escaped repression. This is the case today in families where son and father are open rivals over the question of the family inheritance. Sons find it difficult to wait for their father's disappearance before benefiting from the transfer of family wealth. But the analyst frequently discovers that behind the rationalizations of the overt conflict there lies, hidden yet active, the infantile conflict in which the possession of the mother plays the greatest part.

Avunculate and epiclerate

In Sophocles' play, it is the character of Creon in his relations with Oedipus who is most often subjected to psychological analysis. Let us try to identify his place in the context of the kinship relations.

Thanks to the work of Lévi-Strauss, ethnology and structural anthropology have drawn the attention of a wider public to the interest to be found in the avunculate. The maternal uncle has a variable function according to whether he forms part of a patri- or matrilinear system. In a system in which authority is the prerogative of the father, the maternal uncle has the role of a 'masculine mother' (the expression is Lévi-Strauss's own); while in a matrilinear system he assumes those characteristics of severity, hostility and antagonism towards the son which are more usually associated with the paternal function. Above all, Lévi-Strauss's contribution has shown how these combinations were not the work of chance, but formed a system: 'Thus we see that in order to understand the avunculate we must treat it as one relationship within a system, while the system itself must be considered as a whole in order to grasp its structure' (1968, 46). In short, the structure is simply that of the element of kinship, or more precisely the atom of kinship. But the constellation formed around the atomic nucleus, that is to say, the child – and I give here only the outline of a schematic simplification restricted to the needs of my argument – has a meaning that we do well not to ignore. For although the child is certainly 'indispensable in validating the dynamic and teleological character of the initial step, which establishes kinship on the basis of and through marriage' (Lévi-Strauss, 1968, 47), it seems to me that Lévi-Strauss's demonstration reveals on the other hand an attempt to absorb, at least in part, this dynamic character. How are we to understand this extra charge in the kinship element constituted by the intervention of the uncle – whose symbolic nature is unquestionable – other than as the reintroduction of a term, which, if not excluded, was at least diverted elsewhere by the marriage alliance? It is tempting to say that the present, having begun with the birth of the child, is coadapted by the conditions of possibility produced by this birth, which emerge as an 'as if the exchange had not taken place'. This represents more than a movement of counter-prestation, for, despite the extension of the system by the increase in the number of its relations, the result is nevertheless not equivalent to an attempt to cancel out. To say of kinship systems that 'the initial disequilibrium produced in one generation between the group that gives the woman and the group that receives her can be stabilized only by counter-prestations in following generations' (Lévi-Strauss, 1968, 47) demonstrates precisely that exchange is by no means regulated, and that the prohibition of incest that exogamy tries to engineer is undermined by the return of the relation of consanguinity. Such a conception of exchange reduces almost to nil the rupture caused by generation. This rupture is always retarded by the dependence of the child on his progenitors, but, sooner or later, it will have to be revealed, if only at the moment when it appears to be consumed in its opposite – for example, at the time of initiation, when the son, *de jure* if not *de facto*, becomes the father's equal. However, such a rupture is *originative* – Lévi-Strauss calls it 'initial disequilibrium' – through the potentiality, open since birth, for the child himself to be one day not only an *exchanger*, but a *progenitor*. That the maternal uncle should stand in to fill this gap makes it all the more evident.

It cannot be denied that the familial combinatory exists, and it is inconceivable that kinship should be organized otherwise than as a system. But it is the reinclusion of the excluded – challenging the revolution (what is circulated by exchange) of the alliance – that seems to have the purpose of filling a gap. Of course, this gap has nothing to do with any lack of paternal authority, since the uncle may also play the role of 'masculine mother'; the facts lead one to believe that the uncle intervenes in consequence of the exchange in order to eliminate the rupture of which the mother has herself been the product in relation to the father who engendered her. For if the rule is established against incest, exchange is the effect of a concatenation that is not allowed, but which is not eliminated by its prohibition. The incest prohibition prevents the union of the father and the daughter; by extending itself through the avunculate, the system recovers a mediator in the person of the uncle. The uncle serves the dual function of effacing any assimilation between the mother's father and the child's father (difference of the generations) and of being counted in as a figure of that which is at issue in generation: neither on one side of the family nor on the other, but between them (difference of the sexes). While constitutive of the system, it reveals the inability of the system to rid itself of the thing it wants to contain and prevent.

Lévi-Strauss's use of a theory of exchange in order to cover the field of kinship in a comprehensive way seems to ignore the complexity of the problem of sexuality. What he does not seem to consider is that the kinship system might correspond to a contradiction between organic bisexuality, which has as its consequence sexual reproduction by the union of two single-sexed progenitors, and psychical bisexuality, which implies that the 'psycho-sexual' organization of each of the two single-sexed progenitors involves, at least in a recessive way, the sexual characteristics of the sex to which he does not belong. This is what Freud calls 'double identification', a result of the Oedipus complex, which means that each subject bears within him on emerging from this complex a precipitate formed by the presence of male and female identification, with the father and with the mother. This contradiction would account in a more satisfactory way for the presence and function of the maternal uncle. It is a pity that Lévi-Strauss, who considers at the end of his article other possible variants[5] of the kinship structure within the avuncular relation, did not think of studying his chosen case in relation to that of the epiclerate, another effect of the incest prohibition.

We know what the epiclerate consists of: a father deprived of male descent may make up for this lack by becoming nominally the father of the child that his daughter is allowed to have by a close relation appointed by him, whom she marries. This 'stand-in' is appointed according to a strict order of succession,[6] which usually gives first place to the father's brothers. We see that with this formula it is much less the combinatory that is privileged – and I do not doubt that one may be detected – than the absence of the father in the procreation, which is recognized as having been performed by another man to whom the girl is married; and that the only reason invoked is of a symbolic order, so far as the Greeks are concerned at any rate, and that is the celebration of the funeral rites. Generation and procreation are split, only the Name-of-the-Father (Lacan) being transmitted. This is perhaps proof that although one must recognize that Lévi-Strauss is right when he writes, 'but what confers upon kinship its socio-cultural character is not what it retains from nature, but, rather, the essential way in which it diverges from nature' (1968, 50), one may doubt whether this separation is based upon the combination of exchanges alone. In several places, Lévi-Strauss carries the argument to the extreme of declaring that the mode of intelligibility to which the system of relations refers is that of molecular structure. 'However, it would not be enough to reabsorb particular humanities into a general one. This first enterprise opens the way for others which Rousseau would not have been so ready to accept and which are incumbent on the exact natural sciences: the reintegration of culture in nature and finally of life within the whole of its physico-chemical combinations' (Lévi-Strauss, 1966, 247).

Moreover, it is necessary to distinguish within a given social structure between the real kinship system and its phantasmatic projections.

Frazer's hypotheses, developed in his work on the magical origins of kingship, show how a sociological ensemble attached to matri-linearity (which is merely one of its elements) undergoes significant transformations in mythical narratives (Delcourt, 1944, 159–60).

Father and daughter are united by an epiclerate status, the king being without male descent. In the fairy tales, the daughter marries not the father's closest relation, but an adventurer who is of royal blood, though without patrimony. Usually, this man has been banished from his country for a murder. We should again remember in this ensemble the persecution of a new-born child by the mother's father or uncle and – a point on which I have already commented at length – the divine descent of the exposed new-born children. Lastly – and this is a remarkable detail – the paternal uncle is his niece's lover not out of love, but out of hate. This uncle is, indeed, his brother's enemy, the hero's grandfather. Here a link is effected between legends involving an exposed child and those involving marriage with the princess. The two groups, previously separated, come together and complement one another in the description of the rites of conquest of the betrothed girl.

One may note from these observations:

1. that the hypothesis proposed by Frazer of the correspondence of these tales with a matrilinear system says nothing about the mother in the narratives or alludes to her only through the symbolic incest that she authorizes;[7]

2. that the substitute for the father, legally designated in the

epiclerate, does not marry the daughter, but becomes the lover and persecutor of his niece out of hostility, as if it were a question of signifying that in this situation too much or not enough has been given him, or that he is revenging the mother;

3. that the mother's child is in any case unwelcome in the eyes of the mother's father;

4. that the link between the non-existence of a patrimony and the murder committed by the adventurer is not made explicit, but that the unfortunate suitors are killed by the betrothed girl's father;

5. that certain rites of conquest of the betrothed girl show that a struggle or a combat may be the prelude to or the substitute for erotic possession.

So we see that it is not a question here of a coherent ensemble, immediately perceptible through the network of relations. That is natural enough, since it is a question not of a kinship system, but of a legendary projection. However, the intelligibility of the ensemble seems much stronger when one compares the difference between the social kinship system and what Marie Delcourt calls its 'fictional context', and what Freud was to call his 'family romance'. An understanding of the ensemble is possible only on the basis of the fact that this ensemble splits, from one generation to another, or from one lineage to another, the answer on one level from a question that must be found on another level or on another branch of the genealogical tree. That answer is the result of a repression that designates all the more clearly what it has distorted, for one seeks the thing one is looking for in the thing which is lacking in the system if a meaning is to be produced. (It is not a question of setting methods in opposition to one another, since their points of application are very different, but of comparing approaches.) What is active is not the positive intervention of a term and the place it occupies, masking the one that it conceals, but the mapping of an empty space, that of the distinction between procreation and generation, which is duplicated by a generation gap.

One can understand Lévi-Strauss's hesitations and uncertainties as to the foundation of a separation between nature and culture around the incest prohibition. But how is one to situate, to date it? It is at once the product of institutions and a condition of the production of institutions. For it is as if one could speak about the incest prohibition and record its effects only at the moment when the prohibition has already caused silence to fall over what must remain unsaid,[8] whereas the link is broken that binds the incest prohibition to the Oedipal structure, a link that is revealed only in the traces of the distortions from which it may be inferred.

It will be said that this opens up too wide a speculation, too risky a conjecture to win the support of the scientist. We observe, however, that the marks of exclusion in matters of sex certainly do not bring the advantage of opening the interrogated corpus to questions previously left unanswered, but produce much more strongly the feeling of some truncated coherence.[9] This is certainly what is masked in the minimizations of the incest role in the Oedipus myth.

The minimization of incest and sexual exclusion

I cannot agree with Marie Delcourt when she says of *King Oedipus*: 'The whole play is based on the idea of parricide. Incest is discovered incidentally: from a religious point of view, it plays no role in the play.' How could it be otherwise, since the two sins are linked together and since the discovery of the second is subordinate to the first? Parricide cannot avoid disguise, any more than incest can. When the situation presents father and son directly, the issue is confined to the dispute over ownership or political power; on the other hand, when, as is more often the case, it is a question of the opposition between an old man and a young man, the young man will be in love with the old man's daughter. The theme of the conflict between the generations is compatible with marriage to the princess (Delcourt, 1944, 101), but not with the theme of incestuous realization. 'In almost all the stories, the conquest of the kingdom depends on the conquest of the betrothed and it is impossible to study them separately' (Delcourt, 1944, 163). But why say that, 'from a religious point of view', it plays no part, when in reality it is only the oracle dictated by Apollo himself to Oedipus, the one received by Laius, which leaves out the incest, having been given only by his servants? Oedipus himself makes no attempt to attenuate the gravity of either crime. As for the study of ritual, this would show the direct opposite. Marie Delcourt explains the similarity between marriage rituals and those of the conquest of the kingdom as showing the unitary nature of archaic initiations, from the spring hierogamies that link struggles and contests between young and old kings to the marriage celebration of young people.

Social parricide is recognized for motives that are as much sociological as psychological. The community can no longer feel itself either represented or protected by the old king. Strength, virility and fecundity, not the wisdom of years, are the qualities required in a king. In the context of the legends, the loss of physical strength is accompanied by the loss of fecundating power. We are bound to see here a proof of the indissolubility of political power and sexual potency. Power, *potentia*, is obviously the common element here between kingship and sexuality. That is why contempt, not respect, is shown an ageing king, as if he had returned to childhood: he who is castrated is no longer he who castrates. Georges Dumézil's formula, 'Sovereignty and fecundity are inseparable powers and like two aspects of potency', is more often quoted than followed to its logical conclusion. For sometimes this fecundity is conceived as a mere productivity factor, sometimes as an 'origin', spoken of as one speaks of local roots. It is seldom given its full signification, which links it to the sexual matrix. Thus one can say of the Greek beliefs concerning the union of man and the earth 'that this union has a sexual coefficient and has as its symbolic correspondent union with the mother' (Delcourt, 1944, 192).

This is where the chthonian interpretations of the Oedipus myth have their place. These interpretations are generally intended to exclude the sexual or, more subtly, to include the sexual in a broader conception in which the sexual problematic is submerged. But why suppress the question of sex at all? One possible answer presents itself: in order to conceal castration.

The substitute answers to the question of sex will therefore be those that I shall call the chthonian solution and the political solution. Lévi-Strauss adopts the chthonian solution, Vernant the political solution, while Marie Delcourt, we know, supports the Adlerian thesis of the conflict of the generations.

Let us examine the chthonian solution. For Lévi-Strauss, the point of the Oedipus myth is the negation of man's autochthony (1968, 213ff.). This interpretation, in many ways a remarkable one, shows some signs of a suspension of interpretative discourse. Lévi-Strauss breaks off his commentary at one moment when his gaze turns from the Oedipus myth and moves, in a footnote, towards the Hopi Indians, whose function it is to point out, in its place, the relation between the Oedipus myth and castration. The blinding of Oedipus associated with the suicide of Jocasta – whose absence from the older versions is unexplained – are taken together as accretions that make the myth more explicit, 'since the shift from foot to head is to be correlated with the shift from negated autochthony to self-destruction' (Lévi-Strauss, 1968, 216). But the link that Lévi-Strauss leaves unexplained is that which establishes the relation between the negation of autochthony and 'deformity'. What is concealed behind the notion of over-estimation or under-estimation of the kinship relation in Lévi-Strauss's analysis in relation to the question 'One or two parents?' Is this not to pose the question of sexual difference since, unlike Lévi-Strauss, Freud does indeed speak of the alternative between autochthony and bisexual reproduction?[10] But either this difference is total, so that there is no longer any relation between the terms that it relates, or like all differences it is one referring back, beneath the distinction of the sexes, to the presence of this allusively evoked 'deformity'. Castration is not explicitly named in the myth, it must be admitted. But Marie Delcourt poses the question of the link between the deformed and the impotent (1944, 217). And with the Sphinx, the phallic personage, we meet the question again.

The Sphinx recalls even more the *child protruding woman* of the Hopi Indians, a phallic mother if ever there was one. This young woman was abandoned by her group in the course of a difficult migration, just as she was about to give birth. Henceforth she wanders in the desert as the 'Mother of the Animals', which she withholds from hunters. He who meets her in her bloody clothes 'is so frightened that he has an erection', and she takes advantage of this to rape him, after which she rewards him with unfailing success in hunting.   (Lévi-Strauss, 1968, 231; my italics)

This may be compared with Freud's 'Medusa's Head' (1922), an outline, published posthumously, for a more important work that Freud never wrote:

The terror of Medusa is thus a terror of castration that is linked to the sight of something...The hair upon Medusa's head is frequently represented in works of art in the form of snakes, and these once again are derived from the castration complex. It is a remarkable fact that, however frightening they may be in themselves, they nevertheless serve actually as a mitigation of the horror, for they replace the penis, the absence of which is the cause of horror. This is a confirmation of the technical rule according to which a multiplication of penis symbols signifies castration. The sight of Medusa's head makes the spectator still with terror, turns him to stone. Observe that we have here once again the same origin from the castration complex and the same transformation of affect! For becoming still means an erection.   (Freud, *S.E.*, XVIII, 273)

As for the snake as link between the visible and the invisible, I quote Vernant:

At Aulis, before the departure, the Greeks made a sacrifice at the foot of a plane-tree. Suddenly a terrible sign appeared: Zeus summoned up into the light of day a snake, which emerged from underneath an altar; it threw itself upon a brood of sparrows, which it devoured together with their mother. Immediately the god who had made it appear concealed it from their eyes (literally, made it invisible); in effect, the son of Cronus had suddenly changed it into stone (*Iliad*, II, 318–19)...By transforming it into stone, Zeus, who had for a moment brought it to light, restored it to the invisible.   (1965, 261)

Freud's remarks have since become commonplaces; we scarcely need to consult psycho-analytic works to learn that a liking for snakes on the part of women has something to do with the penis. But in the same work from which Lévi-Strauss derived his observation,

Marie Delcourt's *Œdipe ou la légende du conquérant*, there is an appendix concerning animal stories in Greece in which we find the following:

In order to clarify matters, we should first set aside most of the tales concerning the snake. Marx [the author is referring to Auguste Marx] saw very clearly that the snake is a dead man and represents a mysterious ancestor who is to be feared and honoured. If a snake grants to certain privileged persons the gift of understanding the language of the animals and seeing into the future, it is thanks to its relations with the world beyond the tomb and its secrets. These narratives form a special category that must be studied in terms of various conceptions of the soul. However, in certain stories about snakes, one finds themes common to those concerning other animals.   (1944, 233–4)

Marie Delcourt makes a few final remarks on fairies and 'belts which protect against birth'. Popular beliefs 'concerning the clan animal, which became heterogeneous in the religion of archaic Greece, also became transformed into *Märchen*' (Delcourt, 1944, 237), those German tales in which the witch is a familiar character. The chapter finally closes with H. Jeanmaire's interpretation of the wolf, 'whose task it is to frighten and train novices', the wolf–schoolmaster often met in German tales. Note the sequence: snake as category to be set apart, fairy (and therefore witch), old hag, clan animal, protective belt against birth (the woman giving birth refusing food derived from hunting), the wolf–schoolmaster.

What Lévi-Strauss 'sets aside' is first the relation between the dragon and the snake of Cadmus (for this is how he is usually designated), then the relation between the latter and Python, the snake killed by Apollo, later celebrated as the male snake (Delcourt, 1955, 34–5). The Sphinx is the child of Echidna (the viper) and Orthrus (her own son). Her descent from the snake is proved by this origin. She is, then, the phallic mother, and there is no need to seek among the Hopi Indians what the Greeks said in their own language through images.

What this series of associations reveals is perhaps something that would prevent the setting up of endless permutations, for the monster's place of birth is generally a cave, a matrix (the etymology of which refers back to Delphyne, the name of the female snake). This snake is 'a mouth, a *stomion*' (Delcourt, 1955, 140).

Stoma and *stomion* also designate the vagina...In according so much importance to the phantom exhalations that surrounded the Pythoness, later writers attest to the force of the myth of the *stomion*, which continues to grow in richness in their imagination. Perhaps without being aware of it, they were reviving old beliefs in which prophetic dreams arose from their mother's breast, the earth. And they probably played on both meanings of *stomion*, the organ that emits the voice. Curiously enough, in *omphalos* too one could recognize *omphe*, speech.

(Delcourt, 1955, 141)

We must respect the philologist's prudence, but since comparisons are being made between the Greeks of the archaic period and Hopis, Zunis and Pueblos, is not the most significant moment the one when one ceases to compare? No doubt Lévi-Strauss the botanist deflected the thinking of Lévi-Strauss the anthropologist, since he derives the chthonian preoccupation of the Oedipus myth from the vegetal model of man, which may well throw light on the myth of primitive peoples. But in the article's closing remarks, these observations are extended to a general study of mythical thought. And yet Lévi-Strauss the anthropologist did touch on the essence of the problem when he remarked: 'We recall that Freud considered that *two traumas* (and not one, as is so commonly said) are necessary in order to generate the individual myth in which a neurosis consists' (1968, 228). He then turned away from the implications in Freudian theory of this remark and returned to the thought that decorates the cover of his book, *La Pensée sauvage*.

Deformity, then, is not unconnected with bisexual reproduction, since it will govern all the operations at work in the double male and female identification that Freud links to the developed formula of the Oedipus complex. When Lévi-Strauss causes the chain to slip from the injured foot to the head (Oedipus), and even to the point of total destruction of self (Jocasta), it is as if he wished to miss out the intervening links that Sophocles provides. (The link between the earth and the genital organs is cautiously suggested by Marie Delcourt (1944, 207) in a reference to Louis Gernet: 'It seems that it is by contact with the knees and the genital organs that man gives the earth a hold over him.') Oedipus enters the nuptial chamber and sees Jocasta hanging:

> The King saw too, and with heart-rending groans
> Untied the rope, and laid her on the ground.
>
> (Sophocles, *King Oedipus*, 61)

We are brought back to the chthonian aspect:

> But worse was yet to see. Her dress was pinned
> With golden brooches, which the King snatched out.

We have seen Oedipus untie the knot that hid the body from others' eyes and, seizing these brooches,

> thrust, from full arm's length, into his eyes –

(a chthonian distancing)

Eyes that should see no longer his shame, his guilt,
No longer see those they should never have seen,
Nor see, unseeing, those he had longed to see.

'They', Oedipus' eyes, are at this moment snatched from his body like the brooches from Jocasta's clothes. They are the witnesses of a double evil:

Thus two have sinned; and on two heads, not one –
On man and wife – falls mingled punishment.

The Oedipus complex is the conjoint misfortune of man and woman. That is to say, it affects both the son and the mother: the son *qua* son of a dead father, and the mother in so far as she finds it difficult to resign herself to not recovering by means of coitus the product of her womb. It also means that it affects in each human being the man and the woman who coexist there.

The political solution defended by Vernant is expressed along lines in which the power of the oracle is restored. Vernant declares that the aim of the tragedy is to give us

a feeling of the contradictions that tear apart the divine world, the social and political universe, the domain of values, and thus to reveal man himself as a thauma or daimon, a sort of incomprehensible and confusing monster, both agent and acted upon, guilty and innocent, mastering all nature by his industrious mind, yet incapable of governing himself and blinded by a delusion sent by the gods.   (1972, 7)

The striking thing about this profound proposition is precisely that the revelation of man described in the second half of the sentence applies equally well to the description that our contemporaries give of him. That leads me to say that these characteristics are not the result of the conflicts and contradictions that Vernant describes in the first part of his sentence, but that the contradictions are the means of revealing man in this way. This mediation is inevitable in so far as the system of social representations or institutional forms are themselves the result of an attempt to resolve a contradiction, without revealing the conflict on which they are based. The contradiction is between the irreducibility of unconscious desire and that taming of drives which social life demands.

To say, as Marie Delcourt does, that the inscription of a ritual combat in the family survives when the modes of patrilinear heredity are legalized, that is to say, when there is no longer any question of succession through murder, is a sign that succession to wealth and fame is a compromise in, not the solution of, this conflict. The legends do not preserve a memory of lost institutions, as has been maintained. On the contrary, they recover what the institutions have succeeded in maintaining outside themselves. Quoting Frazer, Freud provides a formula concerning the laws of exogamy in its relation to the incest prohibition: 'They aimed at achieving the result they have in fact achieved' (*S.E.*, XIII, 121).

The expression 'conflict between the generations' is both too wide and too restricted. The reason for the suppression of incest, as opposed to the disguise of parricide, is that, faced with this silent absoluteness of the incest prohibition, no other arrangement is possible except by organizing the signifying system by exchange, which can, so to speak, only maintain the present. In itself the system has no determining value except in so far as it is based on the invocation of the dead father. The signifying outcome of the death of the father tries to fix the effacement of parricide, but it opens, with the category of the 'return', the ways by which the present as memory may also be the object of a process in which political modifications become forms of challenge.

Is not the reason for hesitation and difficulty in precisely situating the place of union with the mother to be found in the observation about the disjunction between liturgies possessing a social and political character and agrarian liturgies (Delcourt, 1944, xiv)? Whereas the first disappear early on, the link between the agrarian legends and their rituals remains close. It is this independence of the social and political that leads Hellenists, because they are more apt to perceive its changes, to make them the primary cause. One is more likely to grasp the forms of political transformations when a term of comparison is given, namely the modifications that have occurred in the reality of social life. But one then tends to shift interest away from what is offered by less overtly transformable material, more centred upon significations whose mystery is deeper because there are so few clues that enable one to dispel it. One then observes the strange fact that these themes of union with the mother appear in sets of signifiers that always present themselves in the form of the pun or the riddle.[11] Since Freud, we know that nothing is gratuitous in the ludic relations of the signifier, since these have the double function of satisfying desire and releasing tension in the unconscious. Or again the theme of incest enters the context of a system, often a dream system, in which the misleading portent is the most striking feature (Delcourt, 1944, 198).

Originally, the agrarian and chthonian rites have a dual nature, linking fecundation and the kingdom of the dead, just as riddles are equally concerned with sexual life and the world of the dead. Both, therefore, link the survivals of the incest prohibition (it is not for nothing that the archaic rites of periodicity represent periodicity in the form of incest between mother and son) and of the prohibition of parricide, the burial of the dead also acquiring the value of a feature distinctive between animality and humanity.

There is no need to look for any particular feelings of hostility in a parricide, says Marie Delcourt. The kinship relation itself is sufficient explanation. Every man is born of a person of the same sex and of a person of the opposite sex. He establishes difference by including himself in the couple that constitutes him and excludes him. He himself excludes the similar and mates with the Other. He couples, therefore he kills. I would agree with Marie Delcourt when she writes: 'The fact that despite their horror of parricide they should so often have represented a real hostility between the men of two generations shows what importance must have been attached to succession through murder in Greek prehistory' (1944, 81).

To make parricide and incest inseparable in the unity of the Oedipus complex, or more precisely in the desire phantasy that sustains it, is to say that parricide is so grave a crime that only the anticipated *jouissance* of incest can explain the jealousy that drives a man to murder his father, or that incest will so certainly involve the killing of the child through the father's resentment that the elimination of the father makes parricide necessary to the survival of the desirer.

What the desire phantasy omits is that the child who constructs this legendary day-dream is unaware that he is among those who no longer *are*.

> He cannot in any event
> Pretend that Laius died as was foretold.
> For Loxias said a child of mine should kill him.
> It was not to be; poor child, it was he that died.
>
> (Sophocles, *King Oedipus*, 49)

Jocasta, who a few moments earlier had said,

> Nor need this mother-marrying frighten you;
> Many a man has dreamt as much   (*King Oedipus*, 52),

is now saying: 'You did not sleep with your mother, since I was the wife of him whom you could not have killed because you were already dead.' (This is reminiscent of the celebrated 'he did not know that he was already dead', which Freud used for the theoretical development of a dream. Later, Lacan gave particular significance to this theme.)

The Sphinx and its riddles

Of all the episodes of the Oedipus myth, the most puzzling, the strangest, and therefore the one most likely to interest the psychoanalyst in search of what has escaped repression, is that of the

Sphinx. Marie Delcourt stresses two points. The Sphinx, she says, has a double reality: the first, the oppressive nightmare, is of a physiological order; the second, the belief in souls represented with wings, is of a religious order. A synthesis would merge the oppressive Sphinx and the psychical Sphinx. This clue is a very valuable one: it will enable us to recognize in this figure a product of condensation and displacement.

The oppressive nightmare expresses the anxiety in the dreamer, who feels himself to be in the grip of a being who is crushing and squeezing him. These dreams, which are common during psychoanalysis, are frequently linked to an impression of being stifled by the mother. One intuits beneath the fear the erotic quality of such a relation. Indeed, Marie Delcourt finds this among the characteristics of the spirits of the dead, 'thirsty for blood and erotic pleasure', as the tradition says vampires are.

The abundant documentation gathered by the author from the plastic arts (Delcourt, 1944, 119–26) proves beyond doubt the sexual character of the relation to the Sphinx. Personally, I do not see any need to set aside the hypothesis of murderous aggression in order to preserve that of the erotic relation. Phantasies frequently show the disguise of one by the other, or their association in a form in which aggressiveness and eroticism are linked, as is frequently the case in the relation to the imago of the phallic mother. In shape, the Sphinx is a composite creature with some feminine attributes and some masculine attributes deriving from its Egyptian origin. In any case, the important thing is the collusion of these monsters with the world of the dead,[12] which leads us to believe that here again we must seek, through the oblique mode of the riddle, an initiate's knowledge of certain mysteries and, behind the trial, an ordeal, as in the preceding episodes of the myth. But is it not possible, for us who know the legend in its entirety, to deduce from that knowledge that the episode of the Sphinx, situated after the murder of the father and before the union with the mother, condenses these two events? It evokes the return of the murdered father, who torments the son through the nightmare, wandering through the underworld, in search of life so as to return to earth. (An additional proof of the presence of the father in the Sphinx is the variant, in a version related by Pausanias, in which the Sphinx is an illegitimate daughter of Laius, and in his service.) As for the union with the mother, it suggests the erotic relation imbued with the dangers that lie in wait for the child from the fact of being under the spell of the mother, on to whom he projects all the desire for pleasure that he expects after the elimination of the father. It is, therefore, a figure of condensation, as we have seen, but it is also a displaced figure because it is situated between parricide and incest. It is also a phantasy, which is expressed through the realization of desire: the conquest of paternal power, which the ghost abandons at daybreak. The submission of the dangerous mother, possessed at last, enables the son to free himself, with the coming of day, and to marry the princess. 'In modern Greek tales,' says Marie Delcourt, 'Oedipus marries the Sphinx, who is really the same character as the mother' (1944, 131). This is a case of scission from the maternal imago that becomes more frequent as one digs back towards the archaic roots of the Oedipus complex.

We still have to specify the essential nature of the monster, that is to say, its questionable nature, the spiritual character of the trial. It is easy to agree with Marie Delcourt when she declares that the primitive content of the legend had to be represented in this respect by a physical combat and not by an intellectual exchange. To point out the taste of the Greek people for riddles and to recall, in other legendary contexts, the theme of the pun followed by a terrible punishment is to make the need for a precise answer more urgent: even if we are brought back once again to initiation ritual. We are getting close when the author relates the solution of the riddles to the conquest of a royal betrothed, the nuptial riddles always having the character of a recourse to the intelligence, that is to say, to the solutions offered by intellectual curiosity, itself produced by sexual curiosity. 'At the festival of the Agrionies, at Chaeronea, the women pursued Dionysus, then gave up, saying that he had gone to hide himself among the Muses; then, after the banquet, they asked each other riddles' (Delcourt, 1955, 104). The term 'initiation' is used of the sexual life of the child, who at a certain age learns the secret of things the adults hid from him and which he had to imagine, that is to say, guess. We can, it is true, see the riddle as a pedagogical device, but this is superficial, except in the sense that pedagogy is the socialization of enigmatic desire.

What interests me in the myth transformed into tragedy is precisely the prime place occupied by the riddle – the solved riddle of the Sphinx and the riddle concealed from the investigation. Certain mythologists find the legend of Oedipus, in this form, too intellectual; it still has to be explained why it developed in this way – in the sense not only of an intellectualization of the legend, but also of an essentialization, that is, a reduction to the essential. Here extreme disguise coincides with extreme truth. It is because sexuality is a riddle that the riddle is also a faithful trace of sexual origin. And this dialogue with the Sphinx, limited to an exchange of questions and answers, is perhaps in itself more erotic than the most suggestive representations of actual sexual union. It is really too naïve to believe that the version of the riddle is an impoverished version of others that gave a combat between monster and hero. It is easy enough to intuit the place of sexuality in this too obvious displacement; it loses its opacity. The fact that the stress is placed on human mystery, where the answer to be given concerns the identity of the questioned and not that of the questioner, forces us to think that the questioner cannot be unrelated to the sexual since she speaks of the limits of the human.[13]

The Sphinx herself is a riddle, in her very nature, even more than in the questions she asks. Her fabulous existence casts a spell on us that almost prevents our grasping that the answer concerns the person to whom the question is addressed. Her composite morphology is a labyrinthine approach to the identity that is to be attributed to her. Her transformation into sculptural forms turns her into a young female incubus, 'that is, a female being who approaches a man in order to lie upon him' (Delcourt, 1955, 118). In classical poetry, she is a 'knowing virgin', and in folk tales about nightmares, which are much later and are to be found in the more remote parts of Greece, she is an old woman. These three aspects inevitably suggest a correspondence with the triple state of man in Oedipus' answer. She is, therefore, a monster, but a tripartite monster: a bird by her wings, a lioness by her body, a snake by her tail. This tripartite division is like the progressive stages of difficulty in a proof; she represents the ultimate point and the moment of the hero's victory. This is seen in a number of legendary contexts. Georges Dumézil has made an illuminating analysis of them.[14]

Between the stages of the trial there is a crossing, a frontier between the world of the living and the invisible, passing through a domain of death. Dumézil notes that, confronted with this tri-formed adversary, the hero is himself a third: 'The third of three brothers, with the peculiarity that his two elder brothers were unsuccessful sketches of himself' (Dumézil, 39). Oedipus is an only son, presumed to be malformed. But Oedipus is also the third and last to hold a power that he shares with Creon and Jocasta. We should not assume that the last two merely have the function of transmitting this power, for this is in contradiction with the authority openly assumed by Jocasta at certain moments of the tragedy. Turning back to the tripartite monster, we may find what eludes signification here. The representation of the Sphinx places the snake in the tail that completes the monster's body. But classical art shows that it is the snake's head that is represented at this place (Delcourt, 1955, 138). The mark of Oedipus' wound was in his heels; his head was both the instrument of his victory and the cause of his perdition.

It becomes clear that the whole tragedy of Oedipus is centred on his role as decipherer of riddles (the thing he prides himself on being); on the false signs given as true signs; on the true signs that seem inconceivable; on this confrontation between the shrewd man and the soothsayer; between the interpreter of the singer and the interpreter of the oracle; between the messenger of death and the shepherd of oblivion.

What the legend tells us is that the myth of Oedipus is a rare case in which the solving of the riddle does not end in the happy reign of the hero (Delcourt, 1955, 152). The case of Oedipus, then, is an exemplum of the power of the signifier to be both instrument of power and, through the deception inherent in it, a cause of misfortune and blindness.

Marie Delcourt is convinced that 'the self-blinding of Oedipus is a Sophoclean invention'. She insists on the fact that, in the whole of Greek poetry it is 'an absolutely unique case of voluntary mutilation' (1955, 215). Oedipus' blindness is a theme on which there is much to be said. (Marie Delcourt refers to textual variants in which the blinding of Oedipus is carried out by his parents – Laius, Jocasta or Polybus.) There is the explanation supplied by Oedipus himself, that he cannot bear the sight of his mother and his father in Hades. There is the punishment for violating an optical taboo:

> No longer see those they should never have seen,
> Nor see, unseeing, those he had longed to see.
>
> (Sophocles, *King Oedipus*, 61)

There is the access to a true inner knowledge after exhausting himself in deciphering fallacious riddles. There is the equivalent of castration. But, above all perhaps, there is the punishment of the eyes that have misled. Oedipus punishes himself for having misled himself. He has been a victim of the god's deception. He has made sinister puns on his kinship relations:

> Incestuous sin! Breeding where I was bred!
> Father, brother, and son; bride, wife, and mother;
> Confounded in one monstrous matrimony!
> All human filthiness in one crime compounded!
>
> (Sophocles, *King Oedipus*, 64)

It is around this deception in the signifier that the ways of knowledge and truth are set up in opposition.

III

Truth and *méconnaissance*

If myth had a pedagogical function, as certain mythologists believe, it would be right to ask oneself whether this was not also the case with tragedy – especially the tragedy of Oedipus, whose entire problematic revolves around the desire to know, and ends with a blinding – the blinding of the hero who does not know how to decipher his first and last riddle. He is blind to the signifier, blinded by the signifier. This essential tragedy has puzzled many minds, reflecting on the essence of the tragedy, and on the question of the riddles that Oedipus takes so long to understand – he, the decipherer of riddles. The prosecution of the enquiry itself should have en-lightened Oedipus much sooner. What strikes one is his inability to bring the concordant clues together. One has only to refer to the text to realize that the details that enable Oedipus to think he is not implicated are slight indeed. There is a moment when every decep-tive gloss must be discarded; it is when the situation enables him to realize that absolutely complementary oracles – oracles that could be said to fit into one another – concern Laius' offspring and the destiny of Oedipus. In the face of this strange concordance, the rest is mere quibbling, above all after Teiresias' prophecy. What are we to say about this?

In this tragedy Sophocles shows us, it is commonly said – what-ever sin of pride is imputed to Oedipus, whose self-importance, not to say megalomania, is obvious enough – the ineluctable fulfilment of the oracles which determine before birth the fate of every man. If we go no further than that, the lesson would indeed be brief and banal. To attack the desire to know would be to fall into an advocacy of obscurantism. Where does the greatness of the tragedy lie?

Freud was right to see the effects of the tragedy in the identifica-tion – the recognition that Aristotle speaks of – that each spectator experiences, seeing in Oedipus, so far as repression allows it, the child he once was. But this judgement – revealing and prophetic at the time when Freud made it – is capable of development. There is in *King Oedipus* a double way of knowledge and truth. (This distinc-tion between knowledge and truth has been well brought out by Lacan, far beyond the indications implicit in the Freudian context.) There is the way of knowledge, the way followed by the investiga-tion. Oedipus seeks material evidence of the crime, then material evidence of the exposure on Cithaeron. But this evidence only brings him cruel, but expected, proof. I would say of this proof that it is not strictly speaking a tragic agent. On the other hand Teiresias, Jocasta and the Messenger from Corinth are bearers of revelations. Teiresias, compelled to point to the guilty one, points to the execu-tioner. Jocasta, wishing to appease Oedipus, tells him about Laius' oracle, the exposure of the child in Cithaeron and the place of the crime: a fork at the meeting of the roads to Delphi and Daulis. This is more than is needed to feel the wind of the wing of destiny. Last, the Messenger brings the happy news of Polybus' death, which exculpates Oedipus, since he has nothing to do with that death.

Believing he is doing what is needed to exculpate him completely, the Messenger goes on to tell him that he is not the son of the King of Corinth, and that he found him as an infant on Cithaeron. Sophocles' power is in mixing the lessons of knowledge and truth as if they were caught up in the same web. Such are the ways of truth that it is encountered where it is neither expected nor desired.

The tragedy brings us face to face with the ineluctability of the oracle. This ineluctability has been displaced on to the punishment, whereas in truth it bears on the offence. This is the meaning of the leap from Aeschylus to Sophocles, for in Aeschylus, what is punished is a violation of the prohibition to procreate. What we are concerned with, then, is the ineluctability of the parricide and incest, the ineluctability of the desire for the death of the father and for *jouissance* with the mother. Oedipus is the man who thought he could escape it through knowledge. The question is not how he could have escaped it, but that he should have wished to. This should have made him extremely wary of any situation that would have brought him into conflict with a man of age to be his father and of any sexual relations with a woman of age to be his mother. This is precisely what he forgot in each of the two situations. And here the ineluctability of the parricide and incest is to be found, for they correspond, not with the fulfilment of the oracle, but with the fulfilment of the hero's desire. This ineluctability is accompanied by the double meanings of the signifier, that force him to curse his clear-sightedness when he falls into his own traps.

> He strode among us. 'A sword, a sword!' he cried;
> 'Where is that wife, no wife of mine – that soil
> Where I was sown, and whence I reaped my harvest!'
>
> (Sophocles, *King Oedipus*, 60)

A woman who is and is not a woman, who is and is not a mother, children who are and who are not children – the Sphinx certainly has a fine subject for a riddle there.

The fatality of incest and parricide through the deception of the signifier does not by itself give the true meaning. One must add interdependently the ineluctability of *méconnaissance*. One must not seek for plausible motives for Oedipus' strange deafness to the concordant set of reasons that make him the guilty party, but attribute it to *méconnaissance* – *méconnaissance* of what lives in him apart, which lies at the origin of the acts of which he is accused; and a return of *méconnaissance* when confronted with the pile of evidence.

The criticism that I make too ready recourse to hypothesis can be based only on what the text says *en clair*. But this is not where the problem lies. Our attention is solicited when it stumbles over what seems inexplicable: the paralysis of the ability to make sense of things and the failure to carry out the oracular prescription at the end of the tragedy. We shall decide after consulting the gods – as if they had not already spoken.

The tragedy bears on the ineluctability of the oracle and the *méconnaissance* of the ineluctability of the realization of desires. The ineluctability of the oracle is bound up with the value of religious practice. This reveals the continuity between ancient rites and the oracle. Ritual practice serves to determine the forms of the formulation of a desire, the rite fixing the conditions of possibility of the realization of the desire. In the rite, obligation is limited to an observance of forms to be respected. In the oracle, this obligation becomes an obligation to subject oneself to its judgement. The oracular answer is transformed into a determining prediction. In the case of Oedipus, this prediction bears on acts that the hero has performed in desire, whereas in the usual votive practices, the expected act comes from the gods, who by their intervention provide the solution to a problem.

The oracle has here, therefore, a retrospective value, not about what is to be done by the gods, but about what has already been done by the hero. In the case of Oedipus, the oracle is a prediction of the past. The answer to Oedipus' question 'Who am I and what must I do?' is, 'You will be a parricide and commit incest. This is ineluctable because you have already been a parricide and committed incest, therefore you are a parricide and a committer of incest.'

To say that the act performed by Oedipus reveals 'its true meaning after the event, turns back upon the agent, throws light on his nature, uncovers what he is, what he has really done without knowing it' (Vernant, 1972, 6), is either covered by the fatality of the oracle, or must be reconciled with what Oedipus does not know about his relation to the unexpressed wish. The tragedy hints at such a wish in the cessation of the activity that has hitherto sufficed to reveal Oedipus to himself – the deciphering of riddles. The ineluctability of *méconnaissance* is therefore not only the mark of an existential misfortune; it is rooted in the recall of the acts that are the subject of a question that was intended as a pure question, asked by the man whose charisma it was to be able to answer them without anyone's help.[15]

Here the psycho-analyst has only to turn to his own experience. He rediscovers in Oedipus' *méconnaissance* the same concealment of the truth that is to be found in the case of the neurotic, who also wishes to know but, although he brings with him – displayed for all to see – the clearest signs that ought to open his eyes, remains stricken blind, deaf and dumb. Does not Oedipus, after blinding himself, regret that he cannot also make himself deaf?

> No! Hearing neither! Had I any way
> To damn that channel too, I would not rest
> Till I had prisoned up this body of shame
> In total blankness.   (Sophocles, *King Oedipus*, 64)

What Freud says is not that Oedipus is a neurotic, but that between the neurotic and us Oedipus stands as our common 'unthought'. Thus the spectator not only has before him the spectacle of the repetition of parricide and incest; he also lives through the repetition of their *méconnaissance*. He may enjoy the spectacle and be purged by it as he weeps over the sad destiny of the Other; this Other operates the safety-valve which 'lets off steam', to use Freud's own words, all the more easily in that he feels he is called to undergo the destiny of a life in which nothing important happens, whereas the acting out of the tragedy is evidence of its importance through the repetition that it reproduces of the acting out of life.

If my hypothesis concerns truth and not knowledge, then the fortune of this tragedy can be explained. The wonder it arouses would appear to be based on its ability to mask its value as truth by its aesthetic value. This homage is also paid to *méconnaissance*, since its most fervent admirers are certainly not those who also recognize the truth of Freudian psycho-analysis. Oedipus' first words to the people of Cadmus are most revealing:

> What is the matter? Some fear? Something you desire?
>   (Sophocles, *King Oedipus*, 25)

Hölderlin: drunken knowledge and the god–man coupling

In a text as illuminating in its beauty as it is worthy of its subject, Hölderlin speaks of the tragedy of Oedipus. Approaching the subject in what would now be called a structural way, he says of works of art: 'Up to now they have been judged not so much by the impression they make as by a calculation of their status and the other means by which the beautiful is produced' (*Anmerkungen zum Oedipus*). Is not the calculation of the status of the work and above all of its effects what Freud intended when he discovered the cause of the impression rather than just allowing himself to experience it passively? And is it not also what Hölderlin meant when he noted the point at which the caesura fell in the rhythmic sequence which in *Oedipus* occurs near the beginning in the progressive structure of the work: the point of balance moving therefore from the end to the beginning, while the reverse is the case in *Antigone*?

Hölderlin situates this caesura in the words of Teiresias, designating the place of the god and the place of time. If we consider the sequence formed by *césure*, *cassure* (break), *coupure* (cut), *castration*, we find that it is here that the development of time is presented to us, since Oedipus, at the end of the tragedy, will prefer the blindness of Teiresias the soothsayer to the clear-sightedness of the decipherer of riddles that he was himself. What does this clear-sightedness signify? Hölderlin says: 'Oedipus interprets the words of the oracle too infinitely...He is tempted in the direction of the illicit.' Oedipus' anger against Teiresias is that of a 'drunken' knowledge. How better can one describe the fact that knowledge is desire and *jouissance*, given that Oedipus 'first incited himself to know more than he could bear or contain'? The blinding, then, is here a renunciation of this *jouissance*, of this excitement, in order to attempt to reach what will be the Colonus stage, that of truthful knowledge. Why does he feel this desire, this *jouissance*? Because this knowledge is destined to satisfy a good conscience. Since Oedipus as soothsayer is the equal if not the superior, he thinks, of Teiresias, then the investigation must prove the prophecy wrong, producing at the same time the denial of a wish to fight a father (Polybus as well as Laius), but also realizing it by weakening the prophetic power of the soothsayer. One sees how the tragic issue is that of a struggle between Oedipus and Teiresias and, by this means, between Oedipus and the god. In a brilliant phrase, Hölderlin speaks of a coupling of god and man, followed by their separation.

Here joining and cut, conjunction and disjunction, are terms equivalent to those in which the figures of Eros and the death drive are revealed.

It is on the basis of a power, therefore, the power that makes Oedipus the son of Fortune, that he will be united with the god, becoming more god than the god himself. And Hölderlin writes: 'Everything is discourse against discourse, each giving place to the other.' The outcome is this separation, this categorical turning away from the god, in which Jean Beaufret hears a Kantian echo. Man's volte-face brings him face to face with the irreversible, time that no longer authorizes bestriding the generations, the pun on kinship relations, the accumulation of powers that leads Oedipus to his mother's bed and to his father's throne. This reciprocal infidelity is the mark of the human condition. The locus of truth is simply time and not the deceiving word. The major signifier is that revealed by the signifier of separation: in other words, to use the Freudian term, the death drive. That Oedipus should interpret things in too unrestrained a way is the mark of the excessive pride that must meet its limit. But parricide and incest can be given only in the context of this 'too much to interpret', in that which signifies them as transgression. For their limit is not that from which one may set out and go forward, but that point to which one returns, yet which is not the same as that from which one set out. This point can be subjected to no interpretation, but founds the interpretations that derive from it. These interpretations come up against this limit and diffuse elsewhere – in an elsewhere that gathers up the excess never abolished, never contained, that the temptation to transgress that limit calls for and which is satisfied only in the illicit. But this is the difficulty that we will have to confront: a ground that eludes any definite interpretation, a nebula that refers back to an indefinitely renewed question. What we have here is not so much an infinity of discourse or its limit as a category of thought – to be thought – that psycho-analysis has perhaps helped to elucidate.

Hölderlin's analysis is profound because it unites in a single logic – the word is his own – the semantics of the work and its syntax. The caesura is the expression of conflict, it is 'antirhythmic suspension', a figure of the orientation of the tragic dynamism, of the force and counter-force that share its field. From this opposition is born not only the conflict of representations, but representation itself: 'Pure speech, antirhythmic suspension, becomes necessary if one is to encounter as an uprooting the change and exchange of representations at such a level that it is then no longer the change of representations, but representation itself that appears.' This admirable formula is inscribed in a movement of analytic thought.

This final image in which god and man meet back to back, separate, each unfaithful to the other, each 'finding himself' in this rupture, is one of the profoundest statements ever made about tragedy. For from this separation is born the regulation of the god/man conflict in man himself, which is apprehended in this opposition. The state of the confident independent mind or free spirit gives way before the strength of the spirit which is contradiction; spirit becomes spirit of the world of the dead.

When representation itself appears, it can no longer therefore be anything but the representation of the death of the hero. The absence of the god, his silence in respect of Oedipus, who communicates with him only through intermediaries, is matched by the absence of the hero's death, which was nevertheless demanded by the god. The mutilation that anticipates punishment takes its place. For this polysemy of the signifier, which I have hitherto insisted on, assumes its meaning only to emerge in the outcome of the tragedy, the death or castration of the hero, which distinguishes it from the comic.

As in tragedy, the polysemy of the signifier operates in comedy to a profound degree, but the outcome is different. Everything sorts itself out and the worst is not always inevitable, as in Claudel's formula. Eros wins, life will go on. In this respect, Plautus' *Amphitryon* is in a sense the model of anti-tragic comedy.

The god–man coupling of which Hölderlin speaks is realized here almost literally through the mediation of Alcmene. And Amphitryon, cuckolded and content, smilingly accepts Hercules as his son. A classic theme of adultery condoned by the husband! And yet, what a topic for a tragedy! Or almost. All that is needed is for Amphitryon to refuse Zeus' duplicity and punish his wife for protesting against the iniquity of the god who makes a fool of a victorious general with a right to be treated like a hero. But no, Eros triumphs and the chubby Hercules who is born of this union is certainly a child of love, happy and powerful. The temptation of the illicit is the culmination of the polysemy of the signifier that strikes Oedipus down like a blasted tree. 'The tragic speech of the Greeks is brutally murderous,' says Hölderlin, 'because the body that it grasps really kills.' But it also kills more insidiously, more slowly; it may be more bruising (*meurtrissante*) than deadly (*meurtrière*), according to a concept found further west. A certain opposition may now be made between the native Greek and the western concept. 'Mental return' becomes a return to the origins, memory. Conflictual memory between the excessively formal and the native informal: 'The unformed bursts into flame on contact with what is too formal.' We find this struggle again between languages of different origin, provenance and date, between differently structured modes of speech. But the primary Logos constantly reasserts its rights against the more reasoning, more reasonable secondary mode.

In his fine preface to the French edition of the *Anmerkungen*, Beaufret shows that, in this confrontation of languages, the traditional opposition between Dionysus and Apollo is not taken by Hölderlin in the usual way. Apollo, like Dionysus, is a figure of fire, as virile a force as that of the Bacchic god, as 'oriental' a figure. That is to say, Apollo has the same spiritual origin as the rituals of Thrace and Phrygia. Speech is tumultuous, just as tumult speaks. The native, the indigenous, the original are constantly covered over by what one might call, in cultural matters, the secondary. What Hölderlin makes us consider is the link between native memory and the turning away that springs from the coupling. Separation from the god is a condition of representation in so far as representation is absent representation: 'The god is present in the figure of death.'

Once again I must turn to psycho-analysis – not only in this desire to know, without which there can be no analysis, any more than there can be without a love of truth, but also in the categorical turning away from the analyst that the analysand experiences. A comparison between the analyst and God may cause a smile, but it was the analysands who first made it – just as they produced their phantasy of coupling with him. The analysand must accept responsibility for this categorical turning away, so that the analysis may proceed, so that the interrogation of the signifier, the testing of polysemy and the advent of difference, like the difference between the sexes, may come into play. The analysand's volte-face is the analysis that follows after the desire to seduce the analyst, to circumvent him, to castrate him. The analysis becomes a tragedy of postponed death. Time is the grand master of analysis: it makes the analysand an apostate, a traitor to his analyst, since he will one day leave him, as one leaves father and mother.

Hölderlin's reflection on tragedy, based on Oedipus and Antigone, is among the most profound that we have; there is little to add to it, despite Hegel, Nietzsche and Heidegger. Like Karl Reinhardt, Heidegger sees *King Oedipus* as an exemplary tragedy, as the tragedy of appearance, and as an illustration of the relation between being and appearance. He sees Oedipus as a great questioner, as essentially a metaphysician.

How can we accept a thesis that moves so far from Hölderlin, more indeed than is intended? If *King Oedipus* is the tragedy *par excellence* the fundamental question is, why is this unremitting, relentless questioning, this passion for knowledge, so indissolubly linked with parricide and incest? Outside these realms, the rest is mere displacement of the question. Why is this unveiling of the latent of which Heidegger speaks the murder of the father and coitus with the mother? Must we admire the work and close our eyes and ears to this content or regard it as trivial? Is the tragedy of Oedipus itself an accident, a simple misunderstanding? It may well be that the destiny of this tragedy is one of misunderstanding, just as misunderstanding gave birth to it. The view that one may admire it for its formal qualities, that one may feel pity for Oedipus, purge oneself of one's crimes and nevertheless consider that the parricide and incest are the result of misfortune, is one that has survived a long time and, despite Freud, still holds its own.

It is precisely what Oedipus himself declares long after the discovery of his crime, in the wood of Colonus. To the chorus he says, I struck, I killed, without knowing:

Was I the sinner?
Repaying wrong for wrong – that was no sin,
Even were it wittingly done, as it was not.

(Sophocles, *Oedipus at Colonus*, 79)

Then to Creon he says:

I am not condemned,
And shall not be, either for my marrying
Or for my father's murder. . .
Such, by the gods' contrivance, was my case.

(*Oedipus at Colonus*, 101–2)

Then to Polynices he says:

They are my sons; you are some other man's.

(*Oedipus at Colonus*, 113)

A classic statement of disavowal![16] For, if it is the truth, why has Oedipus blinded himself? Death is pushed back into the distance, and with life disavowal returns.

Thus each of us is an Oedipus according to Freud, not only because each of us has committed parricide and incest – in desire, if not in act – but also by our fierce determination to deny it after childhood. Each of us and our whole western civilization, which wants to see in Sophocles' Oedipus only the representation of an exceptional destiny.

IV

Freud's eye too many: the Oedipus complex

So Hölderlin is closer to the truth than many of our contemporaries who have the benefit of knowledge derived from Freudian theory. This is no doubt because he was both poet and psychotic and had posed the 'question of the father'[17] in a tragic sense. Oedipus, Hölderlin and Freud all had 'an eye too many'. Yet each of us lives from his own centre of vision what is hidden from other men's eyes. Each of us undergoes a different destiny after it has been given him to see. Oedipus blinded himself, Hölderlin sank into madness, Freud discovered the unconscious. Oedipus and Freud both brought the plague with them. For the ancient world, the misfortune that came from the gods required a guilty man and a radical punishment, a ritual exclusion. In our civilization, one fights epidemics in a different way.

Thus, ever since Freud brought the plague upon us, we have set about vaccinating ourselves. Psycho-analysts were the first to do this, by blunting the Freudian message and diminishing its difference

from other discourses. The public followed, by putting into circulation an inoffensive image of psycho-analysis and the psycho-
analyst that sought to limit all that was disturbing or scandalous in
the revelation of the unconscious. The theorists of culture have
played a considerable part in this development. We have seen how,
confronted by the myth of Oedipus, three contemporary specialists
were unable to take cognizance of the epistemological break operated
by Freud's discourse. Marie Delcourt opted – though her conclusions
are not absolutely clear on this point – for the Adlerian thesis of the
conflict between the generations. In the name of historical psychology
J.-P. Vernant, who has links with the sociological psychology of
Marxism, restricted the scope of the myth to the state of fifth-
century Athenian society. Lévi-Strauss, though he claims allegiance
to Marx and Freud, submerges Freudian theory in the combinatory
of all the versions of the myth, from a viewpoint that is entirely
formalist in character. (In the table that Lévi-Strauss puts forward
(1968, 214) as a way of breaking down the myth, all the relations
studied are dual, with the exception of the initial proposition, which
contains within itself the whole complex: 'Cadmus seeks his sister
Europa, ravished by Zeus.' The reduction, however far it may be
taken, may then be understood as an undertaking intended to wipe
out this initial triangulation.) To invoke the primacy of Freud's
interpretation is merely to rediscover what Lévi-Strauss affirms
when he writes of the myth: 'Its substance does not lie in its style,
its original music, or its syntax, but in the *story* which it tells. Myth
is language, functioning on an especially high level where meaning
succeeds practically in "taking off" from the linguistic ground on
which it started by taxying' (1968, 210).

For Freud, there is no doubt about the non-temporality of the
Oedipus complex, since for him the myth of the primal horde is a
reality, and not just a hypothesis.

To find the starting-point for the psycho-analytic view of religious life we
must go a step further. What is today the heritage of the individual was
once a new acquisition and has been handed on from one to another of a
long series of generations. Thus the Oedipus complex too may have had
stages of development, and the study of prehistory may enable us to trace
them out. Investigation suggests that life in the human family took a quite
different form in those remote days from that with which we are now
familiar. And this idea is supported by findings based on observations of
contemporary primitive races. If the prehistoric and ethnological material
on this subject is worked over psycho-analytically, we arrive at an unexpectedly precise result: namely, that God the Father once walked upon
earth in bodily form and exercised his sovereignty as chieftain of the
primal human horde until his sons united to slay him. It emerges further

that the crime of liberation and the reactions to it had as their result the appearance of the first social ties, the basic moral restrictions and the oldest form of religion, totemism. But the later religions too have the same content, and on the one hand they are concerned with obliterating the traces of that crime or with expiating it by bringing forward other solutions or the struggle between the father and sons, while on the other hand they cannot avoid repeating once more the elimination of the father. Incidentally, an echo of this monstrous event, which overshadowed the whole course of human development, is also to be found in myths.

(Freud, *S.E.*, xvii, 262)

Many people, psycho-analysts among them, would now challenge these statements. Others would reply that this hypothesis should be interpreted as a collective desire phantasy, whose evocative power is such that it acquires a reality value. What we are confronted with here is one of those primary phantasies that for Freud have a structuring role in the social imaginary.[18] However, although one may insist on 'dating' the Oedipus complex – and Freud is not opposed to this *a priori*, since he supposes that this complex had a history and even stages of development – its origin cannot be localized at a particular point in time. As soon as there was a family, there was the Oedipus complex. As long as there is a family, there will be an Oedipus complex. This does not mean that modifications were not brought to it at various periods in history or that social systems did not influence the form it took. But one may well have reservations concerning this relativist attitude. The determining factors that affect the complex are of two kinds. The first are primary; they derive from the prematuration of the infant and its dependence on its parents, which is a biological and social fact. The others are secondary; they depend on the way in which the images of maternal and paternal identification are transmitted and on the way in which the parental roles are assumed by those who perform them in a given culture and period. It is easy to understand, then, that only the secondary determinations are susceptible to the influence of time, or the historico-social context. This is not to deny their importance. These modifications play a fundamental role at the level of the formation of ego-ideals. But the constituents of the complex – the opposition of Eros and the destructive drives, psychical bisexuality, the duality of the pleasure and reality principles, the tension between desire and identification – derive from the primary determinations. Their structuring makes the Oedipus complex a symbolic system. This structuring is the primary nucleus articulated according to an unconscious logic that the entire secondarization will envelop: obeying, in part, a conscious logic.

One can see, then, that we are led directly to answer the other question, that of the universality of the Oedipus complex. This universality is inevitable as long as the prohibition of incest and parricide remains in force. Lévi-Strauss himself stressed the exceptional value of the prohibition of incest: it is the rule among rules.

It constitutes a rule, but a rule which, alone among all the social rules, possesses at the same time a universal character...The prohibition of incest is in origin neither purely cultural nor purely natural, nor is it a composite mixture of elements from nature and culture. It is the fundamental step because of which, by which, but above all in which, the transition from nature to culture is accomplished. In one sense, it belongs to nature, for it is a general condition of nature. Consequently, we should not be surprised that its formal characteristic, universality, has been taken from nature. However, in another sense, it is already culture, exercising and imposing its rule on phenomena which are initially not subject to it... The prohibition of incest is the link between them.

(Lévi-Strauss, 1969, 8–9 and 24–5)

We know that Lévi-Strauss later revised his view of the absolute character of this distinction between nature and culture. This change of direction involved moving the rule towards the laws of transmission of the genetic code (DNA), therefore towards biological heredity rather than social institutions. It should be recalled that as early as 1936 Lacan proposed the term 'social heredity'.

If I constantly come back to the incest prohibition, it is in order to stress its strange, its extraordinary, its absolute character. For one can ground it neither in the danger of consanguinity – a naïve and false hypothesis – nor in the preservation of a combinatory system that requires exchange. In the first case, mankind is credited with a proleptic but doubtful power of scientific observation; in the second, it is endowed with a state of mind similar to that of players in a game. The game can be set out as a list of rules like a logical calculus, but it is first of all a search for pleasure: to the point of ruin and suicide.

What then are we to make of the transgression of this prohibition? The case of Oedipus shows us better than any other. The whole tragedy unfolds like a ritual exclusion. The whole ritual of the tragedy is linked here with the rite from which the tragedy sprang. At the end of the tragedy, Oedipus blinds himself, in the very way that boys subjected to initiation undergo the ordeal only after a greater or lesser degree of mutilation, whose symbolic value is essential. The ritual of initiation is, in tragedy, reduced to participation in the spectacle.[19] This spectacle narrates the exclusion of a man who transgressed the prohibitions, but it also cements the unity of the members of the city through their common participation in a ceremony.

The initiation ritual is one of the oldest forms of institutionalization. It marks the child's entry into the world of sexed beings, through a symbolic castration. The link that binds the members of the community is no longer consanguinity, but shared ritual experience. As George Thomson says, it is no longer birth that qualifies the human being, but rebirth. This rebirth derives its value by representing a coincidence between the symbolic death of the child and the resurrection of the dead ancestor: the father of the father. The ritual signifier is thus put in the place of the dead father. It communicates death and the unveiling of a secret code. It signals the existence of a debt to the ancestor whom it brings back to life and promises everyone a new birth after his death. The inauguration of sex is the mediation that permits this passage, the instrument of generation serving to establish the descent of the child from the father of the father or from the dead father. The extra life accorded the ancestor is invested in the signifying system that permits its celebration. The absence of the dead father becomes a consecrated absence, the seed of all religions. Castration is the counterpart of this extra life. It is also the mark made on the subject for having to remember his death and the limits imposed on his *jouissance*. The signifying system has repressed the 'naturalness' of life, and sexuality has forged its link with death.

In fact, nature is not rejected, but invested by the signifying system. For the rituals of human death are closely bound up with the agrarian rituals of the death and rebirth of vegetation. Winter and old age are put to death by renewal, by the spring of puberty. (Oedipus and Dionysus are cousins, let us not forget, both descendants of Cadmus, who killed the dragon. Both are unwanted children, whose survival is miraculous; both are persecuted. It is remarkable that Dionysus should be the only god who is a suffering god.) We meet incest once again. We also find, behind these agrarian rituals with the earth, the mother, excluded from initiation ceremonies that definitively sever the bond between mother and child.

Thus the image of the mother is linked with the agrarian rituals through the correspondence between sexual union and natural fecundity; the image of the father is bound up with the memory of the ancestor and death. On the one hand we have exogamy and on the other totemism. But both must be constantly reaffirmed, scrupulously observed, indefinitely repeated so as not to allow the desire that transgresses the prohibitions to emerge. According to Thomson, a quasi-universal feature of the ancestral ritual celebrations is the production of a sort of drama in which the actors personify the ancestor, often in a totemic form. Tragedy sprang from these sacred ceremonies, in which indeed the epic and the satyric were joined.

One cannot forget that the sacred, which is the implicit aim of the tragic, is not, in Freudian theory, a primary reference, or an ultimate one, as some people say, but is itself the memory, the recall of an act that it commemorates, the murder of the primal father. The sacred as the fundamental expression of the religious is inseparable from the prohibition that establishes a particular category of objects to which sexual reverence is due because in them the presence of the dead man is signified. The dead man is given once more the power that death took away, a power to which homage must be paid in order to obviate any possible hostile act of revenge on his part. It is a projection on to the dead man of the hostility that motivated his extermination *qua* prohibitor of *jouissance*.

Tragedy may make a double use of this mythical event. Either it repeats it, attributing the punishment of the hero, who represents the father here, to an act of revenge on the part of the gods – the sons purifying themselves of the pollution of the crime by the tribute they pay to these invincible powers who know no mortal limitation to their pleasure. Or, reversing this situation, tragedy allows people to witness the impossible replacement of a father by a son, the first occupying the place of the gods, while the second is represented by the figure of the hero, whose past and present deeds lead to the tragic catastrophe. In both cases, the *jouissance* derived from the spectacle undergoes a masochistic turning round, as Freud stressed in his article, 'Psychopathic Characters on the Stage' (*S.E.*, VII, 306). For in all these cases, identification is with the hero and not with the gods.

That the catastrophe can be made an object of *jouissance* testifies to the supremacy of the pleasure principle, which is capable of a curious triumph over pain, disappointment or the non-satisfaction of desires, and the aim thus attained is not an insignificant result. But it is also a question of giving every opportunity for the projected realization on the stage of phantasies of grandeur, through the possible identification of the spectator with the hero. This spectator 'to whom nothing happens', as Freud says, is ready to pay a heavy price so that the deeds of which he dreams may be enacted in the closed space of the spectacle. The tragic outcome seems to result, then, from a compromise between this realization of desires and the price that it demands as payment. It is worth remembering this passage from Freud's 'Beyond the Pleasure Principle':

Finally, a reminder may be added that the artistic play and artistic imitation carried out by adults, which, unlike children's, are aimed at an audience, do not spare the spectators (for instance, in tragedy) the most painful experiences and can yet be felt by them as highly enjoyable. This is convincing proof that, even under the dominance of the pleasure principle, there are ways and means enough of making what is in itself unpleasurable into a subject to be recollected and worked over in the mind. The consideration of these cases and situations, which have a yield of pleasure as their final outcome, should be undertaken by some system of aesthetics with an economic approach to its subject-matter.

(*S.E.*, XVIII, 17)

These remarks come close to the Aristotelian theory of mimesis. But, for Freud, the final outcome is not so much catharsis as masochistic *jouissance* in repetition, though this repetition is produced, once more, in the name of the pleasure principle rather than in the name of the repetitive tendency of the destructive drives. The combination of these two factors leads to the masochistic *jouissance* obtained from the tragic spectacle.

Interpretation, distortion, repetition

To say that the Oedipus complex is universal is to say that every human being is born of two progenitors, one of a sex identical with his own, the other of a different sex; that he becomes attached to the progenitor, the mother, who provides him with his first objects of pleasure; that the father enables both the boy and the girl to become detached from the maternal object, the first by having to renounce the mother, the second by also having to renounce the father; that both children will see their interests become extraverted outside their own bodies in the social world, far from their primal objects, and that finally each will mate with a being of the other sex in order to be in turn a progenitor. The final choice of the subject cannot fail to be influenced by the two progenitors who gave him birth. This series of commonplaces becomes in man material for phantasy, for personal tragedy, then for tragedy pure and simple. It takes its course through the phantasy, born of a desire that is impossible to satisfy, of fully possessing the object of *jouissance* and of totally eliminating the object of rivalry. The personal tragedy is due, outside the limitations of the phantasy, to the real, physical, biological, psychical impossibility of transgressing the prohibitions. The infant can never be strong enough to kill the father and, even if he committed incest with a consenting mother, his physical immaturity would place him in an objective situation of impotence or sterility. It is this set of conditions that gives the Oedipus complex its importance.

This childhood situation can in itself be taken as an image of the tragic. But one may wonder in what respect the Oedipus myth and the Oedipus complex provide the supreme model for the approach to the tragic. I have partly answered this question already by raising the questions that it implies concerning kinship, birth, sexual union and death. But one may find still other reasons. The essence of the tragic lies, as Aristotle himself remarked, in reversal, or peripeteia. The history of the child at the age of the Oedipus complex is exemplary in this respect. For peripeteia may be conceived in accordance with two models. In the first, the hero of the tragedy is fortunate, his desire seems to have a chance of being realized, he is on the side of the phallus, the possessor of power, of objects of *jouissance*; he will therefore be subjected after the reversal to the fall: that is to say, the loss of his wealth, the disappearance of his power, the bitter taste of disappointment and misfortune. In the second, at the very outset of the tragic action, he is deprived of honours and pleasure, and is a pariah in the city; the development of the tragedy will see him overcoming many difficulties, appearing to prevail over the curse impending on him. Yet, like Sisyphus, his efforts will be in vain and he will rush headlong again down the slope to disaster. In each case, the attainment of happiness is impossible, is missed by a hair's breadth, by the decision of the gods punishing some unknown or unperceived crime.

It is in this situation that the child of Oedipal age finds himself. In phantasy, he has reached the age of being like the father, of replacing him beside the mother, of being, as some mothers say of their sons, 'her little husband'. At certain moments he believes himself to be stronger than the father, at least in his day-dreams. But this outcome is forbidden, barred by the father, who has the last word. The sudden reversal of the phantasmatic peripeteia is not now ordained by divine decree, but by a discovery similar, says Freud, to the fall of the throne or altar: the castration of the mother. With this reminder of earlier experiences – the weaning and toilet training that were their precursors – emerges the category of the forbidden and impossible. But this time the threat is to the object most prized because most narcissistically invested: the penis. One must renounce the object and the fulfilment of desire, explore other ways, create a new field for desire by the inhibition of the aim of the drive and the displacement of interests outside the ways of pleasure. It is not much compensation. In any case, this birth of the superego, the heir of the Oedipus complex, is a tragic birth built on the death of the earliest wishes, those most profoundly inscribed in the subject's flesh.

The complex is at once the most general structure, bound up with the condition of man and so never to be left behind, and the most singular ensemble, each individual living it out in his life as that which pertains to his most inalienable individuality. It is therefore both system and structure, but an individual, that is to say, indivisible, inalienable system and structure. The Oedipus complex is situated on the dual plane of diachrony and synchrony, not only because we regard it as non-temporal and universal, but also because it involves history and structure. It is intelligible only in the trajectory of human existence orientated from birth to death, and according to the combinatory of exchanges that it sets up between child, mother and father. It lies at the source of a double difference: the difference of the generations between parents and children, the difference of the sexes between the parents and between the child and one of its parents. By the crystallizations it makes possible it constantly encourages the more or less complete breaking down of its organizations or their reformulation in signifying constructions that make it possible to approach it. Such an approach is unacceptable because its reductive effect appears to annihilate all discourse. Now discourse is the necessary mediator whether one approaches the Oedipus complex or moves away from it. It always risks stumbling over a naturalness in which the language of the law and that of the body coincide, in which the logos of the body would merge in the loss of discourse.

The Oedipus complex is, therefore, caught between the annihilation of all speech, leaving the field free to the language of the body alone, and the polysemy of the signifier that brought Oedipus to his ruin. The eye too many is the thing in man that condemns him to interpretation. But what we learn from the lesson of Oedipus is that interpretation is a matter not only of possibility, but also obligation, necessity. The relationship of the subject to his progenitor grounds the field of interpretative constraint. It is impossible to keep silent before the mystery of origins, which is shared by the parents alone, excluding the subject himself. But it is impossible to know *exactly* how it was. There is always too much to interpret where the kinship relation is concerned. There is always an eye too many, that of the spectator who is not admitted to observe the scene. However, the weight of repression, its sheer massiveness, as is shown by the extent of infantile amnesia, opens up a second constraint. The truth is elusive, hidden, otherwise it would not be the truth. Nor is it given in a relation of all or nothing. It is always absent and always present: absent in its wholeness or its originality, present behind and through the distortions to which repression subjects it. The truth, said Freud, towards the end of his life, is attained only through its distortions – distortions that are not the result of some falsifier, but which are a necessity for all men who wish to avoid the unpleasure that necessarily accompanies the revelation of the inadmissible. This constraint is the constraint of distortion. Hence the *méconnaissance* when the truth emerges; it is never quite the same, so it cannot be the truth, thinks the subject under its gaze and trying desperately not to recognize it.

The dyad formed by the constraint of interpretation and the constraint of distortion itself generates a third constraint – the constraint of repetition – as well as being generated by it. Doomed to allow itself to be deciphered by interpretation and doomed to erratic distortion, the truth tirelessly repeats itself in order to be recognized and to conceal itself indefinitely. But, here again, this repetition is never a repetition of the identical; at most it is a repetition of the similar, producing with each scanning some gap of difference. So the phantasy is repeated in myth and ritual; together, they are repeated in tragedy – a reiteration, in every movement, of the signifier in a new space. Through these endless retellings, the signified is deformed and eludes any univocal, total, definitive grasp.

Hymn, ritual, epic, tragedy

It is clear that the different modes of presenting the narrative presuppose different modes of participation, from which emerge different types of representation that bear its stamp. In the incantation of the hymn, participation is total, for it involves the active reproduction of the narrative and the desubjectification of the participant in a fusion with the whole group. Representation gives way to the incantatory impulse that takes its place before it can be formulated. It is constantly summoned, but remains captive; and so it is only invoked in a poetic sense. If we bear in mind that a representation is not a static phenomenon, but an unfolding process that is bound by its very transformations to other figures that it generates as it develops, it might be said that all the dynamic possibilities are mobilized by the variations of the effective register of the hymn in its incantation. The whole movement is linked by what remains outside representation, which is not allowed a deployment of its own.

The hymn has its counterpart in ritual, which partly liberates representation by exteriorizing it. But, in doing so, it binds it. Ritualization has the essential characteristic of transmitting the feeling of protection against the transgression of prohibitions concerning the object of desire and of the representations associated with them. It does this through strict observance of practices in which ordinary actions are invested with a great power of signification; sacrilege is displaced from the prohibited desires and their possible fulfilment and on to non-observance of the forms required by the rules governing the ritual. Representation is therefore displaced on to 'the enactment' of the ritual – the representation is subjected to the ritual and cannot detach itself from it. Bound to ritual, representation is in a sense exhausted by the considerable investment required, in the successive stages that make up the ritual, in maintaining a conformity to the model whose form it repeats and which it must respect. The ritual is the perfect example of the case in which the means of representation becomes its end. Representation therefore is localized here, held in the grip of a reduced and displaced history, from which no excursion is possible. The participant assists at the ritual, observing it in both senses of the term: that is to say, watching it and subjecting himself to it.

The epic permits this excursion, forbidden to ritual. Delivered from the present, epic does not repeat a form; it does not commemorate by fixing, but by unfolding a discourse in the expectation of its perpetual development. This liberation from the present affects the time of the epic, which is always that of a past to be recreated by the narrative. It therefore solicits representation; representation comes to the aid of the recitation, which has the power to call it up. Born of the recitation, it anticipates it, opens up to it ways that the narrative might take. Guided by the recitation, representation orientates it in the direction of phantasy, which both hymn and ritual each in its own way stifled. Thus it moves in the direction of unconscious representation. From this we may conclude that the epic is a potential representation.

Tragedy absorbs the narrative fully. It no longer allows the spectator's mind to wander as in ritual; it fixes it by confining it in the space of the stage. But on this stage a complete history, neither displaced nor reduced, is unfolding. What is expected of the spectator is no longer conformity in repetition, but concentration on an articulated narrative, without any possibility of wandering. Similarly, tragedy integrates the hymn, which raises the tone of narrative, displaces the tension of intellectual curiosity that it has aroused on to the affective movement, which allows it a temporary discharge. In tragedy, representation moves in advance of the subject, captivates him, apprehends him. Unlike epic, which spoke in the name of the past, representing the past, tragedy actualizes it, makes it present. The way to phantasy, which the epic invited the listener to take, is now cut off. This has the effect of concentrating the subject on the tragic action. Yet is this not because the tragic action has the mission of being an incarnation of phantasy? On the one hand, the tragic action belongs, like the action of the epic, to the past and therefore has the same power of giving rise to representation. But on the other hand, representation does not take the form of evocation. It is not duplicated by the representation of phantasy that unfolded parallel with the epic narrative. The tragic action sets up the representation on the stage in the actualization of the narrative. By the excess of presence that it introduces into its materialization, it captivates the spectator sufficiently to prevent any wandering off into phantasy. It reinvests the activity of the senses of sight and hearing, which it monopolizes in the perception of a second reality, that of which the stage speaks. But a contradiction remains between this past history, of which the epic was meant to be the evocative testimony, and its presence in tragedy. Now this presence is a deceptive one, in that it tries to eliminate this gap between it and the past, which is the motive and motive-force of this rediscovery of the lost object in which phantasy finds the condition of its genesis.

This schema needs to be applied to the content of the Dionysiac legends from which tragedy sprang. Although we tend nowadays to consider that the satyric chorus was not the only origin of tragedy, that we must also recognize the influence of the epic chorus, it would seem that the fusion of these two genres has posed some problems for specialists. It is as if they found it difficult to admit that the drinkers' songs of the dithyramb might be responsible for the birth of the most noble spectacle of western civilization. What we have here, once again, is the elimination of the sexual, regarded as unworthy to consort with heroic actions. The Ancients did not necessarily have the same prejudices. It gives us an opportunity to recall once more that power is both natural, fecundating power (agrarian rites) and military and political power (political rites) and that this fusion is less surprising than one might think. Certainly the psycho-analyst would not regard it as improbable. The phallic signifier, the eagle with two heads, satyric and epic, the support of the sexual and aggressive drives at the origin of tragedy, is very far indeed from our civilized mode of thought, shaped by two thousand years of sexual exclusion. This is one more reason to mistrust any idealizing or partial interpretation. Equally firmly I would reject the transcendental interpretation that places the mystery of the divine at the origin of tragedy or the political interpretation that makes short work of the indestructibility of the desires that it is the mission of social life to repress – when it has failed to exclude them.

The transitional object and unconscious representation

This conception of tragedy enables us to understand its psychoanalytic and social function. As a manifestation of presence, through its link with representation, in the psychical and theatrical sense of the term, it *is*; but, as a support of a mythical truth passed from hand to hand and from mouth to mouth, before finding its written and performed form, it *is not*. We are forced to conclude, therefore, that it is a collective transitional object that is and is not what it represents. This transitional object existed at only one stage in the history of western civilization. Other forms followed it: the Christian mystery plays, Elizabethan drama, neo-classical tragedy, romantic drama and certain forms of contemporary theatre, in which the names of Artaud, Beckett, Genet, Dubillard and Ionesco would need to be mentioned. Thus the signifier is taken up again and again, endlessly modulating the fundamental signified whose presence is felt so heavily by virtue of its very absence.

Despite the theoretical impossibility of such an undertaking, Freud's achievement was to sustain a discourse on an indefinable signified and to continue unremittingly to add by his discourse to the sum of discourses contained within its limits. Reflection on the tragic cannot proceed otherwise today. What one might say of the Oedipus complex is not, therefore, that it is an inaccessible signified, but that this signified is given only in its absence. This absence is not non-existence, nor an elusiveness evading all apprehension; on the contrary, this absence, never admitted to any presence of itself, is read off as the sum of the difference of the tracks that have been made in its direction, or round about it, which tell of it and which are deployed in the successive statements about it.[20] This absence can be called absence in the relation of difference between or with the progenitors, in the potential space of generation.

It is not, therefore, the same thing to designate this signified as perpetually eluding the grasp of the signifier and to signify it as absence of the naturalness of existence where all discourse vanishes. For it is the absence that is difficult to conceive when one denies that it is non-presence, the survival of an effect in a trace, a subtraction, an inadequacy, a non-existence. In order to conceive it before its conceptualization – I say *before* – we must first draw up its economy. To put it more precisely, the moment of its conceptualization is indissociable from the time of its economy. It may well be that the concept, as absent cause, will emerge from the economy and that it is not necessary to posit the concept before studying its economy.

Perhaps psycho-analysts, who are among those who should be most skilled in speaking of this, do not do so as clearly as they ought, but fall all too easily into abstraction, tempted to be over-subtle, toying with the difficulty rather than confronting it. For phantasy, dream and symptom speak of this absence inhabited by unconscious representation – an absence that is not the reflection of death, but death in life itself, in the replication of lack,[21] in so far as absence bears the trace of death, staggering its effects.

The theatre takes up the challenge of evoking this absence in the most outrageous way, since nowhere else does language maintain the discourse of presence with such brilliance. In this respect, the theatre of representation alone is certainly the temptation to annul this presence, but it is also an acknowledgement of the impossibility of such an attempt. One must seek rather the locus of absence in the theatre in the duplication of respoken speech. The theatre is a differential replication of the exchanges of spoken language. The production of the statements that unfold before us has passed through writing, and a theory of writing for the theatre is therefore inevitable. But such a theory cannot afford to forget that this writing is intended to be spoken again. It is, therefore, a dual theory of writing that is necessary, that of the writing of speech and that of respoken writing. (Both forms of writing belong to a general theory of writing, but one cannot make out a specific defence of the literary literal on the basis of such a theory, since it goes well beyond this aspect. By the writing of speech, I do not mean the practice of writing speech down, but writing as the differential replication of speech. In order to be spoken, speech must first be written. It is, therefore, a differential replication of a writing.) The specific effect of the theatre is perhaps the confusion of the two stages. The spectator is entirely caught up in the work of decoding what – in spoken language – the actor means. He then believes that he has registered the translation of this spoken language, whereas he has encoded its delayed expression. And it is by means of this difference, bearing on reduced statements and forming an integral part of an uninterrupted chain, that the absent signified has slipped into his mind. If this first framework is reduplicated by the convergence or opposition of the voices on the stage and if the ensemble itself is caught up in the movement of successive actions and scenes, one can see opportunities here for unconscious representation to arise – because the necessary movements of the fable must derive, as it approaches its never named fundamental model, from the Oedipus complex, to which it is attached by decomposition, duplication or reduplication. The spectator's question 'What is he saying?' constantly replaces that other question 'What is he talking about?' Here there can be no question of knowing who is speaking, since this question can be posed only when the play has come to an end. The question 'What is happening?' dodges the question as to whether anything is happening other than an 'is'. The 'happening' of the 'What is happening?' has meaning only in so far as it is directed at a 'happening', a passage about which all interrogation must be suspended from a single line of the polyphony.

To accept this passage would be to renounce what Jacques Derrida calls linear writing. But the theatre is precisely the demand of the opposite through its obligation to 'follow' where one must – that is to say, to the catastrope of the polysemy of the signifier, the only effect of the absence of the signified. For the aim of the constitution of the signifier can be only the crushing of all polysemy. The dilemma between the fact that there is too much in life and in the world to be signified and the reduction operated by tragedy creates the alternating movement of the rejection of this reduction, which throws one back into the 'too irreducible', and acceptance of this reduction, which verges on deception – a deception that remains the sole recourse in the alternative that sets it against silence.

We cannot help hearing the little sound that Genet's characters make as they break through the screens as they pass from life into death, and as they break through they find themselves inevitably saying, 'Et on fait tant d'histoires.'[22] Freud, bursting the screen of the tragedy of Oedipus, did the same for us in the matter of sex. It is now for the contemporary public, hesitating to fall into the trap, to say as much for Freud and psycho-analysis.

Notes

Prologue

1 [In French, '*représentation*' covers much the same ground as the English 'representation'. Both words are used to translate the German '*Vorstellung*', a word with a long history in German philosophy and one which Freud took up and developed in his own way. (See entry under 'Idea' in Laplanche and Pontalis, 200–1.) However, the French word also translates 'performance', in the theatrical sense. It is natural, therefore, for Green to play on both senses of the word – the psychological and the theatrical. For this reason I have avoided the word 'performance' in this translation.]

2 [The French '*scène*' translates both 'stage' and 'scene'. Here, however, I felt obliged to use the English 'stage' where this was unequivocally meant. The 'other scene' is the reference to Freud's notion of the dream as 'another scene' ('*ein anderer Schauplatz*').]

3 [For an account of the primary and secondary processes, the reader is referred to Laplanche and Pontalis, 339–41. Broadly speaking, they correspond to unconscious mental activity, governed by the pleasure principle, and conscious mental activity, governed by the reality principle.]

4 [The term '*Familienroman*', or 'family romance', was coined by Freud as a name for phantasies in which the subject imagines that his relationship to his parents is other than it really is (as when he imagines, for example, that he is really a foundling). Such phantasies are grounded in the Oedipus complex. (See Laplanche and Pontalis, 160.)]

5 [In psycho-analysis, the 'turning round upon the subject's own self' is a process whereby the drive replaces an independent object by the subject's own self. It is a form of 'reversal into the opposite'. (See Laplanche and Pontalis, 399.)]

6 [Like many of Lacan's terms, '*Autre*' or '*grand Autre*' is extremely difficult to define. Lacan himself resists such definitions, regarding them as a dead hand on the vital potentiality of language. The best way to understand Lacan's concepts is operationally; that is, seeing them at work in a number of contexts. One of Lacan's best-known formulas is: 'The unconscious is the discourse of the Other.' The Other, says Lacan, is 'the locus of the deployment of speech (the other scene, *ein anderer Schauplatz*, of which Freud speaks in "The Interpretation of Dreams")' (Lacan, 264). 'The Other as previous site of the pure subject of the signifier holds the master position, even before coming into existence, to use Hegel's term against him, as Absolute Master' (305).]

7 [There is no adequate translation in English for the French '*jouissance*'.

'Enjoyment' conveys the sense, contained in '*jouissance*', of 'enjoyment' of rights, of property, etc. Unfortunately, the word has lost much of its Shakespearean power in modern English. In French, '*jouissance*' also has the sexual connotation of 'ejaculation'. ('*Jouir*' is the slang equivalent of 'to come'.) Green is using the term here in the Lacanian sense, in contra-distinction with 'pleasure'. For Lacan, pleasure obeys the law of homoeostasis that Freud evokes in 'Beyond the Pleasure Principle', whereby, through discharge, the psyche seeks the lowest possible level of tension. *Jouissance* transgresses this law and, in that respect, it is beyond the pleasure principle.]

8 In a work like this, my debt to Jacques Lacan is probably more important than any other, after that to Freud himself. This is not the place to explain why my approach, when applied to works of art, tends to push into the background my points of disagreement with Lacan's theory. However, these points will be indirectly present whenever I refer, in my analysis, to other theorizations, whether psycho-analytic or not.

9 The reformulation of Freud's thought is made necessary by knowledge that we have gained since his time. This knowledge cannot simply be added to Freud's work, but requires a re-elaboration of theory. If we are to safeguard the truth of the Freudian heritage we must take care that the Freudian language as a whole does not break down into a number of new dialects.

10 The role of the affect is particularly stressed by Freud in his analysis of Michelangelo's 'Moses'. This analysis is carried out according to the strictest rules of the combinatory, through the examination of the function of detail, but is aroused, solicited, by a powerful affect that keeps Freud rooted to the ground before the 'Moses'. The direction of gazes is then reversed: Freud feels that he is under the gaze of Moses, 'as though I myself belonged to the mob upon whom his eye is turned'. Similarly, Freud insists on the fact that the understanding required by the analyst cannot be an intellectual one: 'What he aims at is to awaken in us the same emotional attitude, the same mental constellation as that which in him produced the impetus to create' (*S.E.*, XIII, 212–13). One could hardly state more clearly the indissolubility of the affect and the representative of the drive.

11 An elucidation of these points is to be found in my article, '*L'objet* (a) de J. Lacan', *Cahiers pour l'analyse*, no. 3.

Chapter 1

1 This chapter was first presented at the Colloque de Cerisy on 'L'Art et la psychanalyse' (1962). The version published in the report of the Colloque (The Hague, Mouton, 1968) has been revised in a number of places, especially in the last part.

2 [There is no single, convenient equivalent in English for '*méconnaissance*'. The sense is of a 'failure to recognize' or 'misconstruction'. The concept is central to Lacan's thinking, since, for him, knowledge ('*connaissance*') is inextricably bound up with '*méconnaissance*'.]

3 I am considering here the definitive version of the myth, in the form given it by the tragic writers and more especially by Sophocles. We must, of course, take account of earlier versions and their variants as Marie Delcourt does in her book, *Œdipe ou la légende du conquérant*. I shall return to this later. Let us admit, however, in so far as it is the tragedy, rather than the myth, that is the object of my study and which has given rise to commentaries and reflections, that the tragedy resembles in a remarkably coherent way the truth of the mythical proliferation thus fixed. The work on the myth operated by the tragedy adds an additional distortion to the mythical thought, but it is through the tragedy that the truth conveyed by the myth is best perceived. This is no doubt because the constant reshaping of the myths by the anonymous community is here mapped out by the individual unconscious of the tragic poet.

4 Cf. the famous dream of Atossa in *The Persians*, which Binswanger comments on in *Dream and Existence*. We should also note the presence in Aeschylus' plays of ghosts (Darius, Clytemnestra), which are not found in Sophocles. These are additional testimony to the closeness of the first great tragic writer to the nocturnal world of the unconscious and death. This cannot be explained on the grounds of archaism alone: is Shakespeare, for example, archaic?

I should note in passing my debt to Clémence Ramnoux's *La Nuit et les enfants de la nuit*. My own work is placed in a doubly complementary perspective, more psycho-analytic than Hellenic and more centred on the emergence of meaning in the dream than on the 'power of darkness' in the *Oresteia*.

5 [Lacan's Name-of-the-Father derives, in a sense, from the mythical symbolic father of Freud's *Totem and Taboo*. In terms of Lacan's three orders, it is not the real father, nor the imaginary father (the paternal imago), but the father in the symbolic order. Freud, says Lacan, was led irresistibly 'to link the appearance of the signifier of the Father, as author of the Law, with death, even to the murder of the Father – thus showing that if this murder is the fruitful moment of debt through which the subject binds himself for life to the Law, the symbolic Father is, in so far as he signifies this Law, the dead Father' (199).]

6 [The secondary elaboration (or revision) is the elimination of the dream's apparent absurdity and incoherence, the filling in of its gaps, the partial or total reorganization of its elements by means of selection and addition. (See Laplanche and Pontalis, 412.)]

7 See my article, 'Sur la mère phallique', *Revue française de psychanalyse*, XXXII (1968), 1–38.

8 These truths concerning Electra are expressed by the chorus and by Chrysothemis. The chorus says to her:

> Remember
> The harm you do yourself –
> Do you not see? – the mischief

Is in your own self-torture.
Hoarder of grief, your sullen soul
Breeds strife unending.   (Sophocles, *Electra*, 75)

While Chrysothemis says:

Do you forget
You are only a woman, and weaker than your enemy?
(*Electra*, 98)

9 Such a thematic, so clearly illustrated by Sophocles' *Electra*, is much less clear in *The Choephori*. Since the plot of the two plays is identical, one is tempted to derive the first from the second. Thus Clémence Ramnoux, who rightly sees the legend of the Atrides as a scenario for a royal ordeal, especially in its first phases (the legend of Pelops), comes to a similar conclusion concerning the Orestes episode in Aeschylus (Ramnoux, 155–63). Personally, I regard this aspect as secondary in Aeschylus to the mother/son relation that links matricide and madness. This does not seem to me to contradict the impregnation of the *Oresteia* by the powers of night, whose defeat is brought about at the end of the trilogy, but which dominates the first two tragedies.

10 See Prologue, n. 6, above.

11 See André Bonnard, *Greek Civilization*, trans. A. L. Sells and R. C. Knight (London: Allen & Unwin, 1957), 150–72. In the same way, students of the Sorbonne performed *The Persians* under the German occupation and Sartre reinterpreted the *Oresteia* with *Les Mouches*.

12 Hegel was particularly struck by this succession; see 709–49.

13 For all these questions, see Marie Delcourt, 1959, ch. I. What follows owes a great deal to this chapter.

14 'Figuration de l'invisible et catégorie psychologique du double: le colossos', in Vernant, 1965, 251–99.

15 [Thomson remarks that the term 'hypocrite' – applied primarily to an interpreter of signs and oracles and, secondarily, to an actor in the theatre – springs from the need to explain to an uninitiated public the rituals (singing and dancing) of a secret society (see 181–3).]

16 [Freud's '*Vorstellungsrepräsentanz*', translated into English as 'ideational representative', is an idea or group of ideas to which the drive becomes fixated in the course of the subject's history; it is through the mediation of the ideational representative that the drive leaves its mark in the psyche. (See Laplanche and Pontalis, 203–5.)]

Chapter 2

1 There has been a lot of discussion as to Othello's exact degree of blackness. It has been said that, as an African from Mauretania, he is scarcely to be called black; his blackness was defended by Bradley in *Shakespearean Tragedy*. See also the opinions of Coleridge and Lamb, and Charlton's vigorous rectification.

2 The building of the first public theatre coincided, to a year (1576/7), with Drake's circumnavigation of the globe. Four years before *Othello*, the East India Company was founded. The mythology concerning these Africans, of which the West had only a recent knowledge at that time, was also conveyed through the chivalric romances of Palmerín (1511–47), which had close links with *Don Quixote*, itself filled with Moorish references (though not translated into English until 1612), and the *Microcosmos* of John Davies (1603). The war between the Republic of Venice and the Turks, which is referred to in *Othello*, was also a point of contact between East and West.

3 This difference seemed so exorbitant that Rymer (1692) and Coleridge (1808), among others, rejected it, accusing Shakespeare of extravagance when he made a negro a general of the Republic at a time when negroes could have been nothing but slaves.

4 [Green notes here the impossibility of conveying the ambiguity of the English line, 'That heaven had made her such a man':] This may be understood in two ways. Either that Desdemona wished that heaven had so arranged things that she had been born such a man (the sense adopted, not without reason, by Jouve), or that heaven had made such a man for her, had intended such a husband for her. There is a clear relation here between being and having, between identification and desire.

5 This has been stressed by many commentators, but above all by Leavis.

6 Especially as the strategic weakness of Cyprus is stressed:

> For that it stands not in such warlike brace,
> But altogether lacks th'abilities
> That Rhodes is dress'd in. (1, 3)

7 This kinship with ancient tragedy was sensed by Charlton, who compares *Othello* with *King Oedipus*, and by Swinburne, who finds the only equal for the feeling with which the tragedy ends in that aroused by the end of the *Oresteia*.

8 This throws some light on the fact that, in the first act, after making us expect the imminent arrival of Brabantio, who has set out angrily in search of his daughter's abductor, Shakespeare brings before us not the 'furious father', but Cassio. This makes Iago reply to Othello's question 'Is it they?' (Othello is expecting the outraged father): 'By Janus, I think no.' 'By Janus' opens up the series of double faces in which Brabantio already suggests his role as the substitute of the image of the father.

9 [The distinction between '*énoncé*' and '*énonciation*' is a common one in contemporary French thinking. Both terms are usually covered in English by 'utterance'. '*Enoncé*', which I translate as 'statement', refers to the actual words uttered, '*énonciation*' ('enunciation') to the act of uttering them. This is not, I admit, a perfect solution.]

Chapter 3

1 'Never did Iphigenia sacrificed at Aulis cost so many tears to the assembled Greeks.'

2 'In Racine's tragedies there is an enigmatic, silent character – the altar – which symbolizes ambivalence itself, because, right up to the last moment, we do not know whether the priest will ascend the altar to celebrate a marriage or to officiate at a sacrifice' (Charles Mauron, *L'Inconscient dans l'œuvre et la vie de Racine*, Gap: Ophrys, 1957).

3 [Green's point is somewhat weakened in the translation of Racine's lines. In the original French, all the keywords contain the root '*cour-*'.]

    In this repetitive insistence of the language, Racine seems to have conveyed the force of the Euripidean evocation that is expressed through the voice of the chorus, the spectator in the Greek camp:

> And I saw the runner Achilles
> Whose feet are like the wind,
> Whom Thetis bore and Cheiron trained –
> As he ran along the shingle in full armour,
> Matching his strength and speed against a four-horse chariot,
> Rounding the post to win.
>
>   (Euripides, *Iphigenia in Aulis*, 374)

4 As Charles Mauron rightly remarks, this is evident in the lines when Achilles fails to persuade Iphigenia to disobey her father:

> Take your heart to your father. I discern
> Much less respect for him than hate for me.   (v, 2:117)

What is at issue, then, is not respect, but the love of which Achilles is deprived and which reverts consequently to Agamemnon. Achilles' action in launching an assault on the altar acquires the value of a rebellion against everything that opposes his desire.

5 This opposition was developed by Georges Bataille (see especially *La Part maudite*, *L'Erotisme* and *Les Larmes d'Eros*). In fact, the war may be understood, according to one's point of view, either as an expression of the force of expenditure, or as an expression of the force of calculation. The expedition against Troy is an adventure from which huge profits may be expected.

6   A righteous fury sweeps across my soul.

> You're going to the altar. I shall fly
> To it. If heaven's athirst for blood, its shrines
> Will reek with more than they have ever known.
> To my blind love all is permissible.
> And my first blow will fall on Calchas' head.
> The block, destroyed and overturned by me,
> Will float in fragments in the killer's blood,
> And if, amidst the horrors of this fray,
> Your father falls and perishes himself. . .
>
>   (Racine, *Iphigenia*, v, 2:118)

Epilogue

1 [In Lacan's terminology, the 'imaginary' is one of the three essential orders of the psycho-analytic field, the other two being the 'real' and the 'symbolic'. It is related to what, in psycho-analysis, is known as 'phantasy'. However, for an initial introduction to this complex, evolving notion, the reader is referred to Laplanche and Pontalis, 210.]

2 On this point, Marie Delcourt expresses surprise that no one has ever thought of comparing the struggle between Oedipus and Laius with that between Zeus and Cronus. Broadly speaking, this is what D. Anzieu did in his article, 'Œdipe avant le complexe', *Temps modernes* (January 1966). However, J.-P. Vernant has challenged the legitimacy of such comparisons in 'Œdipe sans le complexe' (Vernant, 1972).

3 See also Vernant's remark that 'right is never fixed, but is displaced in the very course of the action' (1972, 7), which is always attributed to Aeschylus. On the other hand, *King Oedipus* was written only a few years before the death of Pericles, and he and Sophocles were friends.

4 'In particular, it is strange that the moral problem that principally preoccupied Sophocles, that of the guilt of the man who commits a crime by mistake – should not be posed' (R. Dreyfus, Introduction to *Œdipe-Roi*, Pléiade edition, 630).

5 See Lévi-Strauss, 1968, 48. He considers, side by side with cases in which the avuncular structure is simple, a case in which it appears in a more complex way: 'For instance, we can conceive of a system whose point of departure lies in the elementary structure but which adds, at the right of the maternal uncle, his wife, and, at the left of the father, first the father's sister and then her husband. We could easily demonstrate that a development of this order leads to a parallel splitting in the following generation. The child must then be distinguished according to sex – a boy or a girl, linked by a relation which is symmetrical and inverse to the terms occupying the other peripheral positions in the structure.' Later, the positive and negative symbols are replaced, on the grounds that they are too schematic, by the terms mutuality ($=$), reciprocity ($\pm$), rights ($+$) and obligations ($-$). Curiously enough, the relation of hostility disappears in this suggested notation since only the attitude of 'affection, tenderness, spontaneity' is now taken account of.

6 See this order of succession in Vernant, 1965, 118. The essential function of the son is to celebrate the funeral rites. The concern for preserving the patrimony seems less important: 'But it is a question much less of transmitting wealth to a collateral than of maintaining a home through the daughter.'

7 The ambiguity that reigns over the notion of matrilinearity leads Marie Delcourt to write: 'The union between a father and his daughter must have occurred in societies in which the paternal heredity was unknown and in which the older men kept for themselves the women that pleased them most. This practice has no psychological interest, since the two spouses were unaware of their kinship' (1944, 191).

8 'The prohibition of incest...presents, without the slightest ambiguity,

and inseparably combines, the two characteristics in which we recognize the conflicting features of two mutually exclusive orders. It constitutes a rule, but a rule which alone among all the social rules, possesses at the same time a universal character' (Lévi-Strauss, 1969, 8–9). In a note to *The Savage Mind*, Lévi-Strauss was to challenge the heuristic value of the nature/culture opposition. It is not the rejection of the opposition that is significant, but the difficulty of conceiving of the prohibition of incest.

9 Is not this censorship also to be found in Marie Delcourt's refusal, expressed at the beginning of her book (1944, 25), to situate the theme of the union with the mother on an 'ethical' plane, as a transgression of an incest taboo? One is struck, in this work, by the way in which the theme of the homosexual episode of the seduction of Laius by Chrysippus can find no place. Laius seduced Chrysippus when teaching him to ride the chariot, which is not unconnected with the circumstances of the seducer's death. The fact that two different Laius may be involved should encourage us to seek the reasons for the connection. The sexual crime does not allow the author to disentangle 'the strange potpourri that a scholiast may give of *The Phoenician Women*' (1944, 93). Later, Marie Delcourt also speaks of the 'embarrassing version by Nicolaus Damascenus' in which Epicasta – the first Jocasta – is spared by Oedipus and is also present at the brawl between the father and the son (1944, 187). Epicasta's suicide, which is referred to in the *Odyssey*, is interpreted as a suicide of revenge, since Epicasta invokes Laius, who in a sense took the husband's side. This is exactly what Jocasta does in Sophocles – her participation in the incest being clearly stressed. However, it is in the less coherent text that, paradoxically, we witness the re-establishment of verisimilitude. Thus in Nicolaus Damascenus the sojourn in the mountains follows the murder. But the relation to the showing/hiding re-emerges elsewhere. Thus, in certain versions, Oedipus, after the murder, bears Laius' arms, which signifies that he is claiming, according to custom, the ability to use them – which has been regarded as absurd, since this would have made it possible to identify him on his arrival at Thebes; similar, too, is Oedipus' gesture, in sending Laius' mules to Polybus at Corinth, which seems to indicate that the disguise necessary to the continuance of the fable cannot totally bar the meaning that these acts conceal for the hero in his desire to be recognized as the author of the deed. The only mark of recognition in the tragedy is that of the pierced feet. The version of the scholion of *The Phoenician Women* seems to have the function of conveying the parricide with the story of Pelops, which inserts the father/son relations into the context of the probationary nuptial rites, which are no longer mentioned except in the allusion to the abduction of Pelops' son Chrysippus by Laius. Curiously enough, by the same token, the kinship relation is modified, since Hippodamia is said here to be the wife of Oenomaus, whereas she is traditionally his daughter. A seduction brings together father and son, since Oedipus is calumniated by Hippodamia, but it is while bringing help to

Chrysippus that Oedipus kills Laius. Lastly, we should note that the blinding of Oedipus is performed here by Polybus following the oracle, before any crime has been committed – which we may compare with other versions where Oedipus is blinded by Laius' soldiers. This amalgam, then, is particularly revealing. It testifies with great purity to the fact that the distortions that give the feeling of incoherence operate according to the laws of the primary process, by means of condensation (of several generations) and displacement (bearing on the object of desire). All this would obviously be clearer if one had borne in mind Freud's observation – made in passing, it is true – to the effect that the erotic life of Antiquity gave greater importance to the drive than to the objects, whereas our civilization does precisely the reverse.

10 'Although the Freudian problem has ceased to be that of autochthony *versus* bi-sexual reproduction, it is still the problem of understanding how *one* can be born from *two*: How is it that we do not have only one procreator, but a mother plus a father? Therefore, not only Sophocles, but Freud himself, should be included among the recorded versions of the Oedipus myth on a par with earlier or seemingly more "authentic" versions' (Lévi-Strauss, 1968, 217).

11 On the question of the relations between the riddle and the Oedipus myth, see Lévi-Strauss's inaugural lecture, given on 5 January 1960 at the Collège de France (Paris: Editions Collège de France, 26–35).

12 The double signification bound up with the earth is repeated in the legends of the Sphinx. The Sphinx is bound up with the Hesiodic Phix, the exterminating monster of the Thebans, which derives its name from the gorges of Mount Phikion, or from having given his name to the place of his sojourn. Furthermore, the Sphinx is the result of an incest, between Echidna, a monster who was half-woman, half-snake, and her son Orthrus (Delcourt, 1955, 108).

Concerning the Egyptian origins of the Sphinx, I am indebted to M. Scriabine for many illuminating details. Sorting out the various elements – quasi-universal, Greek and Egyptian – that make up the Oedipus myth, one arrives at the following conclusions. The Sphinx, the riddle and the incest are Egyptian in origin. The role of the riddle and of the soothsayer are Greek. As far as the Sphinx is concerned, there does not exist in Egypt any collection of myths specifically relating to the Sphinx; its role is deduced on the basis of dispersed fragments. In earlier periods, the Sphinx represents variously the king or the queen, the rising sun, resurrection or the guardian of the ways of the beyond. These interpretations rest on the basis of hieroglyphic analysis. There did not exist in Egypt a single representation of the Sphinx. It was the Greeks who seem to have been responsible for its unification in a fixed figure.

As for the Oedipus riddle, it concerns, in the context of Ancient Egypt, the sun, which is designated in hieroglyphic representation as a child (or a scarab) at its rising, an adult at its zenith (Ra), and an old man leaning on a stick at its setting (Aton). Lastly, the incest (a practice, we know, authorized among the Pharaohs) is also connected with the sun legend: every evening the sun is united with its mother. The non-engendered sun engenders itself, a sign of immortality, the prerogative of divinity.

What we find in this mythical context is a neutralization of the father, or a nullification of him. According to Scriabine, the Sphinx is the divine double of Oedipus, whose nature is both divine and human (the symbolic double of the riddle: man, the sun). Traditionally, Oedipus accomplishes his divine destiny only by blinding himself: he then accedes to the divine.

This is not the only interpretation. Indeed, Scriabine maintains that, on the contrary, Oedipus rejects his divinity in the search for his kinship, though he is at one moment declared to be the son of Fortune. In the light of Ancient Egypt, it would be permissible to think that the Oedipus myth testifies to a refusal of man's totality: divine and human and integrating into this totality both the destructive forces (Seth) and the creative forces (Horus), Ra remaining the great creative god. Indeed, the Greek Oedipus wishes at all costs to exculpate himself by ridding himself of the evil that he cannot tolerate in himself and which the Ancient Egyptians accepted as forming part of their nature.

13 On the signification of the riddle, see my article, 'La diachronie dans le Freudisme', *Critique*, no. 238 (March 1967).

14 *Cahiers pour l'analyse*, no. 7, had the happy idea of reproducing a passage from G. Dumézil's book, *Horaces et Curiaces*, to which the author added an afterword on 'Les transformations du troisième du triple'.

15 J.-P. Vernant sets out to defend historical psychology against the erroneous or abusive interpretations of Freud and the psycho-analysts. The name he suggests for this new discipline, 'historical psychology', presents more problems for him than it solves. Vernant criticizes Freud, who ignores the historical, social and intellectual context of fifth-century tragedy, for interpreting the tragedy of Oedipus in terms of data discovered by psycho-analysis which, as it were, seem to have a value unlimited by time and space. But, of course, one may turn the question round: if the tragedy of Oedipus is intelligible only to specialists – Hellenists specializing in the period of Pericles – in what sense is it still of interest to us? Can it be said that our curiosity about Oedipus is simply curiosity about the past, unrelated in any real way with the present? How does it come about that philosophers and thinkers have seen this tragedy as embodying a problematic of a fundamental kind? No one is saying that the full scope of tragedy can be reduced to the Oedipal situation. It can be shown, however, that the problematic of Oedipus in its exemplary character is nuclear and that many other problematics are attached to it or gravitate in its orbit.

Vernant attacks the psycho-analytic interpretation of myths – which he rejects on the grounds that it contains arbitrary and incorrect distortions. As a Hellenist – and we cannot blame him for that – Vernant takes the myth literally. But, for psycho-analysts, the myth, which conceals a nucleus of truth, is a construction in which displacement, condensation and censorship have operated and marked the

definitive results of the mythical version. It is not a question of trans-
lating the myth, but of interpreting it. That is to say, of understanding
why such a content rather than any other became embodied in ritual,
myth and tragedy. The proof of these successive distortions is provided
by the invention of the tragic writers, who made their own contribution
to a pre-existing stock of legends. Is it not Vernant who is being
arbitrary in limiting these distortions to the textual? Especially as the
guarantee of the socio-historical context by no means covers the whole
field explored. Sooner or later, the psychological interpretation arises.
What we then get is a cross between academic psychology and the
offspring that psycho-analysis has spawned in the public domain.
'Oedipus is too self-confident, he is naturally proud, always and every-
where he must be the master...' This tells us nothing about the text;
it simply repeats it. It is when it tries to illuminate the text that the
analysis falls back on what it would like to do without. If Oedipus'
fears concerning the revelation of his origin were simply a matter of
his obscure extraction, why have they given rise to so much commentary? Oedipus, in short, would be the tragedy of a man who was
afraid that he had not been born the son of a king. A disappointing
conclusion if that is all there is to it! What is the sense of falling into
despair at discovering that one's father is not a king? Especially for
someone who claims to be the son of Fortune? When Vernant's fine
analyses are situated at a certain distance from this burning problem,
we learn a great deal more and will no doubt continue to enrich our
knowledge. The rejoinder I am making here to his criticism of the
psycho-analytic interpretation of Oedipus does not prevent me from
recognizing all that I owe to his work.

16 Even more of a disavowal than that of the man who boasts: 'Yes, I
have killed my father and slept with my mother. So what?' Or that of
the man who beats his breast and adds, 'And I have committed many
other sins too' – which has the aim of merging these desires in a single
mass awaiting the Last Judgement and the *jouissance* of the child
who is beaten. ['Disavowal' is a term used by Freud in the specific
sense of a mode of defence consisting in the subject's refusing to
recognize the reality of a traumatic perception. See Laplanche and
Pontalis, 118–21.]

17 See J. Laplanche, *Hölderlin et la question du père* (Paris: P.U.F., 1969).

18 See note 1 of this chapter.

19 Among the Hellenists who have supported the thesis that tragedy had
its origin in initiation rites, particular mention should be made of
George Thomson. See his *Aeschylus and Athens*.

20 These lines were suggested by a reading of the work of Jacques
Derrida.

21 I intend to develop the notion of replication and its relations with
repetition in a later work.

22 [The phrase might be translated, 'And they make such a fuss.' In this
context, however, it is obvious that Green (and Genet, too, no doubt) is
stressing the literal sense, 'And they tell so many stories.']

Select Bibliography

PLAYS

Aeschylus, *Agamemnon, The Choephori, The Eumenides,* in *The Oresteian Trilogy,* trans. Philip Vellacott (Harmondsworth: Penguin Books, 1956, reprinted 1975)
   Seven against Thebes, in *Prometheus Bound and Other Plays,* trans. Philip Vellacott (Harmondsworth: Penguin Books, 1961, reprinted 1975)
Euripides, *The Bacchae,* in *The Bacchae and Other Plays,* trans. Philip Vellacott (Harmondsworth: Penguin Books, 1954)
   Iphigenia in Aulis, in *Orestes and Other Plays,* trans. Philip Vellacott (Harmondsworth: Penguin Books, 1972)
   Iphigenia in Tauris, in *Alcestis and Other Plays,* trans. Philip Vellacott (Harmondsworth: Penguin Books, 1953)
Racine, Jean, *Iphigenia,* in *Phaedra and Other Plays,* trans. John Cairncross (Harmondsworth: Penguin Books, revised edition, 1970, reprinted 1972)
Shakespeare, William, *Othello,* ed. Henry H. Hudson (Edinburgh: T. C. & E. C. Jack, n.d.)
Sophocles, *Electra,* in *Electra and Other Plays,* trans. E. F. Watling (Harmondsworth: Penguin Books, 1953, reprinted 1954)
   King Oedipus, Oedipus at Colonus, in *The Theban Plays,* trans. E. F. Watling (Harmondsworth: Penguin Books, 1947, reprinted 1949)

OTHER WORKS

Aristotle, *Poetics,* trans. L. J. Potts as *Aristotle on the Art of Fiction* (Cambridge University Press, 1953)
Artaud, Antonin, *Le Théâtre et son double* (Paris: Gallimard, 1972)
Barthes, Roland, *Sur Racine* (Paris: Seuil, 1963)
   Critique et vérité (Paris: Seuil, 1966)
Delcourt, Marie, *Œdipe ou la légende du conquérant* (Paris: Droz, 1944)
   L'Oracle de Delphes (Paris: Payot, 1955)
   Oreste et Alcméon (Paris: Les Belles Lettres, 1959)

Select bibliography   257

Derrida, Jacques, *L'Ecriture et la différence* (Paris: Seuil, 1967)
Ferenczi, Sándor, *First Contributions to Psycho-Analysis*, trans. Ernest Jones (London: Hogarth Press, 1952)
Freud, Sigmund, *S.E.*: Standard Edition of the Complete Psychological Works, 23 vols. (London: Hogarth Press, 1953–66)
  The Origins of Psycho-Analysis: letters to Wilhelm Fliess, Drafts and Notes: 1887–1902, trans. M. Bonaparte and J. Strachey (London: Hogarth Press, 1954)
Hegel, G. W. F., *The Phenomenology of Mind*, trans. J. B. Baillie, 2nd ed. (London: Allen & Unwin, 1931)
Hölderlin, Friedrich, *Anmerkungen zum Oedipus*, in *Sämtliche Werke*, v (Stuttgart: Kohlhammer, 1954)
  'In lovely blueness...', in *Poems and Fragments*, trans. Michael Hamburger (London: Routledge & Kegan Paul, 1966)
Kierkegaard, Søren, *Fear and Trembling*, trans. Robert Payne (London: Oxford University Press, 1939)
Klein, Melanie, *Our Adult World and Other Essays* (London: Heinemann, 1963)
Lacan, Jacques, *Ecrits: A Selection*, trans. Alan Sheridan (London: Tavistock / New York: Norton, 1977)
Laplanche, J. and Pontalis, J.-B., *The Language of Psycho-Analysis*, trans. Donald Nicholson-Smith (London: Hogarth Press, 1973)
Lévi-Strauss, Claude, *The Savage Mind* (London: Weidenfeld & Nicolson, 1966)
  Structural Anthropology, trans. Claire Jacobson and Brooke Grundfest Schoepf (London: Allen Lane, 1968)
  The Elementary Structures of Kinship, trans. J. H. Bell, J. R. von Sturmer and Rodney Needham (London: Eyre & Spottiswoode, 1969)
Nietzsche, Friedrich, *The Birth of Tragedy*, trans. W. A. Haussmann (Edinburgh and London: Foulis, 1909)
Ramnoux, Clémence, *La Nuit et les enfants de la nuit* (Paris: Flammarion, 1959)
Thomson, George, *Aeschylus and Athens* (London: Lawrence & Wishart, 1941)
Vernant, Jean-Pierre, *Les Origines de la pensée grecque* (Paris: P.U.F., 1962)
  Mythe et pensée chez les Grecs (Paris: Maspero, 1965)
  'Œdipe sans le complexe', in *Mythe et tragédie en Grèce ancienne* (Paris: Maspero, 1972)
Winnicott, D. W., *Playing and Reality* (London: Tavistock, 1971)

Index

O₃